The Princeton Review®

GRE®

PSYCHOLOGY

PREP

9th Edition

The Staff of The Princeton Review

PrincetonReview.com

W9-DGL-213

Penguin
Random
House

The Princeton Review
110 East 42nd Street, 7th Floor
New York, NY 10017
E-mail: editorialsupport@review.com

Published in the United States by Penguin Random House LLC,
New York, and in Canada by Random House of Canada, a
division of Penguin Random House Ltd., Toronto.

ISBN: 978-0-525-57018-9
ISSN: 2693-6771

GRE is a registered trademark of Educational Testing
Service (ETS). This product is not endorsed or approved by ETS.

The Princeton Review is not affiliated with Princeton University.

The material in this book is up-to-date at the time of publication.
However, changes may have been instituted by the testing body in
the test after this book was published.

If there are any important late-breaking developments, changes, or
corrections to the materials in this book, we will post that information online in the Student Tools. Register your book and check your
Student Tools to see if there are any updates posted there.

Editor: Meave Shelton
Production Editors: Kathy G. Carter and Liz Dacey
Production Artist: Jennifer Chapman
Content Contributors: Anne Goldberg-Baldwin, Sarah A. Kass, and
Christine Lindwall

Printed in the United States of America.

10 9 8 7 6 5 4 3 2 1

Ninth Edition

Editorial
Rob Franek, Editor-in-Chief
David Soto, Director of Content Development
Stephen Koch, Student Survey Manager
Deborah Weber, Director of Production
Gabriel Berlin, Production Design Manager
Selena Coppock, Managing Editor
Aaron Riccio, Senior Editor
Meave Shelton, Senior Editor
Chris Chimera, Editor
Anna Goodlett, Editor
Eleanor Green, Editor
Orion McBean, Editor
Patricia Murphy, Editorial Assistant

Penguin Random House Publishing Team
Tom Russell, VP, Publisher
Alison Stoltzfus, Publishing Director
Amanda Yee, Associate Managing Editor
Ellen Reed, Production Manager
Suzanne Lee, Designer

Acknowledgments

The Princeton Review would like to thank Sarah A. Kass, Christine Lindwall, and Anne Goldberg-Baldwin for their dedication and hard work revising and updating this edition.

We are also grateful to the production team—Jennifer Chapman, Kathy G. Carter, and Liz Dacey—for their careful attention to every page, and to Deborah Weber for her expert oversight.

Special thanks to Adam Robinson, who conceived of and perfected the Joe Bloggs approach to standardized tests and many of the other successful techniques used by The Princeton Review.

Contents

Get More (Free) Content
at PrincetonReview.com/prep

As easy as 1·2·3

1 Go to PrincetonReview.com/prep and enter the following ISBN for your book: 9780525570189

2 Answer a few simple questions to set up an exclusive Princeton Review account. *(If you already have one, you can just log in.)*

3 Enjoy access to your **FREE** content!

Once you've registered, you can...

- Get our take on any recent or pending updates to the GRE Psychology Test

- Access your 2nd and 3rd GRE Psychology practice tests (there is 1 right here in your book and 2 online), plus complete answers and explanations

- Get valuable advice about the grad school admissions process, different psych degrees and areas of concentration, researching schools, and applications and candidacy

- Check to see if there have been any corrections or updates to this edition

Need to report a potential **content** issue?

Contact **EditorialSupport@review.com** and include:

- full title of the book
- ISBN
- page number

Need to report a **technical** issue?

Contact **TPRStudentTech@review.com** and provide:

- your full name
- email address used to register the book
- full book title and ISBN
- Operating system (Mac/PC) and browser (Firefox, Safari, etc.)

Look For These Icons Throughout The Book

 ONLINE PRACTICE TESTS

 PROVEN TECHNIQUES

 STUDY TIPS

Introduction

IF YOU NEED TO KNOW IT, IT'S IN HERE

GRE Psychology Prep has been updated and revised for its ninth edition to reflect the changing needs of prospective graduate students. To put it mildly, getting into graduate school in psychology is much tougher than it used to be. This book is designed to be the only resource you will need, aside from official literature from schools, ETS, and the American Psychological Association (APA). You can tackle admissions and the test without gathering a library of books!

WHAT'S IN THIS BOOK

The material in this book is organized into three parts as follows:

The Test

This section explains how the GRE Psychology Test works and how you can work aggressively toward a high score. Smart strategies will help you get the most out of what you know (and even what you don't know).

Content Review

This section has been meticulously researched to include anything that has appeared on past exams, as well as anything so central it could be expected to show up on a future test.

More Practice Tests!

Two additional practice tests, plus answers and explanations, are available to download from your Student Tools online. See pages vi–vii for instructions on how to access these free entitlements.

The Princeton Review Practice GRE Psychology Test

A full-length practice test represents each area that you must know. You may want to begin your study by taking this test and identifying your strengths and weaknesses using the category-specific Answer Key, before diving into the Content Review.

Part I
The Test

Chapter 1
About the GRE
Psychology Test

WHAT IS THE GRE PSYCHOLOGY TEST?

Graduate programs in some fields require a subject test as part of the admission process. Many (but not all) graduate programs in psychology require the GRE Psychology Test, which is comprised of 205 multiple-choice questions from the field of psychology.

Psychology is a wide field, and the questions on the test cover a range of areas. Basically, if you took the final exam for every psychology undergraduate course offered at a major university and randomly selected 205 questions from these exams, you would have the GRE Psychology Test. Yes, it's a lot of material. Therefore, be sure you need to take the test before you prepare.

Who Writes the Test?

The test is constructed by Educational Testing Service (ETS), the same people who brought you the GRE, the TOEFL, and other favorites. During test development, academic faculty in psychology are consulted about the content of the questions, but the test is ultimately written by ETS. Don't be intimidated! ETS is a business, not an omniscient educational gatekeeper. The test is a hoop to jump through. Period.

Contact Information

Official ETS information about the GRE Psychology Test can be found online at www.ets.org/gre/subject/about/content/psychology. Here's additional contact information:

Address:

GRE-ETS
P.O. Box 6000
Princeton, NJ 08541-6000
USA

Email: www.ets.org/gre/contact/contact_form

Fax: 1-610-290-8975

Phone: 1-609-771-7670 or 1-866-473-4373 (toll free for test takers in the United States, U.S. Virgin Islands, Puerto Rico, and Canada)

Hours: Monday–Friday 8 A.M. to 5:45 P.M. EST

Test Dates

Currently, the GRE Psychology Test is offered at paper-delivered test centers on just three Saturdays throughout the year, in September, October, and April. So it is important to plan to take the test well in advance of any graduate school application to allow yourself the option, if necessary, of retaking the exam.

Note that students claiming special circumstances may request to take the test on the Mondays following each of the Saturday testing dates. Monday testers always receive a different exam, since ETS is always concerned about minimizing any chance of cheating. For more information on requesting accommodations, have a look at this website: www.ets.org/gre/subject/register/disabilities.

Testing Fee

As of press time, the fee is $150 USD worldwide. Remember that this price may increase slightly over time, so be prepared for small increases. There are vouchers available for eligible students.

Test Format

Unlike the General GRE, the GRE Psychology Test is a conventional paper-and-pencil exam. Each of its 205 multiple-choice questions has five answer choices, (A) through (E), which you select by bubbling in the proper oval on the answer sheet. The permitted testing time is 2 hours 50 minutes.

On the Day of the Test

According to ETS, you should be at the testing center no later than 8:30 A.M. or else risk being turned away. Plan to be at the testing center for a total of three and a half hours to allow time for administrative paperwork associated with the exam.

Required/Restricted Items on Test Day

You need a bunch of No. 2 pencils and a big eraser. As far as documentation, once you register for the exam, ETS will remind you of the documentation required on test day. Basically, you'll need the registration card that they send you in advance as well as a photo ID with your signature on it, such as a passport, driver's license, military ID, or national ID. If you don't have one of these, pay extra attention to ETS's fine print when you register for the exam to see what you will need to bring instead; otherwise they will have no problem delaying you outside the testing center.

The list of forbidden items is long and glorious and can be found in the GRE registration materials or on the GRE website. At this point it is necessary only to mention that no calculators, no timers that make noise, and no headsets are allowed.

Testing Centers and COVID-19

At the time of this book's printing, per ETS, health concerns and local restrictions "are preventing many institutions...from being able to provide a safe testing space. The Subject Tests cannot be offered online at this time, so the next opportunity to take a Subject Test—assuming health conditions improve—will be April 2021."

Be sure to check ETS's website for ongoing updates concerning testing and COVID-19: https://www.ets.org/s/cv/gre/the-americas/

Sending Off Scores

When you register for the GRE Psychology Test (and again on the day of the exam), you can list up to four schools that you want ETS to send your scores to. With the ScoreSelect® option, you have the freedom to select which test scores to send to the graduate institutions you designate.

You may order additional score reports for an extra $27 per score recipient. You will designate your initial score recipients at the testing center, and you may list the additional recipients on the GRE website. See the following page for details: www.ets.org/gre/subject/scores/send.

Canceling Scores

You can void the exam at any point during the morning of the test. Voiding essentially results in your answer key getting tossed in the trash, and no record of that day ever appears on any future GRE report. Honestly, you should consider doing this only if you're convinced that things have gone seriously wrong.

Taking the Test More Than Once

While it is possible to take the test more than once, most students who do so don't take it more than twice. Your best bet is to take it just once, if you can. Don't take the test without preparing and as if it were just a practice run. Each additional score on your report makes you look more like a professional test taker and less like a potential graduate student.

How Does the Test Factor into the Application Process?

The subject tests were created to provide graduate admission programs with an indication of an individual's grasp of a particular subject. Of course, for the test you are expected to have only a reasonable undergraduate grasp. You are going to graduate school to learn the most advanced principles. Some schools may use the GRE Psychology Test as an indicator of how well you know psychology, especially if you majored in another field. Other schools may use the test to confirm that you remember what you learned as an undergraduate psychology major. The more competitive schools use the psychology subject test as a factor in screening and competition.

What Does the Test Measure?

The GRE Psychology Test isn't an indicator of how successful you may be as a psychologist. It is an indicator of how many undergraduate psychology classes you took, how well you remember them, and/or how thoroughly you prepared for the test. Furthermore, because a correlation exists between scores on the GRE Psychology Test and scores on other nonsubject standardized tests, it's clear that the GRE Psychology Test measures general test-taking skills as well.

What Material Does It Test?

You will be tested on the concepts, specifics, researchers, studies, and principles associated with particular areas of psychology. Some of the questions will be general and basic, yet others will be specific and obscure. According to ETS, the areas that you must know are the following:

I. Biological (17–21%)
    a. Sensation and Perception (5–7%)
    b. Physiological/Behavioral Neuroscience (12–14%)

II. Cognitive (17–24%)
    a. Learning (3–5%)
    b. Language (3–4%)
    c. Memory (7–9%)
    d. Thinking (4–6%)

III. Social (12–14%)
    a. Social Perception, Cognition, Attribution, Beliefs
    b. Attitudes and Behavior
    c. Social Comparison, Self
    d. Emotion, Affect, and Motivation
    e. Conformity, Influence, and Persuasion
    f. Interpersonal Attraction and Relationships
    g. Group and Intergroup Interaction
    h. Gender and Culture
    i. Evolutionary Psychology, Altruism, and Aggression
    j. Theories and Applications

IV. Developmental (12–14%)
    a. Nature-Nurture
    b. Physical and Motor
    c. Perception and Cognition
    d. Language
    e. Learning, Intelligence
    f. Social, Personality
    g. Emotion
    h. Socialization, Family, and Culture
    i. Theories and Applications

V. Clinical (15–19%)
    a. Personality (3–5%)
    b. Clinical and Abnormal (12–14%)

VI. Measurement/Methodology/Other (15–19%)

> Although ETS refers to this sub-category as "abnormal psychology," this book prefers the term "psychological disorders," which is now more commonly used.

How Does the Test Work?

From your performance on the multiple-choice questions, ETS calculates a raw score, a scaled score, two subscores, and a percentile rank. The scaled score is what schools want.

- **Step 1:** Raw Score

    The total number of correct responses is your raw score. Each correct answer receives one point. It is wonderful news that the test no longer subtracts one-fourth of a point for incorrect answers, so the only points that are gained are for correct answers. Incorrect and blank answers receive zero points.

- **Step 2:** Scaled Score

    Your raw score is plugged into a conversion chart that assigns it a value between 200 and 990. This is your scaled score, and the score that interests graduate schools. The conversion charts vary slightly per test due to small variations in test difficulty.

- **Step 3:** Subscores

    Subscore I reflects your performance on questions from the Experimental and Natural Sciences category. Subscore II reflects your performance on questions from the Social Sciences category. Subscores range from 20–99, although the extremes are very rare. These subscores, though present on your ETS score report, are basically ignored by graduate programs.

- **Step 4:** Percentile Rank

    Your percentile is calculated by comparing your raw score to that of others who took that test and other recent psychology subject tests. Your percentile rank indicates what percentage of students scored lower than you did.

Example: Let's say that after completing all the questions, you answered 125 correctly and 90 incorrectly. Since there is no deduction for incorrect answers, your raw score would be 125. The conversion chart printed on the next page provides approximate conversions to scaled scores and percentiles based on the most recent available data from ETS. From the chart, you would have scored a 550 and a 22 percentile rank.

What Score Do I Need?

GRE Psychology scaled scores fall between 200 and 990. Extreme scores are so rare that a score of about 820 or above places you in the 99th percentile. Generally, schools want to see a scaled score between 600 and 700. The mean score of admitted students, however, is often in the 650–750 range, depending on the program. It is difficult to generalize about scores needed for admission because of the many varying psychology programs. Some programs will accept scores in the 400s and 500s. More competitive schools boast average scores in the high 700s. The program literature for a particular school will clearly state the GRE Psychology Test scores preferred for that program.

Total Score					
Raw Score	**Scaled Score**	**%**	**Raw Score**	**Scaled Score**	**%**
	Above 870	99	119–121	530	18
204–205	870	99	117–118	520	18
201–203	860	99	114–116	510	15
199–200	850	99	112–113	500	15
196–198	840	99	109–111	490	12
194–195	830	99	107–108	480	12
191–193	820	99	104–106	470	9
189–190	810	98	102–103	460	9
186–188	800	98	99–101	450	6
184–185	790	95	97–98	440	6
182–183	780	95	94–96	430	5
179–181	770	91	92–93	420	5
177–178	760	91	89–91	410	3
174–176	750	86	87–88	400	3
172–173	740	86	84–86	390	2
169–171	730	80	82–83	380	2
167–168	720	80	79–81	370	1
164–163	700	73	77–78	360	1
159–161	690	65	75–76	350	1
157–158	680	65	72–74	340	1
154–156	670	58	70–71	330	1
152–153	660	58	67–69	320	1
149–151	650	51	65–66	310	1
147–148	640	51	62–64	300	1
144–146	630	44	60–61	290	1
142–143	620	44	57–59	280	1
139–141	610	38	55–56	270	1
137–138	600	38	53–54	260	1
134–136	590	32	50–52	250	1
132–133	580	32	48–49	240	1
129–131	570	27	45–47	230	1
127–128	560	27	43–44	220	1
124–126	550	22	40–42	210	1
122–123	540	22	0–39	200	1

You can use two ways to determine your score goal. The first way is to take a practice GRE Psychology Test (the best is the real ETS test you can download for free at www.ets.org/gre/subject/prepare) and calculate your score. Then, think realistically about how much time you have to study and create a score goal for yourself. Score improvements vary dramatically depending mostly on study time and familiarity with the material. If this is your plan, after the actual test, you will go shopping for graduate programs based on the score you received.

The second way is to look at the scores for applicants admitted to those programs that interest you. These are the scores that you need. Take an ETS psychology practice test, see where you are, and plan to study accordingly. Though improvement is all about preparation, don't forget to be realistic.

Top 10 Ways to Prepare

Gone are the days when subject tests were perceived as tests of general knowledge. With the keen competition for positions in psychology graduate programs, the GRE Psychology Test has moved beyond functioning as a simple achievement indicator. Yikes! What do you do?

1. Begin your study by taking the official GRE Psychology Practice Test, available for free at www.ets.org/gre/subject/prepare. Use the Answer Key provided to identify your areas of strength and weakness using the raw-to-scaled score formula for each content category. An ETS score will accurately reflect how much you have learned and what areas still need work.

2. Then, study this book, particularly the content review in Part II. You may want to begin with the chapters corresponding with content areas in which you feel less confident.

3. Study frequently. Humans learn best in short, spaced, frequent intervals. Most people take at least six weeks to prepare for the GRE Psychology Test. Just say no to cramming.

4. Practice pop psychology on yourself. Stop imagining the worst and envision the best. Don't let the test make you feel like a deer in the headlights! Study and feel confident that you are prepared.

5. Use the smart test-taking techniques that we teach in Chapter 2. Get points even when you don't know the answer. Take the test, don't let the test take you!

6. Take Practice Test 1 in this book. Use the Answer Key to further identify any lingering areas of weakness, and review them as needed. Repeat the process with Practice Tests 2 and 3, which you'll find online in your Student Tools.

To download Practice Tests 2 and 3, see the instructions on pages vi–vii.

7. Stay away from books not published by ETS that offer endless practice questions. These books contain questions that are either too hard or too easy, or may be downright inappropriate. Your time is best spent studying rather than answering bad questions.

8. Don't be a perfectionist. You cannot know everything. No matter how hard you study, the test will include researchers, terms, and principles that you have never heard of. It's okay. Certain questions are designed to weed people out.

9. Okay, if you must be a perfectionist, then the Internet can help you. In this book, concepts and studies are described in the most economical way possible—that is, with the least amount of detail. If every concept were explained in depth, then this guide would be overwhelming. In general, concepts that are given little attention (perhaps a bullet-point or two) have shown up on some (but not all) recent tests in the form of one question. Concepts that are discussed in more detail usually receive attention on every test administration. If a bullet point or an explanation does not meet your satisfaction, search for the term on the Internet. Many websites related to psychology and research will explain terms in more depth.

Study Tip
Flashcards of key terms, scientists, and experiments are a great place to keep yourself studying in short spurts.

10. Students often ask what in this book is important. Well, everything! Absolutely everything in this guide has appeared on a recent test; in other words, nothing in this book is included just for the fun of it. If you are hoping to cram and squeak by, then study the concepts discussed in detail that comprise the bulk of the content chapters; also notice the relative percentage of coverage that each area typically receives on tests (for example, social psychology is much more important to your score than ethology). If you need to do really well on the subject test, then start early and try to learn everything in this book.

Chapter 2
Strategy

GETTING THE MOST OUT OF WHAT YOU KNOW

On the GRE Psychology Test, the issue is not so much pacing as it is accuracy. Given the 170-minute time limit, most people find that they are able to finish the test. They just wish that more of their answers were correct. With simple techniques, you can maximize what you know.

DO YOU WANT MY BEST GUESS?

Yes! We do want your best guess. The test no longer has a "guessing penalty," which previously subtracted one-fourth of a point for each incorrect answer. Now, incorrect answers and blank answers are both worth 0 points. Therefore, you have nothing to lose and everything to gain by guessing!

Consider the following. Let's say you randomly guessed (D) for 30 questions. Statistically speaking, one-fifth of the 30 questions, or 6 questions, should be (D). This would be added to your raw score. Take a peek at the conversion chart on page 11 and you will notice that 6 points is a roughly 20-point scaled gain. It's a great little boost to your overall score.

If you can eliminate just one choice before taking a guess, do so. Process of Elimination is a very strong tool that can increase the probability of choosing the correct answer. Read on to see how this technique works.

POE is a key strategy that can help you to find the correct answer.

Process of Elimination

Wrong answers are often easier to spot than correct answers. While it is rare to be able to eliminate all four of the incorrect answer choices, you will almost always be able to eliminate at least one of them—and frequently two or more. Process of Elimination (POE) will enable you to answer questions that you don't have time to figure out exactly. It's one of the most important strategies you can use on multiple-choice questions to increase your score.

Try a generic example:

> Which of the following countries uses the peso as its unit of currency?
>
> (A) Russia
> (B) Canada
> (C) Venezuela
> (D) England
> (E) Chile

You can probably get rid of only three of the five answer choices using POE. The answer is clearly *not* Russia, Canada, or England, but most people probably don't know for sure whether the answer is Venezuela or Chile.

Once you eliminate those three choices, you've got the question down to two possibilities. What should you do? A Chilean might flip a peso. You have a fifty-fifty chance of getting this question correct, which is much better than if you had guessed at random. Remember, ETS doesn't care how you arrive at the correct answer, so use this to your advantage.

If Process of Elimination is not possible, pick a Letter of the Day (LOTD). If you choose the same letter for each random guess [i.e., choosing (D) for each choice as in the previous example], you are essentially equalizing that 1 in 5 chance of getting the random questions correct. So, yes—take a guess!

> If you eliminate even one of the choices, you are beating the odds, so GUESS. If you have no idea, use LOTD!

BIG-PICTURE TEST STRATEGY

For purposes of technique, the questions on the psychology test can be divided into three types:

- ones you know the answer to
- ones you sort of know the answer to
- ones you have no idea about

We recommend that test takers use a three-pass system on the GRE Psychology Test. What this means is that you go through the test and first answer all of the questions for which you are sure of the answer. Then, you take another whirl with the leftover questions and use aggressive techniques in order to make an informed and educated guess on the questions you "sort of" know the answers to. Finally, you deal with the questions you have no clue about, and use your Letter of the Day with the questions about which you have no idea or for which you have run out of time. It is senseless to run out of time because you struggled with harder questions while you could have been answering easier ones. Take all the points you can get and then struggle with what's left.

First Pass: You Know the Answer, You See It, You Circle It, You Move On

On your first run through the test, read all of the questions and answer the giveaways. Don't waste time struggling with confusing questions when you could be racking up points. After you finish the easy questions, you'll know how much time is left for the others. As you skip questions, circle the ones you think you can work with. Put a question mark by questions that you have no idea about.

Second Pass: Guess Aggressively (Not Randomly)

On the second pass, you work with the questions that you sort of know the answer to—the ones you circled on the first pass. For these questions, you have a good shot of beating the odds and guessing correctly. You'll need to be active and involved with the question and the answers. Guessing aggressively requires skill.

- **Process of Elimination** is your best friend here. Even if you don't figure out what the right answer is, by ruling out choices that you know are incorrect, you increase the probability that your guess will be correct.

- **Use common sense.** Luckily, psychology is a relatively modern field with relatively practical principles. Subject tests do not try to trick you. (Sometimes you can even find unintended hints to the answer within the question and answer choices.) The subject material on the test is considered important (not wacky or random) by faculty consultants. Psychology terms often mean what they sound like. Use this to your advantage. If you do not know the answer to a question but can make a logical guess, go for it! Here's how this works:

> 56. According to Maslow's hierarchy of needs, the most basic human needs are
>
> (A) food and water
> (B) a safe place to live
> (C) the love and esteem of others
> (D) self-actualization
> (E) intellectual challenge

Some questions are this basic, yet seem difficult because you're not up on your Maslow. But Maslow fan or not, a good guess is that our most basic needs are (A) food and water.

> 47. Which of the following are newborn infants unable to see?
>
> (A) Simple shapes
> (B) Vivid colors
> (C) Weak light
> (D) Intense contrasts
> (E) Intricate detail

Because the question implies that babies do not have great eyesight, think about sight logically. Of the five answer choices, what would be the easiest things to distinguish? Probably (A), (B), and (D), so eliminate those. (If you guess now, you have a 50 percent chance of getting the right answer.) Between (C) and (E), do you have a guess as to what would be the more difficult thing to see? If you guessed (E), you're right.

- **EXCEPT, LEAST, or NOT Questions**

> One of these things is not like the others.
> One of these things is not the same.
> Well, can you guess which thing is not like the others?
> That's how we play this game.
>
> —*Sesame Street*

Sesame Street is so educational that it will even help you on your subject test! Some questions on the test will be what we call "EXCEPT" questions. They are easy to spot because they contain EXCEPT, LEAST, or NOT in big letters. The key to answering these questions is to think of the answer you want as the odd man out. It will be out of step somehow with the other four choices. So even if you don't know the answer to the question, you can guess aggressively using the Sesame Street technique. Let's play:

107. Damage to the hypothalamus would
     be likely to impair each of the following
     EXCEPT

     (A) sexual behavior
     (B) aggression
     (C) vision
     (D) temperature control
     (E) hunger

So you didn't get around to learning your physiology for the test. What do you do? Look for one thing different from the rest! Choices (A) and (B) both seem like basic elements of instinct or survival. Not the case with (C). Choices (D) and (E) seem necessary for survival. Choice (C) is the oddball and, for our purposes, the answer we want.

- Go with what you know. The GRE Psychology Test is not a trick! It is supposed to measure your knowledge about important principles in the field, not about unimportant hocus-pocus. The rule is simple: if all else fails, just choose the answer you have heard of.

Third Pass: POE and LOTD

Spend time on questions that you have no idea about only after you have answered all of the questions you know and sort of know. If time is remaining, take another look at the questions that you put question marks next to. If you can eliminate at least one answer choice, take a guess. If it is a blind guess, use a Letter of the Day (LOTD). This ensures that roughly 1 in 5 of your guesses will be correct, thus giving your raw score an extra boost.

MORAL OF THE STORY

You do not have to know everything to get a good score on the psychology test! First, take another look at the conversion chart. You can answer 60 questions wrong or leave 75 questions blank and still score higher than a 650! Second, you don't have to know the answer to a question in order to answer it correctly. Using the techniques that we've provided, you can beat the odds and guess correctly. Finally, use your LOTD to guess on any remaining questions and don't leave anything blank. Every little bit counts!

Part II
Content Review

Chapter 3
Sensation and Perception

This chapter discusses the basic concepts and prominent theories concerning *sensation* (our awareness of external stimuli through the senses) and *perception* (the way we interpret this sensory information). It covers thresholds for stimulus detection, the function and basic structural components of the major senses (vision, hearing, taste, smell, and touch), as well as other sensory systems, such as the vestibular and kinesthetic processes that help us maintain balance, equilibrium, and awareness of body movement. It also discusses various principles of perceptual organization.

> **DEFINED: Sensation is the feeling that results from physical stimulation, while perception is the way we organize or experience the sensation.**

Sensation involves three steps:

- **Reception** takes place when **receptors** for a particular sense detect a stimulus. The **receptive field** is the distinct region of sensory space that can produce a response when stimulated. Receptive fields are found on the body surface and in the muscles, joints, eyes, and internal organs.

- **Sensory transduction** is the process in which physical sensation is changed into electrical messages that the brain can understand. Sensory transduction is at the heart of the senses.

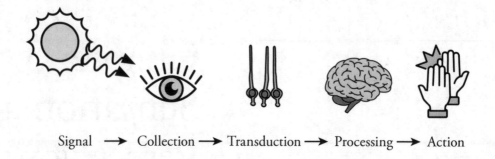

Signal → Collection → Transduction → Processing → Action

- The electrical information travels down **neural pathways** to the brain, where the information is understood.

Obviously, we sense many more things than we process each second. Also, other factors come to bear on how we understand the sensory information that we receive.

THE BASICS

Different theories exist about the workings of perception:

- **Nativist theory** asserts that perception and cognition are largely innate and genetically based. Human beings are born with all their perceptual capacities, even though some abilities are not present at birth and develop as the individual matures. Nativist theory lies in contrast to **empiricist theory,** which holds that perception is basically learned and develops as the individual adapts to his or her environment.

- **Structuralist theory** asserts that perception is the sum total of sensory input: one can understand the mind by understanding its basic components. This theory focuses on **bottom-up processing,** which starts with sensory data and works upward to the brain's integration of that data.

- **Gestalt psychology** asserts that people tend to see the world in terms of organized wholes rather than constituent parts. It focuses upon **top-down processing,** which starts with higher-level cognitive processes and works downward to sensory information.

- Current thinking, not surprisingly, is that perception is partially innate/sensory and partially learned/conceptual.

THRESHOLD AND STIMULUS DETECTION

Threshold addresses minimum levels of stimulation that are needed for detection. Important types of threshold are as follows:

- **Absolute threshold** is the minimum amount of a stimulus that can be detected 50 percent of the time.
- **Differential threshold** (also known as **just noticeable difference** or **JND**) is the minimum difference that must occur between two stimuli, in order for them to be perceived as having different intensities. This was defined by **E. H. Weber.**
- **Terminal threshold** is the upper limit above which the stimuli can no longer be perceived. For example, the lowest pitch sound a human can hear is the absolute threshold, whereas the highest pitch sound a human can hear is the terminal threshold.

Psychophysics is the study of the quantitative relations between psychological sensations and physical stimuli. Gustav Fechner is believed to have coined the term in 1860 with the publication of his text *Elements of Psychophysics.*

Psychophysical explanations for perception of intensity:

- **Weber's law** applies to all senses but only to a limited range of intensities. The law states that a stimulus needs to be increased by a constant fraction of its original value in order to be perceived as noticeably different. This formula is shown as

$$\textbf{K (the constant fraction)} = \frac{\Delta \textbf{I (increase in intensity needed for jnd)}}{\textbf{I (original intensity)}}$$

- **Fechner's law** is built on, and more complicated than, Weber's law. In general, it says that the strength of a stimulus must be significantly increased to produce a slight difference in sensation. The law is written as

S (sensation strength) = k log R (a logarithm of the original intensity)

J. A. Swet's Theory of Signal Detection (TSD) suggests that subjects detect stimuli not only because they can but also because they want to. TSD factors motivation into the picture, which changes the idea of purely mathematical equations and explains why subjects respond inconsistently. Individuals are partly motivated by rewards and costs in detection. This is **response**

bias. The interplay between response bias and stimulus intensity determines responses:

- A **false alarm** is saying that you detect a stimulus that is not there.
- A **hit** is correctly sensing a stimulus.
- A **miss** is failing to detect a present stimulus.
- A **correct rejection** is rightly stating that no stimulus exists.
- **Receiver operating characteristic (ROC)** curves are graphical representations of a subject's sensitivity to a stimulus.

	Response present	Response absent
Stimulus present	Hit	**Miss** (Type II Error: False Negative)
Stimulus absent	**False alarm** (Type I Error: False Positive)	**Correct rejection**

VISION

We see objects because of the light that they reflect. Light is composed of **photons** and **waves** measured by brightness and wavelengths. **Hue** (also known as color) is the dominant wavelength of light. **Brightness** is the physical intensity.

Vision results from the work of many different eye parts:

- The **cornea** is the clear protective coating on the outside of the eye.
- The **lens** is located behind the cornea. **Ciliary muscles** allow it to bend **(accommodate)** in order to focus an image of the outside world onto the retina.
- The **retina,** located on the back of the eye, receives light images from the lens. It is composed of about 132 million photoreceptor cells and of other cell layers that process information.
- **Receptor cells** (rods and cones) on the retina are responsible for sensory transduction (converting the image into an electrical message the brain can understand). This happens through the chemical alteration of **photopigments.**
- **Rods** are particularly sensitive to dim light and are used for night vision. They are also concentrated along the sides of the retina, making them extremely important for peripheral vision.
- **Cones** are concentrated in the center of the retina (in the area called the fovea). The **fovea** is the area of the retina with the greatest **visual acuity**—meaning it is the best at seeing fine details. Cones are particularly sensitive to color and daylight vision. Cones see better than rods because there are fewer cones per ganglion cell than rods per ganglion cell.
- After light passes through the receptors, it travels through the **horizontal cells** to the **bipolar cells** to the **amacrine cells.** Some information processing probably takes place along the way. Finally, the information heads to the **ganglion cells,** which make up the optic nerves.

- The eyes are connected to the cerebral cortex by a visual pathway. This visual pathway consists of one **optic nerve** connecting each eye to the brain. Along the pathway is an **optic chiasm** in which half of the fibers from the optic nerve of each eye cross over and join the optic nerve from the other eye. Thus, the pathways are 50 percent crossed. This ensures that input from each eye will come together for a full picture in the brain. Because of this layout, a stimulus in the left visual field is processed in the right side of the brain, and vice versa. After the optic chiasm, the information travels through the **striate cortex** to the **visual association areas** of the cortex.

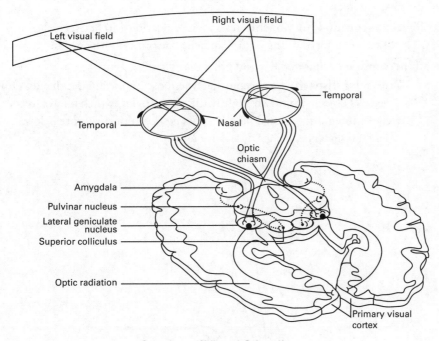

Sensing of Visual Stimuli

Different theories exist for the details of vision:

- **Opponent-color** or **opponent-process** is a theory for color vision proposed by **Ewald Hering.** It suggests that two types of color-sensitive cells exist: cones that respond to blue-yellow colors and cones that respond to red-green. When one color of the pair on a cone is stimulated, the other is inhibited. This is why we don't see reddish-green colors. If an object seems red to us, then our ability to see green in that object is inhibited. This is also why if you look at something red for a long time, and then focus on a white image, you'll see a green **afterimage.**

- The **trichromatic theory** (aka the **component theory**) was proposed by **Thomas Young** and **Hermann von Helmholtz.** This theory suggests that there are three types of receptors in the retina: cones that respond to red, blue, or green.

- Research shows that the **opponent-process theory** seems to be at work in the lateral geniculate body, whereas the **trichromatic theory** seems to be at work in the retina.

- **Lateral inhibition** allows the eye to see contrast and prevents repetitive information from being sent to the brain. This complex process is the idea that once one receptor cell is stimulated, the others nearby are inhibited.

- **David Hubel** and **Torsten Wiesel** discovered that cells in the visual cortex are so complex and specialized that they respond only to certain types of stimuli. For example, some cells respond only to vertical lines, whereas some respond only to right angles, and so on.

VISUAL PERCEPTION

- The **visual field** refers to the entire span that can be perceived or detected by the eye at a given moment.
- The **figure and ground relationship** refers to the relationship between the meaningful part of a picture (the figure) and the background (the ground).
- **Depth perception** has monocular and binocular cues:
  - **Binocular disparity** has been called the most important depth cue. Our eyes view objects from two slightly different angles, which allows us to create a three-dimensional picture. This is shown in the figure below, where d = distance, n = near, and f = far.

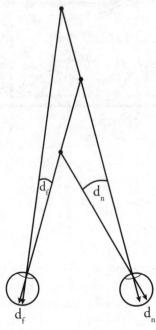

  - **Apparent size** gives us clues about how far away an object is if we know about how big the object should be.

o   **Interposition** or overlap of objects shows which objects are closer. When one object appears to obscure another, the partially covered object is perceived as being farther away due to the interposition effect.

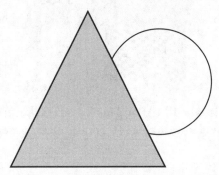

o   **Linear perspective** is gained by features we are familiar with, such as two seemingly parallel lines that converge with distance.

Photo by Ryan Stone, Unsplash.com

o   **Texture gradient** refers to the way we see texture or fine detail differently from different distances. The closer the object, the more coarse and distinct the features appear. More distant objects appear finer and smoother in texture.

o   **Motion parallax** is the way movement is perceived through the displacement of objects over time, and the way this motion takes place at seemingly different paces for nearby or faraway objects. Ships far away seem to move more slowly than nearby ships moving at the same speed.

- **Eleanor Gibson** and **Richard Walk** developed the **visual cliff** apparatus to study whether depth perception is innate. The visual cliff was a thick layer of glass above a surface that dropped off sharply. The glass provided solid, level ground for subjects to move across in spite of the cliff below. Animals and babies were used as subjects, and both groups avoided moving into the "cliff" area regardless of the glass.

Gibson and Walk's visual cliff (A) originated as market testing for glass-bottom boat excursions; **(B)** provided valuable information about depth perception in infants.
Answer: (B).

- **Afterimages**, also known as the **McCollough effect**, are perceived because of **fatigued receptors**. Because our eyes have a partially oppositional system for seeing colors, such as red-green or black-white receptors, once one side is overstimulated and fatigued, it can no longer respond and is overshadowed by its opposite. This explains why you see a dark afterimage after staring at a white light.

- **Dark adaptation** is the result of regeneration of retinal pigment.

- A **mental set** is a framework for assessing a problem and identifying solutions based on our experience: we tend to try what has worked for us in the past. For example, a psychiatrist might be inclined to view symptoms like lethargy and loss of appetite as symptoms of depression, while an oncologist might immediately associate them with cancer.

- **Pragnanz** is the overarching **Gestalt** idea that experience will be organized as meaningful, symmetrical, and simple whenever possible. The following are specific Gestalt ideas:

  o **Closure** is the tendency to complete incomplete figures.

  The Gestalt principle of closure suggests that you will see a rectangle above, not a series of line segments.

o **Proximity** is the tendency to group together items that are near each other.

The Gestalt principle of proximity suggests that you will see one block of dots on the left but two columns of dots on the right.

o **Continuation**, or **good continuation**, is the tendency to create a whole or detailed figures based on our expectations rather than what is seen.

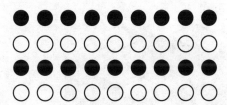

The Gestalt principle of good continuation suggests that you will see the above figure as two intersecting lines, not four line segments.

o **Similarity** is the tendency to group together items that are alike.

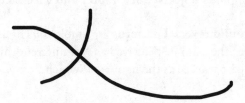

The Gestalt principle of similarity suggests that you will see rows of alternating dots—shaded and unshaded—in the figure above (not one continuous block of dots).

o **Symmetry** is the tendency to group together items that are alike.

o **Constancy** is the tendency of people to perceive objects in the way that they are familiar with them, regardless of changes in the actual retinal image. A book, for example, is perceived as rectangular in shape no matter what angle it is seen from. **Size constancy** is knowing that an elephant, for example, is large no matter how it might appear. **Color constancy** is knowing the color of an object even with tinted glasses on, for example.

o **Minimum principle** is the tendency to see what is easiest or logical to see.

• **Classic illusions:**

  o **Ambiguous figures** can be perceived as two different things depending on how you look at them.

Ambiguous objects: duck/rabbit and vase/faces

  o **Figure-ground reversal patterns** are ambiguous figures, such as the Rubin vase. They can be perceived as two different things depending on which part you see as the figure and which part you see as the background.

  o **Impossible objects** are objects that have been drawn and can be perceived but are geometrically impossible. **Multistability** is when the perception of an object can alternate between two or more possible interpretations, i.e., that our perception of an object flips from one "stable" interpretation to another.

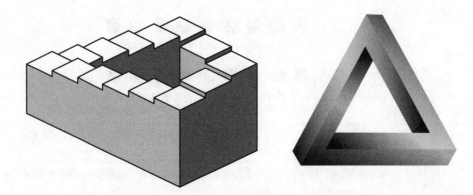

  o The **Moon illusion** shows how context affects perception. The Moon looks larger when we see it on the horizon than when we see it in the sky. This is because the horizon contains visual cues that make the Moon seem more distant than the overhead sky. In the overhead sky, we cannot correct for distance when we perceive the size of the Moon because we have no cues to work with.

o The **phi phenomenon** is the tendency to perceive smooth motion. This explains why motion is inferred when there actually is none, often by the use of flashing lights or rapidly shown still-frame pictures, such as in the perception of cartoons. This is **apparent motion.**

- The **Müller-Lyer illusion** is the most famous of all visual illusions. Two horizontal lines of equal length appear unequal because of the orientation of the arrow marks at the end. Inward facing arrowheads make a line appear shorter than another line of the same length with outward facing arrowheads.

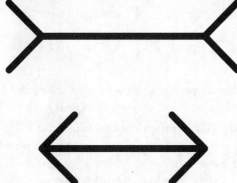

- The **Ponzo illusion** occurs when two horizontal lines of equal length appear unequal because of two vertical lines that slant inward.

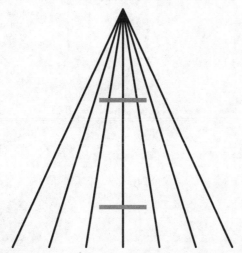

- **Autokinetic effect** is the way that a single point of light viewed in darkness will appear to shake or move. The reason for this is the constant movements of our own eyes.

- **Purkinje shift** is the way that perceived color brightness changes with the level of illumination in the room. With lower levels of illumination, the extremes of the color spectrum (especially red) are seen as less bright.

- **Pattern recognition** is most often explained by **template matching** and **feature detection.** In order to pick the letter o out of a page of letters, we would probably first concentrate only on letters with rounded edges and then look for one to match a typical o.

- **Robert Fantz** found that infants prefer relatively complex and sensical displays.

HEARING

Humans are sensitive to loudness and pitch in sound.

- The **amplitude** or physical intensity of a sound wave largely determines **loudness.**
- **Frequency,** the pace of vibrations or sound waves per second for a particular sound, determines **pitch.** Low frequency is perceived as low pitch or low tone, and vice versa. Frequency is measured in **hertz (Hz),** and humans best hear frequencies around **1,000 Hz.**
- **Timbre** comes from the complexity of the sound wave.

There are three major parts of the ear:

- **Outer ear** consists of the parts that you see called the **pinna** and the **auditory canal.** Vibrations from sound move down this canal to the middle ear.
- **Middle ear** begins with the **tympanic membrane** (also known as the eardrum), which is stretched across the auditory canal. Behind this membrane are the **ossicles** (three small bones), the last of which is the **stapes.** Sound vibrations bump against the tympanic membrane, causing the ossicles to vibrate.

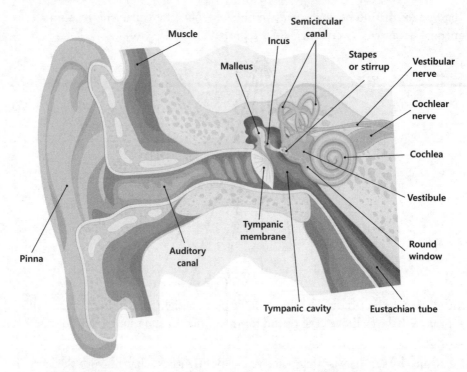

- The **inner ear** is responsible for both hearing and balance. It begins with the **oval window,** which is tapped upon by the stapes. These vibrations then activate the fluid-filled, snail-shell-like **cochlea,** which contain the ear parts for hearing (the **basilar membrane** and the **organ of corti**). The movement of the cochlear fluid activates the hair-cell receptors on the basilar membrane and the organ of corti. This movement on the basilar membrane is called the **traveling wave.** The **vestibular sacs** (which also respond to hair movement) are sensitive to tilt and provide our sense of balance.

- Receptor cells in the inner ear activate nerve cells that change the information into an electrical message the brain can process. The auditory system that leads to the auditory cortex consists of the **olivary nucleus,** the **inferior colliculus,** and the **medial geniculate body.**

Other details:

- **Hermann von Helmholtz** is also famous for the **place-resonance theory** of sound perception, in which different parts of the basilar membrane respond to different frequencies.

- **Sound localization** is achieved in different ways. The degree to which one of our ears hears a sound prior to and more intensely than the other can give us information about the origin of the sound. Specifically, high-frequency sounds are localized by intensity differences, whereas low-frequency sounds are localized by phase differences.

- **Dichotic presentation** is often used in studies of auditory perception and **selective attention.** In these tasks, a subject is presented with a different verbal message in each ear. Often subjects are asked to **shadow,** or repeat, one of the messages to ensure that the other message is not consciously attended to.

OLFACTION

Smell is an extremely primitive sense. Hair receptors in the nostrils send their messages to the **olfactory bulb,** which lies at the base of the brain. Smell has been strongly connected to memory and the perception of taste.

GUSTATION

Humans distinguish five basic tastes: **sweet, bitter, sour, salty,** and the recently discovered **umami,** which means meaty or savory. Most taste receptors lie on the tongue. Saliva mixes with food, so that the flavor can flow easily into the tongue's taste receptors. These taste receptors are called **taste buds** (or **papillae**).

SOMATOSENSES

Somatosenses give us information about the physical body apart from the major sensory organs. They provide sensory data concerning touch, heat, pain, pressure, balance, vibration, orientation, and muscle movement.

Cutaneous/Tactual

Human skin senses touch, pain, cold, and warmth.

- **Free nerve endings** in the skin detect pain and temperature changes.
- **Meissner's corpuscles** are receptors in skin that detect touch or contact.
- **Pacinian corpuscles** are touch receptors that respond quickly to displacements of skin.
- The size of the **two-point threshold** for touch is largely determined by the density and layout of nerves in the skin.
- **Physiological zero** is the temperature that is sensed as neither warm nor cold.
- **Ronald Melzack and Patrick Wall's Gate Control Theory of Pain** looks at pain as a process rather than just a simple sensation governed in one center in the brain. Melzack and Wall assert that pain perception is related to the interaction of large and small nerve fibers that run to and from the spine. Pain may or may not be perceived depending on different factors, including cognition.
- **Phantom limb pain** occurs when amputees feel sensations of pain in limbs that have been amputated and no longer exist.
- **Endorphins** are neuromodulators that kick in to reduce or eliminate the perception of pain.
- The **orienting reflex** is the tendency to turn toward an object that has touched you.

THE VESTIBULAR SENSE

The **vestibular sense** allows us to orient ourselves in space and maintain balance. The main components are found in the inner ear in the **vestibular labyrinth,** a series of interconnected structures continuous with the cochlea. The vestibular labyrinth contains three tubes called **semicircular canals,** which detect head motion and help to maintain equilibrium.

THE KINESTHETIC SENSE

The **kinesthetic sense** involves awareness of the body's movement. **Spindles,** which are tiny receptors in the muscles throughout the body, provide "muscle memory," allowing us to sense how our limbs are moving in space without visual confirmation. A related concept is **proprioception,** which refers to the cognitive awareness of where our bodies are in space at any given time.

Kinesthetic sensation and proprioception are closely related concepts but are not the same. Proprioception deals with sensing one's own bodily *position* in space, while kinesthetic sensation deals more with bodily *movement*. The latter has more of a *behavioral* component: kinesthetic sensation is what allows us to learn complex physical actions such as performing a dance routine or effectively swinging a baseball bat.

ATTENTION

Selective attention is the process of tuning in to something specific (such as what your date is saying) while ignoring all of the other stimuli in the background (such as the conversation that the people at the table next to you are having about a funny television show).

- Models of selective attention:
    - The **spotlight model** suggests that humans focus on one particular task while all the other tasks remain in the background until the spotlight focuses on a different task. **William James** described this, saying attention has a **focus, fringe,** and a **margin.** The focus is the primary area attended to, the fringe is on the periphery, and the margin is the limit.

    - **Donald Broadbent's filter model of attention** says that any information not attended to is filtered out and decays. This theory is meant to explain why we are not constantly bombarded with sensory inputs. The sensory input goes from our sensory stores through a selective filter, which blocks unattended messages. Only the information attended to makes it into our working memory.

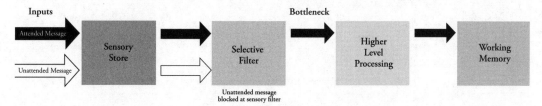

    - **Anne Treisman's attenuation model of attention** altered Broadbent's model to account for phenomena such as the **cocktail party effect,** in which a person involved in a conversation can detect their name or something equally salient from across a crowded room. Treisman said that sensory input flows into our sensory stores, as in Broadbent's model, but instead of going through a selective filter, the information goes through an attenuating filter, turning the volume down or up on the information. Rather than decaying, the unattended information still goes through higher level processing and into working memory, so it is available on this other channel if need be.

    - **Divided attention,** or **multitasking,** occurs when a person's attention is split among multiple tasks, such as reading a book while listening to music, or doing homework while watching television. Research on divided attention shows that when people multitask, they are more likely to make mistakes and/or move more slowly through their task because of the enormous **cognitive load**, the amount of mental effort involved. The **resource model of attention** addresses this issue, suggesting humans have a limited amount of attention at any given time.

Study Tip

Dress appropriately when going to take the GRE Psychology Test. Being too warm causes people to feel sleepy and too relaxed. It's always a good idea to wear layers. Also, rumor has it that wearing certain scents, such as peppermint and rosemary, can enhance attention and concentration.

OTHER IMPORTANT TERMS IN SENSATION AND PERCEPTION

- **Simulations** use perceptual cues to make artificial situations seem real.
- **Subliminal perception** is the perceiving of a stimulus that one is not consciously aware of, such as the unattended message in dichotic presentation or visual information that is briefly presented.
- **Osmoreceptors** deal with thirst.

Chapter 4
Physiological and Behavioral Neuroscience

This chapter discusses the basic concepts concerning physiological and behavioral neuroscience. It covers neurons and neural transmission, the nervous system, the endocrine system, and the essential processes associated with the sleep cycle.

DEFINED: **Physiological psychology is the study of the essential biology involved in the study of the mind.** The GRE Psychology Test favors questions about the nervous system, the brain, and neural activity.

THE NERVOUS SYSTEM: BIG PICTURE

- **Central nervous system (CNS).** The CNS is made up of two parts:
  - brain
  - spinal cord
- **Peripheral nervous system (PNS).** The pathway that runs to and from the CNS. **Afferent** fibers run toward the CNS, and **efferent** fibers run away from the CNS (remember afferent is like affect, which means feel, so it goes toward the CNS, and efferent is like effect, so it goes away from the CNS to cause the effect the brain wants). The PNS is made up of two parts:

  - **Somatic nervous system** interacts with the external environment by controlling voluntary movements of striated muscles.

  - **Autonomic nervous system (ANS)** interacts with the internal environment and is responsible for the "fight or flight" response. It controls the involuntary functions including movement of smooth muscles, digestion, blood circulation, and breathing. The ANS has two parts:

    - **Sympathetic nervous system** controls arousal mechanisms such as blood circulation, pupil dilation, and threat and fear response. Lie detector tests rely on the premise that lying activates the sympathetic nervous system and causes things like an increase in heart rate, blood pressure, and respiration.

    - **Parasympathetic nervous system** is responsible for recuperation after arousal by doing things like lowering heart rate, blood pressure, and respiration.

THE SPINAL CORD

The spine consists of an inner core of gray matter (cell bodies and dendrites) and an outer covering of **white matter** (nerve fibers, axon bundles, and myelin sheathing) that go to and from the brain.

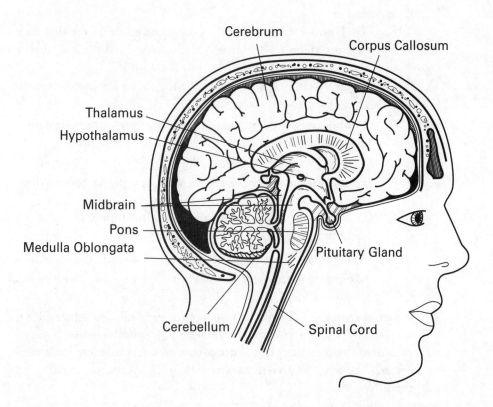

Labels: Cerebrum · Corpus Callosum · Thalamus · Hypothalamus · Midbrain · Pons · Medulla Oblongata · Pituitary Gland · Cerebellum · Spinal Cord

THE BRAIN

The brain, which is an extension of the spine, has evolved over time and through species. In general, the brain has developed from the base to the front. You should learn the separate parts of the brain in the general evolutionary order.

- **Hindbrain**
  - **Myelencephalon** (aka the medulla)—Mainly controls reflexes but also controls sleep, attention, and movement.
  - **Metencephalon**—Contains the pons (connects brain parts to spine) and cerebellum (controls muscle coordination, balance, and posture).
  - **Reticular formation** (The base is located in the hindbrain, and the rest is located in the midbrain. The functions of the reticular formation are similar in both locations.)—Considered the **oldest part** of the brain; controls alertness, thirst, sleep, and involuntary muscles such as the heart.

- **Mesencephalon (midbrain)**
  - **Tectum**—Controls vision and hearing.
  - **Tegmentum**—Houses the rest of the reticular formation. It is also involved in the sensorimotor system, and the analgesic effect of opiates.

- **Forebrain**—Can be divided into diencephalon (thalamus and hypothalamus) and telencephalon (essentially the rest of the forebrain).
  - **Corticospinal tract**—Connections between brain and spine.

- o **Diencephalon**
  - **Thalamus**—Channels sensory information to the cerebral cortex.
  - **Hypothalamus**—Controls ANS biological motivations, such as hunger and thirst, and the pituitary gland.
- o **Pituitary gland**—The "master gland" of the endocrine/hormone system.
- o **Telencephalon**
  - **Limbic system**—A group of structures around the brainstem involved in the four F's (fleeing, feeding, fighting, and fornicating—to be polite).
  - **Hippocampus**—Involved in memory, specifically transferring short-term memory into long-term memory. Recent research indicates that new neurons can form in the hippocampus of the adult mammalian brain.
  - **Amygdala**—Controls emotional reactions such as fear and anger.
  - **Cingulate gyrus**—Links areas in the brain dealing with emotion and decisions.
- o **Cerebral cortex**—The outer half-inch of the cerebral hemispheres. It's the seat of sensory and intellectual functions and is split into lobes. Ninety percent of the cerebral cortex is **neocortex** (new in evolution, six-layered cortex). The other 10 percent has fewer than six layers and is more primitive.
  - **Frontal lobe**—Controls speech, reasoning, and problem solving. Houses Broca's area for speech.
  - **Occipital lobe**—Responsible for vision.
  - **Parietal lobe**—Responsible for the somatosensory system.
  - **Temporal lobe**—Responsible for hearing. Also includes Wernicke's area, which is related to speech.
  - **Gyri** (bumps) and sulci (fissures) are seen on the cortex surface.

Other Important Terms Related to the Brain

- **Meninges** are tough connective tissues that cover and protect the brain and spinal cord.
- The **blood-brain barrier** protects the brain by making it extremely difficult for toxic substances to pass from the blood into the brain, since the cells that make up the blood vessels in the brain are very tightly packed.
- **Ventricles** are chambers filled with cerebrospinal fluid that insulate the brain from shock.
- **Superior colliculus** (controls visual reflexes) and **inferior colliculus** (controls auditory reflexes) appear as bumps on the brainstem.
- **Basal ganglia** control large, voluntary muscle movements. Their degeneration is related to motor dysfunction in Parkinson's and Huntington's diseases.
- **Cortical association areas** are areas on the cortex that correspond to certain functions. The larger the area, the more sensitive and highly accessed is the corresponding function. Damage to particular areas results in the loss of specific abilities.

Brain Damage

Damage to certain areas of the brain produces specific types of dysfunction. The following are notable conditions that result from disease or injury to the brain.

- **Aphasia** is the loss of the ability to speak or understand language in spoken or written form. **Broca's aphasia** is caused by damage to **Broca's area** of the brain, which is located in the left frontal lobe. Someone with Broca's aphasia can understand speech but has difficulty speaking (often speaking slowly and laboriously and omitting words). **Wernicke's aphasia** is caused by damage to **Wernicke's area** of the brain, which is located in the left temporal lobe. Someone with Wernicke's aphasia can speak but no longer understands how to correctly choose words. The person's speech is fluent but nonsensical.

- **Agraphia** is the loss of the capacity to write due to problems with language processing, an inability to spell, disruption of motor functions or visualization skills that prevent the physical act of writing, or a combination of any of these. A dozen areas of the brain are associated with writing and the type of **agraphia** depends on which area is affected. Damage to the language areas of the brain, such as Broca's and Wernicke's areas, results in **phonological agraphia** in which the individual cannot write due to an inability to sound out words.

- **Alexia** is the loss of the capacity to read due to an inability to comprehend written words, read aloud, or both. It is an acquired reading disorder, distinguishable from learning disabilities such as developmental dyslexia. It is often associated with damage to the left angular gyrus.

- **Acquired apraxia** is the inability to plan and coordinate specific motor movements (e.g., walking, speaking, moving one's extremities), depending upon which particular ability or area of the body is affected. This inability is due to brain injury (specifically, injury to the posterior parietal cortex), not to any other physical injury or abnormality that would also impair that function. Individuals with acquired apraxia cannot perform certain learned purposeful movements on command.

- **Agnosia** involves an inability to process sensory information even though the sensory apparatus is intact. It usually involves damage to the occipital or parietal lobe. Only one sense, such as speech, vision, etc., is generally affected. **Prosopagnosia** is a specific type of **visual agnosia** in which the individual cannot recognize faces, even those of family and close friends.

The book *The Man Who Mistook His Wife for a HAT and Other Clinical Tales*, by Oliver Sacks, M.D., derives its title from a famous case of a patient with visual agnosia. "Dr. P." could recognize neither faces nor familiar objects, despite having normal vision. When getting up to leave after consulting with Dr. Sacks, "Dr. P." famously grabbed his wife's head instead of his hat!

Chronic Concussion and Damage to the Brain

The brain can sustain serious irreversible damage even when the injury appears extremely minor or goes undetected. Repeated blows to the head, such as occur in sports like football and boxing, can result in a progressive form of brain degeneration known as **Chronic Traumatic Encephalopathy** (CTE). For those who develop this condition, multiple **concussions** (mild traumatic brain injuries), even ones that don't cause unconsciousness, eventually induce dementia-like symptoms that mimic those seen in Alzheimer's and Parkinson's diseases.

Instruments of Measurement for the Brain

- **Functional magnetic resonance imaging (fMRI)** measures oxygen flow in different areas of the brain. It is used most frequently in cognitive psychology research to measure activity in different brain regions during certain tasks.
- **Positron emission tomography (PET)** scans glucose metabolism to measure activity in various brain regions.
- **Stereotaxic instruments** are used to implant electrodes into animals' brains in experiments.

THE NEURON

The **neuron** is the basic unit of the nervous system and has various parts:

- **Dendrites** are neuron branches that receive impulses. Their branching patterns change throughout life.
- The **cell body,** also known as **soma,** is the largest central portion and makes up **gray matter.** It has a **nucleus** that directs the neuron's activity.
- The **axon hillock** is where the soma and the axon connect.
- The **axon** transmits impulses of the neuron. Bundles of these are nerve fibers, also known as **white matter.** The wider a nerve fiber, the faster its conduction of impulses.
- The **myelin sheath** is a fatty, insulating sheath on some axons that allows faster conduction of axon impulses. It looks like beads on a string.
- The **nodes of Ranvier** are the dips between the "beads" on the myelin sheath. They help send the impulse down the axon.
- **Terminal buttons** are the jumping-off points for impulses. They contain **synaptic vessels** that hold **neurotransmitters** (chemicals that stimulate nearby cells).
- The **cell membrane** covers the whole neuron and has selective permeability. Sometimes it lets positive charges (**ions**) through.
- A **synapse,** or **synaptic gap,** is the space between two neurons where they communicate:
  - The **presynaptic cell** is the end of one neuron (the terminal buttons).
  - The **postsynaptic cell** is the beginning of another neuron (the dendrites).
- **Glial cells** are the other type of cell in the nervous system. They mainly help to support neurons. There are multiple types of glial cells, two of which are listed below.
  - **Oligodendrocytes** provide myelin in the central nervous system.
  - **Schwann cells** provide myelin in the peripheral nervous system.

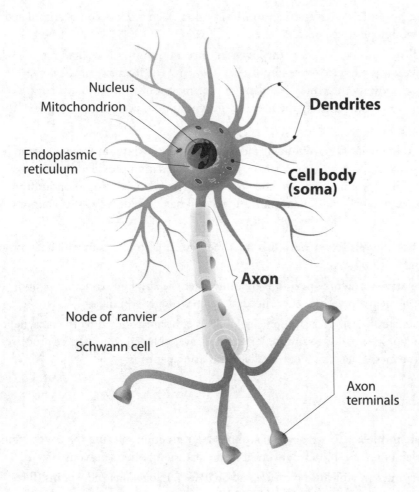

Nucleus

Mitochondrion

Dendrites

Endoplasmic
reticulum

**Cell body
(soma)**

Axon

Node of ranvier

Schwann cell

Axon
terminals

Neural Transmission

Neurons communicate with each other through these steps:

1. **Resting potential** is the inactivated state of a neuron. The neuron is negatively charged at this point, and the cell membrane does not let positive charges (**ions**) in.

2. A **presynaptic cell** fires and releases neurotransmitters from its terminal buttons as a messenger to other neurons.

3. **Postsynaptic receptors** in the **postsynaptic cell** detect the presence of neurotransmitters and cause the ion channels to open.

4. **Postsynaptic potentials** are changes in a nerve cell's charge as the result of stimulation. There are two forms:

    *   **Excitatory postsynaptic potential (EPSP).** In this case, positive charges from the outside are allowed into the cell in a process called **depolarization.** They increase the chance that a cell will fire.

    *   **Inhibitory postsynaptic potential (IPSP).** In this case, the few positive charges in the cell body are let out, and the cell becomes **hyperpolarized** (or even more negative compared to the outside). They decrease the chance that a cell will fire.

5. **Action potential,** or the **nerve impulse,** begins when a cell becomes stimulated with enough positive ions and "fires."

6. The **all-or-none law** refers to the fact that once a minimum threshold for stimulation is met, the nerve impulse will be sent. The intensity of the nerve impulse is always the same, regardless of the amount of stimulation. Intensity of stimulation is indicated by the number of signals fired, not by the strength of the signals.

7. The action potential travels down the axon, frequently "jumping" from one node of Ranvier to the next because of the increased insulation provided by the myelin sheath (this jumping from one node to the next is called **saltatory conduction**). At the terminal buttons, neurotransmitters will be released. Now, this neuron is the presynaptic cell for the next connection.

8. **The absolute refractory period** is the time after a neuron fires in which it cannot respond to stimulation.

9. **The relative refractory period** is the time after the absolute refractory period when the neuron can fire, but it needs a much stronger stimulus.

10. After a neurotransmitter has done its job, it is either reabsorbed by the presynaptic cell in a process called **reuptake,** or it is deactivated by enzymes. These processes keep the messenger from continually stimulating neurons.

Some important neurotransmitters:

- **Acetylcholine** is released at the neuromuscular junction to cause the contraction of skeletal muscles. It is also involved in the parasympathetic nervous system.

- **Endorphins** are linked to pleasure and analgesia. Exogenous endorphins (like morphine or heroin) are highly addictive.

- **Monoamines** comprise two classes of neurotransmitters:
  - Indolamines, which include **serotonin.** A lack of serotonin is linked to depression.
  - Catecholamines, which include **dopamine.** Too little dopamine is associated with Parkinson's disease, and too much dopamine is associated with schizophrenia (see Chapter 12, Clinical Psychology and Psychological Disorders). Dopamine is also involved in feelings of reward, and it is therefore linked to addiction.

- **Amino acids** are frequently present in fast-acting, directed synapses. Two important amino acids are:
  - **Glutamate** is the most abundant excitatory neurotransmitter in the nervous system.
  - **Gamma-aminobutyric acid (GABA)** is the most abundant inhibitory transmitter in the nervous system.

- Most drugs used in psychology, as well as recreational drugs like cocaine, alter the transmission of neurotransmitters.

- **Neuromodulators** are like neurotransmitters, but they cause long-term changes in the postsynaptic cell.

- **Agonists** of a specific neurotransmitter increase the effects of that neurotransmitter. For example, selective serotonin reuptake inhibitors (SSRIs), which are used to treat depression, increase serotonin activity.

- **Antagonists** decrease the effects of a specific neurotransmitter. Botox is an acetylcholine antagonist that decreases muscle activity where it's administered.

THE ENDOCRINE SYSTEM

The **pituitary gland,** which is controlled by the hypothalamus, is involved in the regulation of hormones in the body. Hormones have numerous effects throughout life, which are characterized as either organizational or activational.

- **Organizational**
    - The presence of **H-Y antigen** during development causes a fetus to develop into a male (the absence causes the fetus to develop into a female).
    - The increase in the release of **androgens** (i.e., testosterone) in males and **estrogen** in females during puberty causes the genitals to mature and secondary sex characteristics to develop (i.e., facial hair, breast development, etc.).
    - In females **menarche,** the onset of the menstrual cycle, occurs during puberty.
- **Activational**
    - The female menstrual cycle is associated with changes in hormone levels throughout the month, specifically estradiol, progesterone, **luteinizing hormone (LH),** and **follicle stimulating hormone (FSH).**
    - LH and FSH regulate the development of ovum and trigger ovulation (the release of an egg cell) in females. In males LH and FSH regulate the development of sperm cells and the production of testosterone.
    - **Oxytocin** is released from the pituitary and facilitates birth and breast feeding. It is also involved in pair bonding (i.e., a mother to child or romantic partners).
- Other important hormones released from the pituitary
    - **Vasopressin** helps to regulate water levels in the body and therefore also helps to regulate blood pressure.
    - **Thyroid stimulating hormone** activates the thyroid.
    - **Adrenocorticotropic hormone (ACTH)** is a stress hormone that increases the production of androgens and cortisol.

SLEEP

Electroencephalograms (EEGs) measure brain-wave patterns and have made it possible to study waking and sleeping states. Sleep has two distinct components.

- **Non-REM** (Rapid Eye Movement) sleep.

  o **Stage W:** The Wake Stage is recorded when the brain is producing more than 50 percent of **alpha waves** (about 7–14 Hz). When the eyes are opening and closing, the brain is producing both **beta** (15–30 Hz) and alpha waves. When the eyes are closed, the brain is producing primarily alpha waves.

  o **Stage N1:** Stage N1 (the first stage of NREM sleep) occurs as the person is transitioning into sleep. This stage consists primarily of **theta waves** (4–7 Hz) and lasts about 1–7 minutes.

  o **Stage N2:** Stage N2 is characterized by both theta waves as well as episodes of alternations between **sleep spindles** and **K complexes.** This is the stage during which physiological functions including heart rate and respiration begin to slow, and temperature begins to drop.

  o **Stage N3:** Stage N3 sleep is characterized by a predominance of slow **delta waves** (up to 4 Hz). This stage is the deep restorative sleep, where growth hormones are secreted. It is also where most **parasomnias** occur. It also has the largest arousal threshold—if you wake a person in N3 sleep, they will usually appear confused or disoriented.

- **Stage R:** Stage R is **Rapid Eye Movement (REM)** sleep. It occurs about 90–110 minutes after sleep onset and comprises about 20-25 percent of sleep time over the course of the night. Brain waves during this stage are small and irregular, while the eyes are displaying quick bursts of activity (hence the name). Stage R sleep is also known as **paradoxical sleep,** as a person's physiological signs resemble wakefulness but the voluntary muscles are essentially reduced to the point of paralysis. The **rebound effect** occurs when people are deprived of Stage R sleep and will compensate for it by spending more time in Stage R sleep later in the night. This is the stage where dreams and nightmares occur.

Study Tip

Don't burn out on studying. Though you need a consistently diligent study regimen, taking time off can be important. When you feel really saturated, or the test begins to take on too much of a negative twist, rebel with some time off.

People complete four to six complete sleep cycles each night. Altogether, it takes about 90–110 minutes to complete one entire sleep cycle. Early in the night, most of the time is spent in Stage N3. Stages N2 and R sleep predominate later on in the night.

- An infant sleeps about 16 hours a day, in contrast to an elderly person who sleeps only about six hours.

- While Stage R sleep comprises about half of total sleep at birth, it eventually decreases to only 25 percent.

Circadian rhythms are cyclical bodily, mental, and behavioral changes that greatly affect our sleep patterns. Inside the hypothalamus is the **suprachiasmatic nucleus (SCN),** a biological "master clock" composed of thousands of neurons that secrete **melatonin,** a hormone that makes us sleepy. The SCN gets direct input from the eyes and secretes more melatonin when it is dark and less when it is light. This produces a circadian rhythm in which the body needs to remain awake during the day and sleep at night for optimal performance and functioning. When this rhythm is disturbed, as with people who routinely work nights, adverse physical and psychological effects can occur.

Jet lag **(desynchronosis)** and its negative effects occur as the result of disrupted circadian rhythms. When we travel from one time zone to another, our bodies remain stuck in the previous zone for a few days until we adjust to the change, causing symptoms such as fatigue, nausea, and irritability. It might be 10:00 P.M. in France but our bodies still think we're in California (where it's only 1:00 P.M. and nowhere near bedtime).

OTHER STATES OF CONSCIOUSNESS

Drug-Induced States

Psychoactive drugs alter the mental processes of the user by affecting neurotransmitter activity. They can do so by increasing or decreasing the amount of a neurotransmitter released at the synapse, preventing neurotransmitter reuptake by presynaptic cells, or by affecting the receptors on postsynaptic cells. Recreational drugs generally fall into one of four categories, each of which affects the brain differently:

- **Hallucinogens** (e.g., Lysergic acid diethylamide (LSD), mescaline) cause distortions in perception and thinking that can closely resemble psychosis. They produce hallucinations (most notably visual and auditory), intensified feelings, and an altered sense of time.

- **Stimulants** (e.g., caffeine, methamphetamine, cocaine) stimulate the central nervous system. They cause euphoria, increased energy and alertness, and a heightened sense of pleasure.

- **Sedatives** (e.g., alcohol, barbiturates, Xanax) slow down the central nervous system. They cause euphoria, relaxation, and loss of inhibition.

- **Narcotics** (e.g., heroin, oxycodone) reduce or eliminate pain. They cause euphoria, relaxation, and drowsiness.

The effect that a drug has depends also on the circumstances under which it is used. The emotional, psychological, and physical states of the user are important, as are his or her experience with that substance and resultant expectations about what the drug will do.

Hypnosis

Hypnosis is a trancelike state in which the individual is highly suggestible. It is artificially induced by a hypnotist who encourages sleepiness and focuses on the sensations the subject should be experiencing as relaxation progresses. Hypnosis is, however, distinct from sleep, as the brain waves do not follow the same reliable pattern. Some individuals are more easily hypnotized than others, and some cannot be hypnotized at all. For those who can, the technique can be used to treat various psychological and medical problems and has shown to be effective in controlling pain. A **posthypnotic suggestion** involves instructing the individual while in the trance to act in a certain way after recovery from the hypnotic state (e.g., to have an aversion to smoking cigarettes). Contrary to popular misconceptions, however, a hypnotic subject cannot be forced to act against his or her will, nor be made to behave in a way that violates his or her moral code.

Meditation

Meditation refers to a variety of techniques, many of which have been practiced for thousands of years, and which usually involve the training of attention and awareness. Meditators may focus intensely on one object of attention, such as their breathing, or they may broaden their attention and be aware of multiple stimuli, such as anything in their auditory field. Meditation has been utilized successfully to manage pain, stress, and anxiety disorders. **Mindfulness-based stress reduction (MBSR)** is a protocol commonly used in the medical setting to help alleviate stress. Meditators have increased alpha and theta waves while they are meditating (and to some extent an increase above baseline after they stop), with more experienced meditators showing greater improvements.

Chapter 5
Learning

This chapter discusses the basic concepts concerning behaviorist learning theories (including associative learning (classical and operant conditioning) as well as nonassociative learning), observational learning, insight and latent learning, as well as other cognitive theories of learning. This chapter also discusses motivation and performance as well as educational psychology.

DEFINED: Learning is the relatively permanent or stable change in behavior as the result of experience.

BEHAVIORIST THEORIES

Associative Learning: Classical Conditioning

Classical conditioning is one of psychology's most famous learning principles. **Ivan Pavlov,** who first gained fame winning a Nobel Prize for work on digestion, stumbled onto the concept now known as classical conditioning while doing further work investigating dogs and digestion. Classical conditioning, pioneered by Pavlov, is often called **Pavlovian conditioning.** This type of conditioning involves pairing a neutral stimulus with a not-so-neutral stimulus; this creates a relationship between the two. As discussed above, Pavlov noticed that his dogs salivated when they heard the footsteps of his assistant. To test his theory that the dogs had inferred a relationship from these temporal events, Pavlov attempted to teach his dogs to salivate to an even more neutral stimulus: a light or a bell. In order to set up a relationship between food and a particular light, Pavlov arranged for a certain light (or bell) to be turned on (or rung) just prior to the dogs' being fed. After consistent pairings of these two stimuli (the neutral stimulus of the light or bell and the unconditioned stimulus of the food), the dogs would salivate in the presence of either. Of course, food still elicited saliva, but more importantly, the dogs began to salivate even when just the light was turned on or the bell was rung.

Classical conditioning is pretty easy to understand, but unfortunately, all of the vocabulary is not. Classical conditioning lingo is both important and plentiful on the GRE Psychology Test. These following five concepts are crucial.

Unconditioned Stimulus (UCS)

The not-so-neutral stimulus. In Pavlov's dog experiments, the UCS is the food. Without conditioning, the stimulus elicits the response of salivating.

Unconditioned Response (UCR)

The naturally occurring response to the UCS. For Pavlov's dogs, it was salivation in response to the food. The UCS and UCR are called unconditioned because they do not have to be learned. Often they are reflexive or instinctual behaviors.

Neutral Stimulus (NS)

A stimulus that does not produce a specific response on its own. In Pavlov's experiments, this was the light or bell before he conditioned a response to it.

Conditioned Stimulus (CS)

The neutral stimulus once it has been paired with the UCS. The CS has no naturally occurring response, but it is conditioned through pairings with a UCS. In classical conditioning, a CS (the light) is paired with a UCS (food), so that the CS alone will produce a response.

Conditioned Response (CR)

The response that the CS elicits after conditioning. The UCR and the CR are the same (salivating to food or a light, for example).

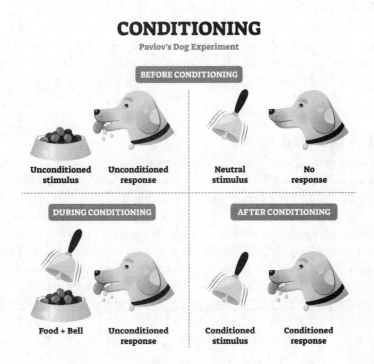

CONDITIONING

Pavlov's Dog Experiment

BEFORE CONDITIONING

| Unconditioned stimulus | Unconditioned response | Neutral stimulus | No response |

DURING CONDITIONING | **AFTER CONDITIONING**

| Food + Bell | Unconditioned response | Conditioned stimulus | Conditioned response |

Next, we have a barrage of words that relate to the different orders and ways in which one could present the UCS and CS within classical conditioning.

Simultaneous Conditioning

The UCS and NS are presented at the same time.

Higher-Order Conditioning/Second-Order Conditioning

A conditioning technique in which a previous CS now acts as a UCS. Using Pavlov's dogs as an example, for higher order conditioning the experimenter would use the light as a UCS after the light reliably elicited saliva in the dogs. Food would no longer be used in the experiment, but now the light would be the UCS. The light could be paired with a bell (CS) until the bell alone elicited saliva in the dogs.

Forward Conditioning

Pairing of the NS and the UCS in which the NS is presented before the UCS. Two types of forward conditioning are delayed conditioning and trace conditioning:

- **Delayed conditioning.** The presentation of the NS begins before that of the UCS and lasts until the UCS is presented.
- **Trace conditioning.** The NS stimulus is presented and terminated before the UCS is presented.

Backward Conditioning

The NS is presented after the UCS is presented. For Pavlov's dogs, they would have been presented with the food and then with the light. Backward conditioning has proven to be ineffective. In fact, it accomplishes only **inhibitory conditioning,** which means that later the dogs would have a harder time pairing the light and the food even if they were presented in a forward fashion.

Taste Aversion Learning

Taste aversion learning is a special type of classical conditioning. It occurs when food or drink becomes associated with an aversive stimulus such as nausea or vomiting, even if the food or drink itself did not actually cause the nausea or vomiting. It differs from traditional classical conditioning in two important ways: 1) the response usually takes one pairing (think about when you got food poisoning!) as opposed to the longer acquisition periods required in other types of classical conditioning, and 2) the response takes a very long time to extinguish, if it ever does. In regular classical conditioning, the extinction period begins as soon as you remove the unconditioned stimulus. Taste aversion learning is thought to be evolutionarily adaptive and appears in many species in order to ensure that the human or animal does not eat poisonous food and die.

Other Early Behaviorist Theories

- **E. L. Thorndike** suggested the **law of effect,** which was the precursor of operant conditioning. The law of effect postulated a cause-and-effect chain of behavior revolving around reinforcement. Individuals do what rewards them and stop doing what doesn't bring some reward.
  - Thorndike called his theory **"connectionism"** because he believed learning occurs through the formation of connections between stimuli and responses. His famous **"Puzzle Box"** experiment showed that cats can learn complex tasks through trial and error. When the cat made a correct move, what Thorndike would call a "satisfying response," the connection was "stamped" in, and the cat solved the puzzle faster in the next trials.

- **Kurt Lewin** developed the **theory of association,** which was a forerunner of behaviorism. Association is grouping things together based on the fact that they occur together in time and space. Organisms associate certain behaviors with certain rewards and certain cues with certain situations. This idea is basically what Ivan Pavlov later proved experimentally. (See also Chapter 9, Social Psychology.)

- **John B. Watson** expanded the ideas of Pavlov and founded the **school of behaviorism.** Watson's idea of learning, like his idea of all behavior, was that everything could be explained by stimulus-response chains and that conditioning was the key factor in developing these chains. Only objective and observable elements were of importance to organisms and to psychology.

- **Clark Hull** created a **hypothetico-deductive model** designed to try to deduce logically all the rules that govern behavior. He created an equation involving not only input variables leading to output variables, but also included intervening variables in between that would change the outcomes.

- **Radical behaviorism** is the school of thought where it is believed that all behavior, animal and human, can be explained in terms of stimuli and responses, or reinforcements and punishments. It makes no allowances for how thoughts or feelings might factor into the equation.

> Watson is possibly most famous for his "Little Albert" experiment, in which he conditioned a fear response in an 11-month-old boy. Watson believed that anyone could be conditioned to do anything given the right circumstances. For more on this experiment, see Chapter 10, Developmental Psychology.

Associative Learning: Operant Conditioning

B. F. Skinner conducted the first scientific experiments to prove the concepts in Thorndike's law of effect and in Watson's idea of the causes and effects of behavior. This idea of behavior being influenced primarily by reinforcement is now called **operant conditioning.** Skinner practically created the now classic stereotype of psychological study; he used rats and pigeons and a device that he created called the **Skinner box.** Experimentally, Skinner proved that animals are influenced by reinforcement. Later, Skinner went even further in his famous books *Walden Two* and *Beyond Freedom and Dignity* by discussing the control of human behavior rather than rat behavior.

Skinner's operant conditioning, also called **instrumental conditioning,** aims to influence a response through various reinforcement strategies. Basically, it's the idea that we do what reaps rewards and don't do things that don't reap rewards. Skinner is most famous for his initial studies, in which he used rats or pigeons and his device, the Skinner box. This box was essentially bare on the inside except for a lever and a hole through which food pellets were inserted. The floor had an electrified grid. Though many different reinforcement schedules were used, the basic idea is that the rats repeated behaviors that won them rewards and gave up on behaviors that did not.

In Skinner's experiments, the goal was to condition the rats or pigeons to perform an unnatural behavior: pressing the lever in the Skinner box. The plan was to accomplish this through reinforcement of such behavior. The first problem was getting the rats to press the lever.

Through a process called **shaping,** the experimenter rewarded the rats (with food pellets) for even being near the lever and then rewarded them again for touching the lever. The rats were rewarded for behaviors that brought them closer and closer to actually pressing the bar. Thus, another term for shaping is the **differential reinforcement of successive approximations.** Eventually, this led the rats to the desired behavior of pressing the bar. At that point, only bar pressing was rewarded. These rats were successfully operantly conditioned.

Skinner and others since have tested various reinforcement strategies. Here's some operant vocabulary that you should know.

Primary Reinforcement

A natural reinforcement; something that is reinforcing on its own without the requirement of learning. Food is a primary reinforcer.

Secondary Reinforcement

A learned reinforcer. Money is the perfect example. Every day, we work to be rewarded with money, but for someone on a desert island, money would do very little. Secondary reinforcements are often learned through society. Other examples of secondary reinforcements are prestige, verbal praise, or awards. They are also instrumental in token economies (see page 58).

Positive Reinforcement

Adding something desirable to increase the likelihood of a particular response. Rewarding a dog with a treat stimulates the response of obeying in the future. Some subjects are not motivated by rewards because they don't believe or understand that the rewards will be given.

Negative Reinforcement

Negative reinforcement is not punishment. It is not the delivery of a negative consequence. Rather, it is reinforcement through the *removal of a negative event*—i.e., taking away something undesirable to increase the likelihood of a particular behavior. If a monkey in a cage were subjected to a blaring noise at all times, except when the monkey rode a tricycle, the monkey would learn to ride the tricycle more often in order to stop the noise. So negative reinforcement and positive reinforcement both aim to increase the likelihood of a behavior, but positive reinforcement works by giving someone something that he or she likes, while negative reinforcement works by taking away something that he or she dislikes.

Continuous Reinforcement Schedule

In this schedule, every correct response is met with some form of reinforcement. This type of reinforcement strategy facilitates the quickest learning, but also the most fragile learning; as soon as the rewards stop coming, the animal stops performing.

Partial Reinforcement Schedules

In these schedules, not all correct responses are met with reinforcement. These strategies may require a longer learning time, but once learned, these behaviors are more resistant to extinction. There are four distinct types of partial reinforcement schedules:

1. **Fixed ratio schedule.** In this schedule, a reinforcement is delivered after a consistent number of responses. If the ratio is 6:1, after every 6 correct responses, there is a reward. The power of drug addiction has been proven using this schedule. Drug-addicted rats in a Skinner box-type apparatus will press a bar vigorously and consistently upon discovering that after every few pressings a drug is delivered. Because the rat has to perform the behavior in order to receive the reward, the rat will learn, but there is a small pause after the reinforcement (a satiated rat is not so interested in a food pellet) thought to be analogous to procrastination.

2. **Variable ratio schedule.** In this schedule, the learning is less likely to become extinguished. A variable ratio is different from a fixed ratio schedule in that reinforcements are delivered after different numbers of correct responses. The ratio cannot be predicted. Slot machines are the perfect example of this strategy. The gambler is rewarded every so often, but there is no way to tell if the reward is only one coin away or two days away. Las Vegas was built on the variable ratio strategy. The learning is very powerful with this schedule as the gambler continues to perform the behavior not because the behavior has been rewarded but rather that they know the behavior *could* be rewarded on the next try.

3. **Fixed interval schedule.** With interval schedules, rewards come after the passage of a certain period of time rather than the number of behaviors. So, for example, if the fixed interval is five minutes, the rat will get rewarded the first time it presses the lever after a five-minute period has elapsed, regardless of what the rat did during the preceding five minutes. So, it can be argued that a fixed interval schedule does little to motivate an animal's behavior since the rat gets the same reward for taking a five-minute nap and then waking up and pushing the lever once as it does for pushing the lever continuously for five minutes.

4. **Variable interval schedule.** In this schedule, rewards are delivered after differing time periods. Variable interval schedule is the second most effective strategy in maintaining behavior. The length of time varies, so one never knows when the reinforcement is just around the corner. Waiting for a bus is a good example. Even though there's nothing we can do to make the bus arrive earlier, we tend to wait because we never know when the bus might arrive. This schedule provides slow and steady learning.

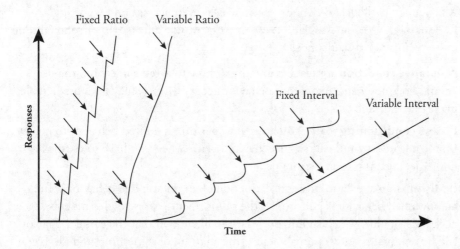

Behavior Response Patterns to Each of the Four Reinforcement Schedules

Token Economy

An artificial mini-economy is usually found in prisons, rehabilitation centers, or mental hospitals. Individuals in the environment are motivated by secondary reinforcers, tokens in this case. Desirable behaviors are reinforced with tokens, which can be cashed in for more desirable reinforcers, such as candy, books, privileges, or cigarettes.

Other Important Classical and Operant Conditioning Terms

- **Stimulus** refers to any event that an organism reacts to. The stimulus is the first link in a stimulus-response chain.

- **Stimulus discrimination** refers to the ability to discriminate between different but similar stimuli. Every day, we react to discriminated stimuli. A doorbell ringing means something different from a phone ringing. An ice cream truck's tune means something different from a stereo heard from a passing car.

- **Stimulus generalization** is the opposite of stimulus discrimination. To generalize is to make the same response to a group of similar stimuli. Though not all fire alarms sound alike, we know that they all require the same response. **Undergeneralization** is the failure to generalize a stimulus.

- **Response learning** refers to the form of learning in which one links together chains of stimuli and responses. One learns what to do in response to particular triggers. An example of response learning is leaving a building in response to a fire alarm.

- **Aversive conditioning** uses punishment to decrease the likelihood of a behavior. The most common example is the drug antabuse, which is used to treat alcoholism. When taken with alcohol, antabuse can cause severe nausea and vomiting. Eventually the person associates these unpleasant side effects with alcohol and no longer wants to drink alcohol.

- **Avoidance conditioning** teaches an animal how to avoid something the animal does not want. Avoidance behavior occurs when you avoid a predictable, unpleasant stimulus.

- **Escape conditioning** teaches an animal to perform a desired behavior to get away from a negative stimulus. Escape behavior occurs when you have to escape an unpredictable, unpleasant stimulus.

- **Punishment** is meant to promote extinction of an undesirable behavior. After an unwanted behavior is performed, the punishment is presented. This acts as a negative stimulus, which should decrease the likelihood that the earlier behavior will be repeated. Positive punishment is the addition of something undesirable to the situation to discourage a particular behavior. Negative punishment is taking away something desirable in order to discourage a particular behavior. Primary punishments, such as pain, are punishments that most species do not have to learn about its unpleasant consequences. Secondary punishments are those that one must come to understand as a negative consequences. For example, if you don't drive, taking away the car keys will have little effect on your behavior. But if you drive everywhere all the time, taking away the car keys will discourage whatever behavior that led to the punishment from ever happening again. Of course, punishment has received mixed reviews. Some animal experiments have shown that severe punishment effectively extinguishes undesirable behavior. Many, including Skinner himself, argue that punishment is not effective in the long run because it carries with it too many negative effects. Skinner preferred to extinguish behavior by stopping reinforcement as opposed to applying a punishment.

- **Autonomic conditioning** refers to evoking responses of the autonomic nervous system through training.

- **Extinction** is the reversal of conditioning. The goal is to encourage an organism to stop doing a particular behavior. This is generally accomplished by repeatedly withholding reinforcement for a behavior or by disassociating the behavior from a particular cue. Using operant conditioning, parents can reduce temper tantrums in children by not giving into, or reinforcing, the child's behavior. In operant conditioning, one might also see an **extinction burst** when first beginning to extinguish a behavior where the behavior initially increases before it begins to diminish. A child's tantrum might get bigger at first when it is not reinforced before the child stops having tantrums. In classical conditioning, extinction begins the moment the UCS and NS are no longer paired. Using classical conditioning, you could teach your dog to disassociate the car from the vet by taking it on frequent car trips to the park.

- **Spontaneous recovery** is the reappearance of an extinguished response, even in the absence of further conditioning or training.

- **Superstitious behavior** occurs when someone "learns" that a specific action causes an event, when in reality the two are unrelated. For example, a football fan that always wears the same shirt when his favorite team plays its major rival may do so because he noticed that every time he wore the shirt his team won the game, and whenever he wore a different shirt his team lost the game. Therefore, he continues to wear the shirt because of the association he learned, even though the clothes he wears at home could not possibly impact the outcome of a game he is watching on TV.

- **Chaining** is the act of linking together a series of behaviors that ultimately result in reinforcement. One behavior triggers the next, and so on. Learning the alphabet is an example of chaining. Twenty-six letters are required to complete the chain, and each letter stimulates remembering the next letter.

- **Autoshaping** refers to experiments in which an apparatus allows an animal to control its reinforcements through behaviors, such as bar pressing or key pecking. The animal is, in a sense, shaping its own behavior.

- **Overshadowing** is a classical conditioning concept referring to an animal's inability to infer a relationship between a particular stimulus and response due to the presence of a more prominent stimulus.

- **John Garcia** performed classical conditioning experiments in which it was discovered that animals are programmed through evolution to make certain connections. The concept that certain associations are learned more easily than others is called **preparedness.** Garcia studied "conditioned nausea" with rats and found that invariably nausea was perceived to be connected with food or drink. Garcia was unable to condition a relationship between nausea and a neutral stimulus (like a light). This extremely strong connection that animals form between nausea and food has been used to explain why humans can become sick only one time from eating a particular food and are never able to eat that food again; the connection is automatic, so it needs little conditioning. This phenomenon is called the **Garcia effect** and is especially strong in children.

NONASSOCIATIVE LEARNING

- **Habituation** is the decreased responsiveness to a stimulus as a result of increasing familiarity with the stimulus. For example, when you first enter a room where an overhead fluorescent light is buzzing nonstop, you are constantly aware of the noise; however, after you are in the room for a while, you eventually stop noticing it.

- **Dishabituation** occurs when you remove the stimulus to which the organism had become habituated. But if you reintroduce the stimulus, the organism will start noticing it again.

- **Sensitization** is increasing sensitivity to the environment following the presentation of a strong stimulus.

- **Desensitization** is decreasing sensitivity to the environment following the presentation of a strong stimulus. Desensitization is often used as a behavioral treatment to counter phobias.

OBSERVATIONAL LEARNING

- **Social learning theory** or **social cognitive theory** posits that individuals learn through their culture. People learn what are acceptable and unacceptable behaviors through interacting in society. **Albert Bandura** developed this theory, also known as **observational learning,** to explain how we learn by **modeling**— that we do not require reinforcements or associations or practice in order to learn. For example, a child who cradles a new doll like a baby did not have to get rewarded to learn to hold the doll that way, nor did she have to practice. She likely had a role model.

  o Because this type of learning had been observed in the world, but not demonstrated experimentally, Bandura and his colleagues devised the now-famous **Bobo doll.** In this study, children who watched adults take out their frustrations on a blowup clown doll in a playroom proceeded to do the same during their playtime with the Bobo doll; children who did not witness the aggression did not behave in this way.

- **Vicarious reinforcement** results when a person witnesses someone else being rewarded for a particular behavior so that encourages them to do the same. For example, if a boy sees his sister get extra money in her allowance for making her bed, he will be more likely to make his bed.

- **Vicarious punishment** is when a person witnesses someone else being punished for a behavior, and that punishment discourages the likelihood of the witness engaging in that behavior. For example, a boy sees his brother get into trouble for breaking curfew and that causes him to not break curfew.

- Observational learning is often cited as the basis for arguments claiming that violent television shows, movies, and video games lead to violence in the real world. While there is much experimental evidence supporting a correlation between the two, causation has not been definitively proven.

**Bandura's widely cited "Bobo doll" study (A) provided support for the views of social learning theorists; (B) taught children to defend themselves against killer clowns.
Answer: (A).**

INSIGHT LEARNING

- **Insight learning** occurs when the solution to a problem appears all at once rather than building up to a solution. **Wolfgang Köhler** demonstrated insight learning in his work with chimpanzees. He designed experiments in which the chimps would have to try to get bananas that were out of reach. In one instance, the chimps were in a room with boxes on the floor, none high enough to reach the banana. Köhler noticed that the chimps spent most of their time frustrated by their inability to reach the tasty treat. Then, all of a sudden, they realized they could stack the boxes, climb up, and reach the banana.

- Insight is the key element in **Gestalt psychology** (see Chapter 3, Sensation and Perception) because a person can perceive the relationships between all the important elements in a situation and finding a solution greater than the sum of its parts. Gestalt psychology describes how people **organize** elements in a situation and think about them in relation to one another.

LATENT LEARNING

- **Latent learning** describes learning that happens but does not demonstrate itself until it is needed later on. For example, maybe you have watched someone play chess many times. The fact that you are learning while watching may not be evident, but when you play chess later, you find that you have learned some new tricks.

- **Edward C. Tolman** and his colleagues demonstrated latent learning with three groups of rats running a maze. The first group always found food at the end of the maze, so they always ran to the end. The second group had no food at the end of the maze, and thus wandered around, but did not necessarily go to the end of the maze. For the first 10 days, the third group got no food at the end of the maze, so they acted like the second group. On the 11th day, they were presented with food at the end of the maze. The rats quickly learned to run to end of the maze and soon were doing it as well as the Group 1 rats.

- **Incidental learning** is like accidental learning. Unrelated items are grouped together during incidental learning. For example, pets often learn to dislike riding in cars because it means they are going to the vet. Though it is actually the vet that the animal fears, pets associate cars with the vet experience. Incidental learning is the opposite of **intentional learning.**

OTHER COGNITIVE THEORIES OF LEARNING

- **Donald Hebb** created an early model of how learning happens in the brain— through the formation of sets of neurons that learn to fire together (see Chapter 7, Memory).

- **Perceptual** or **concept learning** refers to learning about something in general rather than learning-specific stimulus-response chains. An individual learns about something (history, for example) rather than any particular response. **Tolman's** experiments with animals forming **cognitive maps** of mazes rather than simple escape routes are an example of this. In Tolman's experiments, in which he showed rats mazes but then blocked routes to the end, he discovered that they could figure out another route based on having an internal sense of where the end was, rather than using trial and error. He described the rats' behavior as **purposive**.

- **Harry Harlow** demonstrated that monkeys became better at learning tasks as they acquired different learning experiences. Eventually, monkeys could learn after only one trial. Harlow called this "**learning to learn**" (see Chapter 10, Developmental Psychology).

MOTIVATION AND PERFORMANCE

An animal must be motivated in order to learn and to act. Individuals are at times motivated by **primary** or **instinctual drives,** such as hunger or thirst. Other times, they are motivated by **secondary** or **acquired drives,** such as money or other learned reinforcers. Still other types of drive, such as an **exploratory drive,** may exist. Experiments have shown that individuals are motivated simply to try something new or to explore their environment. Various theories of motivation exist:

- Some theories assert that humans are primarily motivated to maintain physiological or psychological **homeostasis. Fritz Heider's balance theory, Charles Osgood** and **Percy Tannenbaum's congruity theory,** and **Leon Festinger's cognitive dissonance theory** (see Chapter 9, Social Psychology) all agree that what drives people is a desire to be balanced with respect to their feelings, ideas, or behaviors. These theories, along with **Clark Hull's drive-reduction theory,** are called into question by the fact that individuals often seek out stimulation, novel experience, or self-destruction.

- **Hull** proposed that **Performance = Drive × Habit**. This means that individuals are first motivated by drive, and then they act according to old successful habits. They will do what has worked in the past to satisfy the drive.

- **Edward Tolman** proposed that **Performance = Expectation × Value**. This is also known as the **expectancy-value theory.** The idea here is that people are motivated by goals that they think they might actually meet. Another factor is how important the goal is. **Victor Vroom** applied this theory to individual behavior in large organizations. Individuals who are lowest on the totem pole do not expect to receive company incentives, so these incentives do little to motivate them.

- **Henry Murray** and later **David McClelland** studied the possibility that people are motivated by a **need for achievement (nAch).** This may be manifested through a need to pursue success or a need to avoid failure, but either way, the goal is to feel successful. Also, **John Atkinson** suggested a theory of motivation in which people who set realistic goals with intermediate risk sets feel pride with accomplishment, and want to succeed more than they fear failure. But because success is so important, these people are unlikely to set unrealistic or risky goals or to persist when success is unlikely.

- **Neil Miller** proposed the **approach-avoidance conflict**. This conflict refers to the state one feels when a certain goal has both pros and cons. Typically, the further one is from the goal, the more one focuses on the pros or the reasons to approach the goal. The closer one is to the goal, the more one focuses on the cons or the reasons to avoid the goal.

- **Hedonism** is the theory that individuals are motivated solely by what brings the most pleasure and the least pain.

- **The Premack principle** is the idea that people are motivated to do what they do not want to do by rewarding themselves afterward with something they like to do. For example, a young child may be rewarded with dessert only after he eats his spinach.

For more on Maslow's pyramid, see Chapter 11.

- **Abraham Maslow,** a humanistic psychologist, proposed a model for motivation—**Hierarchy of Needs,** indicating that not all needs are created equal. Maslow used a pyramid to demonstrate that physiological needs take precedence. Once those are satisfied, a person will work to satisfy safety needs, followed by love and belonging needs, self-esteem needs, and finally the need to self-actualize.

- **M. E. Olds** performed experiments in which electrical stimulation of pleasure centers in the brain were used as positive reinforcement. Animals would perform behaviors to receive the stimulation. This was viewed as evidence against the **drive-reduction theory.**

Arousal is a part of motivation, and an individual must be adequately aroused to learn or perform. **Donald Hebb** postulated that a medium amount of arousal is best for performance. Too little arousal or too much arousal could hamper performance of tasks. Specifically, for simple tasks, the optimal level of arousal is toward the high end. For complex tasks, the optimal level of arousal is toward the low end, so that the individual is not too anxious to perform well. The optimal arousal level for any type of task, however, is never at the extremes. The above relationship is the **Yerkes-Dodson effect**. On a graph, optimal arousal looks like an inverted U-curve, with lowest performance at the extremes of arousal.

OTHER IMPORTANT TERMS IN LEARNING

- **State dependent learning** refers to the concept that what a person learns in one state is best recalled in that state. State, here, is obviously referring to a physiological state, not the united 50.

- **Continuous** motor tasks are easier to learn than **discrete** motor tasks. An example of a continuous task is riding a bicycle. This is one continuous motion that, once started, continues naturally. A discrete task is one that is divided into different parts that do not facilitate the recall of each other. Setting up a chessboard is a good example. Placing the different pieces in their proper positions involves different bits of information. This is not one unbroken task.

- **Positive transfer** is previous learning that makes it easier to learn another task later. Previous learning that makes it more difficult to learn a new task is called **negative transfer.**

- **Age** has been shown to affect learning. Humans are primed to learn between the ages of 3 and 20 (the school years). From the age of 20 to 50, the ability to learn remains fairly constant. After the age of 50, the ability to learn drops.

- The **learning curve** was first described by **Hermann Ebbinghaus** and refers to the fact that when learning something new, the rate of learning usually changes over time. For example, when learning a foreign language someone may quickly learn a bunch of vocabulary words and basic sentence structure, but as they try to learn more complex grammatical constructions, the rate of learning may decrease. Later, other people described different types of learning curves, including a positively accelerated curve—in which the *rate* of learning is increasing—and a negatively accelerated curve—in which the *rate* of learning is decreasing.

The Effects of Technology on Cognition

Our phones are getting smarter—but are we? Many experts fear that our modern reliance on the Internet, computers, smartphones, and other technological conveniences is actually diminishing our ability to think for ourselves. Studies have demonstrated that our capacity to analyze situations, solve problems, and recall information is adversely affected by our relegating these functions to machines, although some data suggests that these negative effects are only transient. Similarly, our attention spans and ability to concentrate for extended periods have decreased as well due to the constant barrage of cognitive stimulation to which we've become accustomed.

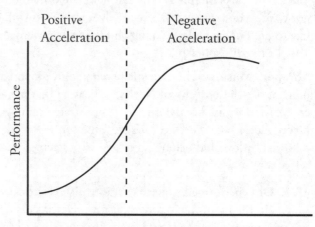

Number of Attempts at Learning

EDUCATIONAL PSYCHOLOGY

The branch of educational psychology is concerned with how people learn in educational settings. Educational psychologists examine things like student and teacher attributes and instructional processes in the classroom. Educational psychologists are frequently employed by schools and help when students have academic or behavioral problems.

- **Thorndike** is credited with writing the first educational psychology textbook in 1903. He developed various methods to assess students' skills and teaching effectiveness.

- **Aptitude** refers to a set of characteristics that are indicative of a person's ability to learn.

- **Cooperative learning** involves students working on a project together in small groups.

- **Lev Vygotsky** described learning through the zone of proximal development, in which a lower achieving student in a particular subject is placed with someone who is just a bit more advanced. The lower-achieving student thus raises their game through the interaction. Vygotsky also discussed using **scaffolding learning,** which occurs when a teacher encourages the student to learn independently and provides assistance only with topics or concepts that are beyond the student's capability. As the student continues to learn, the teacher aids with less to encourage the student's independence. Vygotsky's theories on education are in use in many classrooms throughout the world.

Study Tip
Not surprisingly, people change their attitudes about activities or interests once these interests become a paying job. According to the overjustification effect, getting paid for something you enjoy often leads to reduced enjoyment. Before you apply to graduate school, do some work in the field. This will both help your application and let you see how your interests hold up as a job.

Chapter 6
Language

This chapter discusses components of language, theories of language acquisition and development, language comprehension, and language in the brain. The chapter also explores the relationship of language and thought, as well as language in animals.

DEFINED: Language is the meaningful arrangement of sounds. Psycholinguistics is the study of the psychology of language. Luckily, psycholinguistics is a highly specialized area of research in which only a limited number of concepts relate to general psychology. For this reason, the language topics that might be covered on the GRE Psychology Test are predictable.

COMPONENTS OF LANGUAGE

- **Phonemes.** Discrete sounds that make up words but carry no meaning, such as *ee*, *p*, or *sh*. Infants first make these sounds when learning language. Phonics is learning to read by sounding out the phonemes. All words in a language are created from basic phonological rules of sound combinations.

- **Morphemes.** Made up of phonemes; the smallest units of meaning in language. Words or parts of words that have meaning are morphemes. The word *boy* and the suffix *-ing* are morphemes.

- **Phrase.** A phrase is a group of words that when put together function as a single syntactic part of a sentence. For example, "walking the dog" is a noun phrase that could function as the subject of a sentence if it were followed by a verb.

- **Syntax.** The arrangement of words into sentences as prescribed by a particular language.

- **Grammar.** The overall rules of the interrelationship between morphemes and syntax that make up a certain language.

- **Morphology or morphological rules.** Grammar rules; how to group morphemes.

- **Prosody.** Tone inflections, accents, and other aspects of pronunciation that carry meaning. Prosody is the icing on the cake of grammar and meaning. Infants can more easily differentiate between completely different sounds than between different expressions of the same sound.

- **Phonology.** The study of sound patterns in languages.

- **Semantics.** The study of how signs and symbols are interpreted to make meaning.

THEORIES OF LANGUAGE ACQUISITION

- **Behaviorist theory.** B. F. Skinner developed one of the earliest theories of language acquisition, applying the principles of operant conditioning. Children learn language based on which words are reinforced (the child receives praise for the word or sees its communicative value in getting what the child wants) and which are punished (the child is punished for using the word or it does not display communicative value).

- **Social interactionist theory.** Lev Vygotsky and others suggested language was learned through social learning and interaction with others.

Noam Chomsky

Noam Chomsky is undoubtedly the most important figure in psycholinguistics. You will see at least one or two questions about his work. Chomsky's **transformational grammar** differentiates between surface structure and deep structure in language. **Surface structure** is the way that words are organized. Each of the following sentences has a different surface structure:

> I studied the material for hours.
> The material was studied for hours by me.
> For hours, I studied the material.

But the **deep structure,** or the underlying meaning, of the above sentences is the same. Each of those sentences has the same active declarative kernel sentence (subject = *I*, verb = *studied*, object = *material*).

Probably Chomsky's most famous contribution to psycholinguistics was his idea of an innate **language acquisition device (LAD).** After studying children and noticing how they made small errors ("I founded the toy") often based on grammar rules rather than large structural errors, Chomsky proposed that humans have an inborn ability to adopt generative grammar rules of the language that they hear. The rules are then used to make millions of novel sentences.

One reason that the LAD is so important and controversial is that it is a nativist, or genetic, interpretation. According to Chomsky, children need only be exposed to a language in order to easily apply the LAD. They do not simply imitate, memorize, or learn through conditioning. The LAD also explains why children who are learning different languages progress similarly.

LANGUAGE DEVELOPMENT

Research has shown that the ability to understand language precedes the ability to produce language.

- **Pre-linguistic stage:** infants use facial expressions, eye contact, crying, and body language to communicate.
- **Cooing:** appears at about 2–3 months old and consists solely of vowel sounds—for example, "Ahhhhh" or "Eeeeeee"
- **Babbling:** appears at about 4–6 months old and now incorporates consonant sounds as well as vowels—for example, "BahBahBah" or "MahMahMah"

- **Other language acquisition milestones:**
  - o 1 year   speaks first word(s)
  - o 2 years   > 50 spoken words, usually in two- (and then three-) word phrases
  - o 3 years   1,000-word vocabulary, but use has many grammatical errors
  - o 4 years   grammar problems are random exceptions

- **Overextension** is generalizing with names for things. This is often done through chaining characteristics rather than through logic. For example, a two-year-old may call any furry thing a *doggie*. Overextension usually occurs in children 12 months to 2–3 years old.

- **Holophrastic speech** is the use (by a young child) of one word **(holophrase)** to convey a whole sentence. "Me" may mean "give that to me."

- **Telegraphic speech** refers to speech without the articles or extras, similar to the way in which it would appear in a telegram, such as "Ship arrived New York."

- **Overregularization** is the overapplication of grammar rules. For example, children realize that past tense is indicated by the suffix *-ed*. Then they add this to verbs that don't actually need it, as in the sentence "I founded the toy." Also, children think that plural always requires *-s*, as in *sheeps*. Even after a child correctly learns an adult speech pattern, such as saying *sheep* instead of *sheeps*, he periodically slips back into old errors. This error is typical in children approximately 2–5 years old.

Study Tip
Verbalization (saying things out loud) helps learning.

Other Important Terms in Language Development

- **Girls** are faster and more accurate with language learning than boys are.
- **Bilingual children** are slower at language learning.
- **Reading and writing** are processed in the same regions of the brain as producing and understanding speech. However, there are slight differences, as there are people who are unable to read (alexia) or write (agraphia) but have no problems speaking or understanding speech.
- **Children** usually use nouns first, then verbs. The first phrases children usually speak consist of one noun and one verb (i.e., "me want") or two nouns (i.e., "mommy shirt").

- **Roger Brown** researched the areas of social, developmental, and linguistic psychology. He found that children's understanding of grammatical rules develops as they make hypotheses about how syntax works and then self-correct with experience.

- **Katherine Nelson** found that language really begins to develop with the onset of **active speech** rather than during the first year of only listening.

LANGUAGE COMPREHENSION

- **Parsing:** A grammatical exercise in which language is broken down into its component parts, called **constituents**, to get to the meaning of a message.

- **Ambiguity:** Occurs when a word **(lexical ambiguity)** or text **(linguistic ambiguity)** is open to multiple interpretations or has multiple meanings.

- **A garden path sentence:** Begins by luring the reader into believing the sentence will mean one thing when it actually means something else.

- **Online versus offline measurement:** Two methods of measuring language processing. Online measurement does not require interrupting the speaker to get their understanding of what they are saying, while offline measures stop the speaker at various points to get their interpretations.

LANGUAGE AND THOUGHT

- **Benjamin Whorf** (from studies of Hopi language) posited that language, or how a culture says things, influences that culture's perspective. This **Sapir-Whorf hypothesis,** also known as the **linguistic relativity hypothesis,** has been used as an argument for the importance of nonsexist language. It has been found, however, that cultures that don't have words for certain colors can still recognize them, so it is unclear to what extent language really affects our perceptions.

> ### Other Important Terms in Language
> **William Labov** studied "Black English," now known as African American Vernacular English (AAVE), and found that it had its own complex internal structure. His groundbreaking book, *Language in the Inner City* (1972), demonstrated that African American vernacular is not merely slang but a separate and independent dialect of English.

- **Lev Vygotsky** and **Alexander Luria,** Russia's best-known psychologists, studied the development of word meanings and found them to be complex and altered by interpersonal experience. Also, they asserted that language is a tool involved in (not just a byproduct of) the development of abstract thinking.

- **Charles Osgood** studied semantics, or word meanings. He created **semantic differential charts,** which allowed people to plot the meanings of words on graphs (like near "good" but far from "relaxed"). The results were that people with similar backgrounds and interests plotted words similarly. This indicates that words have similar **connotations** (implied meaning) for cultures or subcultures.

LANGUAGE AND THE BRAIN

- **Broca's area** is located in the dominant hemisphere (usually left) of the frontal lobe of the brain and is associated with speech production. Damage to Broca's area results in nonfluent aphasia, in which a person can understand language but cannot produce it.

- **Wernicke's area** is located in the posterior section of the temporal lobe in the dominant hemisphere of the brain (the left for most people) and is associated with the comprehension of speech and written language. Damage to Wernicke's area results in fluent aphasia, in which a person cannot understand language, but can produce sounds with the rhythm and prosody of language.

LANGUAGE AND ANIMALS

Research into how animals communicate has shown that animals do indeed communicate with one another, and sometimes even with humans. However, whether their communication actually qualifies as a language has not yet been definitively established.

- **Washoe and Koko:** Beatrice and Alan Gardner conducted research with Washoe, a chimpanzee, teaching her to communicate using American Sign Language. Washoe knew 300–400 signs and could combine them to make sentences. Koko, a gorilla, learned ASL from her caregiver, and reportedly used more than 1,000 signs.

- **Lana:** Lana was a chimpanzee who was part of an experiment on communicating with lexigrams, which was an artificial language using symbols on a keyboard. Lana was able to use the keyboard to communicate her desires to her caregivers.

- **Dolphins:** Researchers have studied the communication patterns of dolphins for many years. Much research points to dolphins' ability to understand language, but not necessarily using true language to communicate themselves.

Chapter 7
Memory

This chapter will discuss the basic concepts concerning memory, including encoding, storage, and retrieval, as well as memory effects and memory in the brain.

DEFINED: Studying memory involves understanding how things are remembered and why things are forgotten.

STORES OF MEMORY

According to the Atkinson-Shriffin model of memory, there are three stores of memory—sensory, short-term, and long-term.

Sensory Memory

- Lasts only for seconds (iconic input decays in less than one second, echoic input decays in 2–4 seconds)
- Forms the connection between perception and memory.
- **Iconic memory** is the sensory memory for vision studied by **George Sperling.** He found that people could see more than they can remember. In his classic experiment, subjects were shown something like this for a fraction of a second:

GPRZ
ILTH
TBAE

Then they were instructed to write down the letters of a particular line. Although subjects were able to do this, they invariably forgot the other letters in the time that it took to write the first ones down. This **partial report** shows that sensory memory exists, but only for a few seconds.

- **Ulric Neisser** coined the term **icon** for brief visual memory and found that an icon lasts for about one second. In addition, he found that when subjects are exposed to a bright flash of light or a new pattern before the iconic image fades, the first image will be erased. This is **backward masking,** and it works for the auditory system as well. A mask is more successful if it is similar to the original stimulus.

- The concept of sensory memory explains why, if you wiggle a pen back and forth, you see trails or a ghost pen in all positions. The sensory information remains briefly in your awareness, and because the pen moves quickly, the information all runs together.

- **Echoic memory** is the sensory memory for auditory sensations.

Short-term Memory (STM)

- Temporary; lasts for about 15–30 seconds.
- Encoding from sensory memory to short-term memory requires paying attention to the sensory stimulus.
- **Working memory** is the temporary memory that is needed to perform the task that someone is working on at that moment.
- **George Miller** found that short-term memory has the capacity of about seven items (+ or – two items).
- **Chunking** (grouping items) can increase the capacity of STM.
- STM is thought to be largely auditory, and items are encoded **phonologically.**
- **Rehearsal** (repeating or practicing) is the key to keeping items in the STM and to transferring items to the long-term memory (LTM). **Primary (maintenance) rehearsal** simply involves repeating material in order to hold it in STM. **Secondary (elaborative) rehearsal** involves organizing and understanding material in order to transfer it to LTM.
- **Displacement theory** suggests there are a limited number (7 +/– 2) slots that can be filled at any given time, so if there is no room for new information, old information is displaced.
- **Baddeley's model of working memory** starts with a central executive that controls the flow of information and oversees the memory processes. Information from the central executive flows to the two slave systems (called that because they are service to the central executive). The phonological loop is a short-term auditory store and the visuospatial sketch pad is a short-term store for visual and spatial information. Also part of this model is the episodic buffer, which integrates information across domains. Information then flows from these systems into long-term memory.

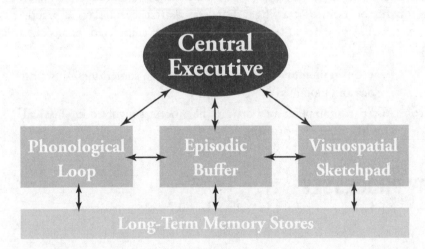

Long-Term Memory (LTM)

- Capable of permanent retention.
- Most items are encoded semantically, for meaning.
- Long-term memory retention is measured by recognition, recall, and savings.
  - **Recognition** simply requires subjects to recognize things learned in the past. Multiple-choice tests tap recognition.
  - **Recall** requires that subjects generate information on their own. **Cued recall** uses various cues, often sensory or verbal; fill-in-the-blank tests are an example. **Free recall** is remembering with no cue.
  - **Savings** measures how much information about a subject remains in LTM by assessing how long it takes to learn something the second time as opposed to the first time.
- LTM is subject to the **encoding specificity principle,** which means that material is more likely to be remembered if it is retrieved in the same context in which it was stored.

Explicit (Declarative) Versus Implicit (Nondeclarative) Memory

- **Explicit (or declarative) memory** is knowing something and being consciously aware of knowing it, such as knowing a fact. There are two types of explicit memory:

See the section on storage on the next page.

  - **Episodic memory** consists of a person's experiences of the world, including details, events, and discrete knowledge.
  - **Semantic memory** consists of facts and information—general knowledge of the world.
- **Implicit (or nondeclarative) memory** is knowing something without being aware of knowing it. For example, HM's (an amnesia patient described below) performance on a mirror-drawing task increased after several days of practice; however, each day he would report that he had never completed the task before. Implicit memory requires no conscious awareness.
  - **Procedural memory** is knowing "how to" do something—physical actions and motor skills.
  - Also part of implicit memory are the processes involved in **classical conditioning** and **priming.**

MEMORY PROCESSES

Memory involves three main processes: encoding, storage, and retrieval.

Encoding

The process of transforming information into a form more easily stored in the brain.

- **Mnemonics** are memory cues that help learning and recall. For example, the word OCEAN can be used as a mnemonic to help you remember the Big Five factors of personality: openness, conscientiousness, extraversion, agreeableness, neuroticism.

- **Clustering** is the brain's tendency to group together similar items in memory whether they are learned together or not. Most often, they are grouped into conceptual or semantic hierarchies.

- **Rehearsal** is the repetition of information over and over. Think about what one rehearses: a speech, lines in a play, or a phone number.

- Encoding into long-term memory uses systems of **organization,** usually semantically or categorically.

- **Elaborative encoding** is an organizational strategy that uses meaning and the creation of associations to remember.

- **Allan Paivio** suggested the **dual coding theory,** which states that items will be better remembered if they are encoded both visually (with icons or imagery) and semantically (with understanding). One such technique is the Method of Loci—visualizing a place you know very well with something you are trying to remember and then creating associations between the two.

- **Self-reference** refers to making information personally relevant in order to remember it. TIP: When you are trying to remember information for the GRE Psychology Test, think of situations that happened to you or someone you know (or even to characters in films or books) that exemplify the concept in order to make the information relevant to you.

Storage

- **Karl Lashley** found that memories are stored diffusely in the brain.

Retrieval

- **Frederick Bartlett** found that memory is **reconstructive** rather than rote. Using the story "War of the Ghosts," he discovered that people are more likely to remember the ideas or semantics of a story rather than the details or grammar of a story.

- **Fergus Craik** and **Robert Lockhart** asserted that learning and recall depend on the **depth of processing.** Different levels of processing exist from the most superficial phonological (pronunciation) level to the deep semantic (meaning) level. The deeper an item is processed, the easier it is to learn and recall.

- **Elizabeth Loftus** found that memory of traumatic events is altered by the event itself and by the way that questions about the event are phrased. "How fast were the cars going when they crashed?" will elicit higher speed estimates than "What was the rate of the cars upon impact?" This finding is particularly important for law-psychology issues, such as the questioning of witnesses.

- The **generation-recognition model** suggests that anything one might recall should easily be recognized. This is why a multiple-choice (or recognition) test is easier than an essay (or recall) test.

- The **tip-of-the-tongue phenomenon** is being on the verge of retrieval but not successfully doing so.

- **Elizabeth Loftus** and **Allan Collins** suggested that people have hierarchical semantic networks in their memory that group together related items. The more closely related two items are, the more closely they are located in the hierarchy, and the more quickly a subject can link them (i.e., faster reaction time, decreased latency). For example, subjects can answer "true" more quickly to the sentence "A canary is a bird" than they can answer "false" to the sentence "A toaster is a bird."

FORGETTING

- **Hermann Ebbinghaus** was the first to study memory systematically. He presented subjects with lists of nonsense syllables to study the STM. He also proposed a **forgetting curve** that depicts a sharp drop in savings immediately after learning and then levels off, with a slight downward trend. However, some psychologists doubt that results obtained from having subjects memorize lists of nonsense syllables (which were convenient) generalize to other types of memory.

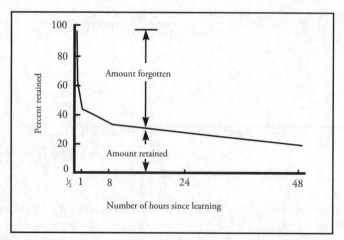

- Two main theories suggest the origin of forgetting: decay theory and interference theory. **Decay theory** (also known as **trace theory**) posits that memories fade with time. This theory has been called too simplistic because other activities are known to interfere with retrieval. **Interference theory** suggests that competing information blocks retrieval. If, for example, two groups learned a list of words, and then one group sleeps while the other group solves riddles, the group that slept is more likely to remember more from the word list. For both groups, the passage of time was the same, but for the riddle group, competing information existed.

  o Disrupting information that was learned before the new items were presented, such as a list of similar words, is **proactive interference.** This is problematic for recall and thus causes **proactive inhibition.** Disrupting information that was learned after the new items were presented is called **retroactive interference.** This is also problematic for recall and thus causes **retroactive inhibition.**

MEMORY AND LEARNING

- **Behaviorists** explain memory through **paired-associate learning.** One item is learned with, and then cues the recall of, another.

- **Donald Hebb** posited that memory involves changes of **synapses and neural pathways,** making a "memory tree." Hebb described the process of **Long-Term Potentiation** ("what fires together, wires together"): when neurons consistently fire in particular sequences, those sequences (patterns) become enhanced or strengthened. **E. R. Kandel** had similar ideas from studying the sea slug aplysia. Also, brain studies of young chicks show that their brains are altered with learning and memory.

- Types of verbal learning and memory tasks:
  - **Serial learning.** A list—such as the presidents of the United States—is learned and recalled in order **(serial recall).** Feedback on the correct responses in the correct order is given after the entire list is recalled. This type of learning is subject to **primacy** and **recency effects**—how the first and last few items learned are easiest to remember, whereas the ones in the middle are often forgotten. First items are remembered because they benefit from the most rehearsal/exposure; last items are easy to remember because there has been less time for decay. The **serial-position curve** (a U-shaped curve on a graph) shows this savings effect.
  - **Serial-anticipation learning.** This type of learning is similar to serial learning; however, instead of being asked to recall the entire list at once, the subject is asked to recall one item at a time. For example, when learning the order of the U.S. presidents, the subject would be presented with George Washington and then be expected to say John Adams. A few seconds later, the subject would be presented with John Adams (and would then know that her previous answer of John Adams was correct) and be expected to say Thomas Jefferson.
  - **Paired-associate learning.** We use this type of learning when we study foreign languages. For example, when studying Spanish, we remember that *coche* means "car" and *hombre* means "man." We pair the Spanish word with the English word.
  - **Free-recall learning.** A list of items is learned, and then must be recalled in any order with no cue.
- The following factors make items on a list easier to learn and retrieve:
  - **Acoustic dissimilarity**
  - **Semantic dissimilarity**
  - **Brevity** (both in the length of the term and in the length of the list of terms to be remembered)
  - **Familiarity**
  - **Concreteness**
  - **Meaning**
  - **Importance to the subject**

Study Tip

According to what we know about levels of processing, elaborative rehearsal, and the **dual coding theory,** test material will be better retained if you take time to truly understand it. Rote memorization depends only on one link in memory and is therefore highly susceptible to decay.

- **State-dependent memory** is like state-dependent learning. Retrieval is more successful if it occurs in the same emotional state or physical state in which encoding occurred. This explains why depressed individuals cannot easily recall happy memories and why alcoholics often remember details of their last drinking session only when under the influence of alcohol. (See also the encoding specificity principle on page 76.)

- In a recall task involving the **order of items on a list,** subjects can more quickly state the order of two items that are far apart on the list than two items that are close together. For example, in a list of numbers, subjects can recognize that 7 occurs before 593 more quickly than they can recognize that 133 occurs before 136.

- **Incidental learning** is measured through presenting subjects with items they are not supposed to try to memorize and then testing for learning.

MEMORY AND THE BRAIN

- **Anterograde amnesia** occurs when a person is unable to form new memories after a brain injury.
- **Retrograde amnesia** occurs when a brain injury causes a person to lose the ability to recall information learned prior to the onset of the injury.
- Memory is encoded in the brain via the limbic system. When presented with sensory input, the thalamus relays the information to the appropriate cortex (occipital for visual input and temporary for aural input), which sends it to the **prefrontal cortex.** For encoding into long-term memory, the input would then be relayed to the hippocampus and then sent to the appropriate sensory cortex for storage. The **hippocampus** is also next to the amygdala, another part of the limbic system associated with emotion. The **amygdala** is thought to play a role in the strength of the memory.
- **Brenda Milner** wrote about patient "HM" who was given a lesion of the **hippocampus** to treat severe epilepsy. While he remembered things from before the surgery, and his short-term memory was still intact, he could not store any new long-term memories.

OTHER IMPORTANT MEMORY TERMS

- **Eidetic imagery** is photographic memory. This is more common in children and rural cultures.
- **Flashbulb memories** are recollections that seem burned into the brain, such as "What is your memory of the World Trade Center collapsing?" or "Where were you when you found out John F. Kennedy, Jr., was dead?"
- A **tachtiscope** is an instrument often used in cognitive or memory experiments. It presents visual material (words or images) to subjects for a fraction of a second.
- **Source monitoring errors** are misremembering the source of information—for example, "I remember hearing this in a class, but I can't remember which class or who said it."
- The **Zeigarnik effect** is the tendency to recall uncompleted tasks better than completed ones.

Chapter 8
Thinking

This chapter discusses the basic concepts concerning thinking, including schemas and heuristics, problem solving, as well as obstacles to problem solving, and reasoning and creativity. Also included are discussions of decision-making and information processing.

DEFINED: Cognitive psychology is the study of thinking, processing, and reasoning, including problem solving, memory, intelligence, and language.

BASIC CONCEPTS

- **Concepts** are used to represent the relationship between two things. We organize our world through concepts. "A bird is an animal that has wings and flies."

- **Hypotheses** are ideas used to test relationships and then to form concepts. "Animals with wings are the ones that fly."

- A **schema** is an organized bunch of knowledge gathered from prior experiences that includes ideas about specific events or objects and the attributes that accompany them. New events and objects are categorized based on how well they match the existing attributes of schemas. Jean Piaget called that process assimilation. For example, a schema about birds might include wings, feathers, flying, and worms, but when someone learns that penguins are birds that swim instead of fly and eat fish instead of worms, that person may have to adjust his or her schema of birds. Piaget called that process accommodation.

- **Scripts** are ideas about the way events typically unfold. "When people go to the movies, they sit in their seats and are quiet."

- **Prototypes** are the **representative** or "usual" type of an event or object. "A scientist is someone who is good in math and does not write poetry."

- **Metacognition** refers to the process of thinking about your own thinking. It might involve knowing what solving strategies to apply and when to apply them, or knowing how to adapt your thinking to new situations.

PROBLEM SOLVING

- **Problem space** is the sum total of possible moves that one might make in order to solve a problem.

- **Algorithms** are problem-solving strategies that consider every possible solution and eventually hit on the correct solution. This may take a great deal of time for humans, but computers use algorithms and process them very quickly.

- **Heuristics** are problem-solving strategies that use rules of thumb or short-cuts based on what has worked in the past. A heuristic cannot guarantee a solution but is faster than an algorithm.

- **Trial and error** is a problem-solving strategy in which someone tries various combinations at random until they find the solution or give up trying. This can also take a great deal of time.

- **Mental set** is the preconceived notion of how to look at a problem. This may help future problem solving. "A bird cage is good for housing birds."

- **Insight** is having a new perspective on an old problem: the *a-ha! experience.*

- **Mediation** is the intervening mental process that occurs between stimulus and response. It reminds us what to do or how to respond based on ideas or past learning.

- **Computer simulation models** are designed to solve problems as humans do. **Allen Newell** and **Herbert Simon** introduced the first of these (called the **logic theorist**) and then revamped it (the **general problem solver**).

Obstacles to Problem Solving

- **Functional fixedness** is the idea that people develop closed minds about the functions of certain objects. From this, they cannot think of creative uses or think divergently. "A bird cage is good only for housing birds."

- **Logical reasoning errors:**
    o **Atmosphere effect.** Drawing a conclusion based on the way information is phrased.
    o **Semantic effect.** Believing in conclusions because of what you know or think to be correct rather than what logically follows from the information given.
    o **Confirmation bias.** Remembering and using information that confirms what you already think.

REASONING AND CREATIVITY

- **Convergent thinking** is the type of thinking used to find the one solution to a problem. Math is an example. Convergent and divergent thinking were first defined by **J. P. Guilford.**

- **Divergent thinking** is used when more than one possibility exists in a situation. Playing chess or creative thinking are examples. In a group, the presence of a dissenter leads to divergent thinking.

- **Deductive reasoning** leads to a specific conclusion that must follow from the information given. "All coats are blue. She wears a coat. Therefore, her coat must be blue."

- **Inductive reasoning** leads to general rules that are inferred from specifics. "Most of the PhD students I know studied hard for their GRE. Therefore, studying hard probably helps one do well on the test and then get into graduate school."

DECISION MAKING AND HEURISTICS

- **Decision making** is working on solving a problem until an acceptable solution is found. Research indicates that the process of reaching a solution is usually based on some sort of assumption, which could either be rational or irrational, and the solution is usually found by relying on reasoning and/or emotion. Common decision-making techniques include making a list of pros and cons, flipping a coin, divination (i.e., tarot cards), and consulting an expert.

- **The availability heuristic** relies on using examples that immediately come to mind rather than facts to make a decision. For example, if news of a plane crash is on constantly, a person might think they are more likely to die in a plane crash than by heart disease or cancer, which are statistically far more likely. But because they can call the example of the plane crash to mind, they declare death by plane crash more likely.

- **The representativeness heuristic** uses an existing prototype to make a decision. For example, if our prototype of surgeon is a male, wearing scrubs, and wielding a scalpel, we will not necessarily envision that the woman in a business suit with a cup of coffee can also be a surgeon. With the representativeness heuristic, we are comparing one scenario to our prototype in our minds.

- **Loss aversion** suggests that people are more willing to take risks when they are afraid of losing. Loss or punishment is a stronger incentive than gain or reward.

- **Utility theory** suggests that people make choices based on their personal preferences.

INFORMATION PROCESSING

- **Reaction time** is most frequently used to measure cognitive processing. This is also called **latency**. Response speed for all types of tasks declines significantly with age.

- **Allan Collins** and **Ross Quillian** assert that people make decisions about the relationship between items by searching their cognitive semantic hierarchies. The farther apart in the hierarchy, the longer it will take to see a connection. The searching and cognitive semantic hierarchies have been termed parallel distributive processing (or connectionism).

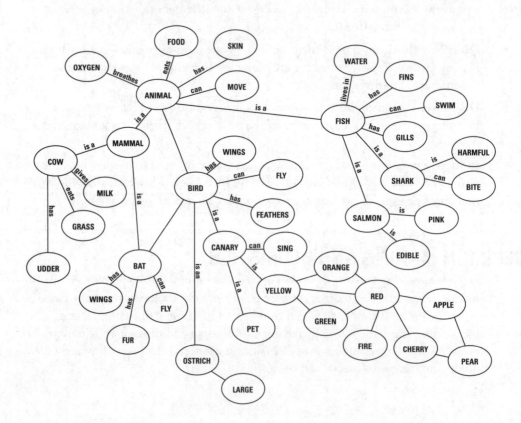

- It takes longer to make associations between pictures than between words, probably because pictures must mentally be put into words before associations can be made.

- **Semantic priming** in a word-recognition task is the presentation of a related item (such as "test") before the next item (such as "GRE"). Semantic priming decreases reaction time because it activates the node of the second item in the semantic hierarchy. In contrast, it would take longer for subjects to recognize the acronym "GRE" if it were preceded by the word lobster rather than by the word test.

- **Stroop effect** explains the decreased speed of naming the color of ink used to print words when the color of ink and the word itself are of different colors, such as when the word yellow is printed with blue ink.

- **Bottom-up processing** is recognizing an item or pattern from data or details **(data driven)**. This is opposed to **top-down processing,** which is guided by larger concepts.

- **Automatic processing** occurs when a task is effortlessly done because the task is subsumed under a higher organization process.

- **Eye movements** and **gaze durations** are indicators of information processing while reading. Eye movements from one fixation point to another are called **saccades.**

- **Intelligence** has a definition that is frequently debated; however, most people tend to agree that intelligence is the capacity to use knowledge to improve achievement in an environment. Many different types of intelligence have been proposed including linguistic, logical, spatial, musical, body movement, and emotional. (For more information on intelligence, see Chapter 14, Measurement and Methodology.)

Study Tip
Slow down on EXCEPT/ LEAST/NOT questions. It takes longer to process the negative versions or denials of statements. Put a big circle around the entire EXCEPT/LEAST/ NOT question and its answer choices. Some students forget that they're dealing with an EXCEPT question by the time they get to choice (E). Slow down and be careful.

Chapter 9
Social Psychology

This chapter will discuss various concepts in social psychology including social perception and cognition, attribution, the self, social comparison, and social influence and persuasion. Also discussed are attraction and aggression, groups and the influence of others, as well as stereotypes, prejudice, and discrimination. The chapter also contains a discussion of industrial and organizational psychology.

DEFINED: Social psychology is the study of how people relate to and influence each other. Social psychology is one of the most heavily weighted sections on the test, so learn your research studies! Some have alleged that social psychology is simply common sense about what we see every day. Let that help you. Use your common sense when choosing answers about social psychology findings.

KEY CONTRIBUTORS

The field of social psychology overflows with big-wig researchers and their studies. They have been subdivided into research areas below—know them all. Three founding contributors:

- **Norman Triplett** conducted the first official social psychology type experiment in 1897 on social facilitation. He found that cyclists performed better when paced by others than when they rode alone.

- **Kurt Lewin** is considered by many to be the founder of the field of social psychology. He applied Gestalt ideas to social behavior. He conceived **field theory,** which is the total of influences upon individual behavior. A person's **life space** is the collection of forces upon the individual. **Valence, vector,** and **barrier** are forces in the life space (see Chapter 5, Learning).

- **Fritz Heider** was the founder of:
  - **Attribution theory,** or the study of how people infer the causes of others' behavior. People will actually attribute intentions and emotions to just about anything—even moving geometrical shapes on a screen!
  - **Balance theory,** or the study of how people make their feelings and/or actions consistent to preserve psychological homeostasis.

SOCIAL PERCEPTION, COGNITION, ATTRIBUTION, BELIEFS

- The **representativeness heuristic** refers to the use of a shortcut about typical assumptions to guess at an answer rather than relying on actual logic. For example, one might assume that a woman who is six feet tall and beautiful is more likely to be a model rather than a lawyer, even though there are many more lawyers than models.

- The **availability heuristic** refers to a process in which people think there is a higher proportion of one thing in a group than there really is because examples of that one thing come to mind more easily. For instance, if someone has read a list of names, half of which were names of celebrities and the other half of which were names randomly selected from a phone book, the person would later report that there were more celebrities than phone book names on the list, because the celebrity names were easier to remember.

- **Anchoring** is the use of a predetermined number or position as a starting point and then making adjustments from there. A lawyer may use anchoring when they start negotiating a settlement for a client.

- **Schemas** are mental frameworks we use to process the enormous amount of information we encounter. We try to match what we are experiencing with our schemas in order to help determine our response.

- **Automatic processing** is processing of the data in the world without conscious awareness. **Controlled processing** is processing of data with systematic, logical, thoughtful awareness.

- **Optimism bias** occurs when a person anticipates more positive outcomes than they do negative outcomes.

- **Planning fallacy** is a type of optimism bias that suggests we believe that a task will take far less time than it actually does.

- **Overconfidence bias** refers to the making of predictions and judgments about ourselves without considering relevant facts.

- **Counterfactual thinking** is "what if things had been different" thinking. For example, a person may wonder, "What if I had actually come to every class and done every assignment? Maybe then I might not have failed my class."

- **Magical thinking** happens when a person imagines something will happen but is unlikely when examined realistically. Believing in superstitions is a type of magical thinking.

- **Terror management** involves our efforts to control an uncontrollable world and keep our fear of death at bay.

- **Nonverbal communication** refers to all the ways people communicate without words. **Body language** includes our gestures, body positions, and how/if we touch others. **Facial expressions** involve both expressions of emotions and **microexpressions,** which are fleeting (they can be less than a second long) expressions that may give us clues about a person's true feelings or if they are lying. **Paralanguage** involves the tone, pitch, and rate of speech.

- Detecting **deception** involves attending to a person's microexpressions, exaggerated facial expressions, or changes in linguistic style.

- **Paul Ekman** has argued that humans have six basic universal emotions: **sadness, happiness, fear, anger, surprise,** and **disgust.** He drew this conclusion from cross-cultural studies that show that individuals in a variety of different cultures were able to recognize facial expressions corresponding to the six aforementioned emotions. Researchers code facial expressions for emotion using the Facial Action Coding System, or **FACS coding.** Such coding can help determine whether a smile is genuine (derived from happiness and therefore engaging the upper cheek) or whether it is fake (a smile is made with the mouth but the eyes and whole face are less involved).

- **Harold Kelley** thought that the **attributions** we make about our actions or those of others are usually accurate. He said we base this on the consistency, distinctiveness, and consensus of the action.

- We either attribute a person's behavior to **dispositional, or internal,** causes (something about their character) or **situational, or external,** causes (something about what is happening in that moment).

- **Fundamental attribution error (correspondence bias)** refers to the attributing of a person's bad behavior to a character flaw rather than to the situation.

- **Actor-observer attributional divergence** is the tendency for the person who is doing the behavior to have a different perspective on the situation than a person watching the behavior.

- **Self-serving attributional bias** is interpreting one's own actions and motives in a positive way, blaming situations for failures and taking credit for successes. We like to think we are "better than average."

- **Self-presentation,** particularly positive self-presentation, is an important influence on behavior. We act in ways that are in line with our attitudes or in ways that will be accepted by others.

- **Impression management** involves all the ways we craft our self-presentation to convey particular messages about ourselves, often based on social norms. For example, on social media, we pick and choose what we post in order to portray ourselves as smart or funny or fun-loving or as having a lot of friends. We edit out what does not serve our image.

When we use schemas and heuristics to interpret the world, we also make mistakes.

- **Illusory correlation** is assuming that two unrelated things have a relationship.

- **Slippery slope** is a logical fallacy that says a small, insignificant first step in one direction will eventually lead to greater steps that will eventually have a significant impact.

- **Hindsight bias** is believing after the fact that you knew something all along.

- **Halo effect** is thinking that if someone has one good quality, then they have many/only good qualities.

- **False consensus bias** is assuming most other people think as you do.

- **Lee Ross** studied subjects who were first made to believe a statement and then later told it was false. The subjects continued to believe the statement if they had processed it and devised their own logical explanation for it.

- **Richard Nisbett** showed that we lack awareness for why we do what we do.

- **Base-rate fallacy** is overestimating the general frequency of things we are most familiar with.

- **M. J. Lerner's just-world bias** is the belief that good things happen to good people and bad things happen to bad people. It is uncomfortable for people to accept that bad things happen to good people, so they blame the victim.

- **Ellen Langer** studied the **illusion of control,** or belief that you can control things that you actually have no influence on. This illusion is the driving force behind manipulating the lottery, gambling, and superstition.

- **Oversimplification** is the tendency to make simple explanations for complex events. People also hold onto original ideas about cause even when new factors emerge.

THE SELF, ATTITUDES, SOCIAL COMPARISON, AND BEHAVIOR

- An **attitude** is a positive, negative, or neutral evaluation of a person, issue, or object.

- **Self-fulfilling prophecy** occurs when one's expectations somehow draw out, or in a sense cause, the very behavior that is expected. In the beginning, there is a false definition of a situation, which evokes a new behavior, which then makes the original false definition true.

- **Leon Festinger's cognitive dissonance theory** suggests that people feel tension, or dissonance, when they hold two thoughts that do not match. So, they try to change their thoughts or behaviors to relieve the unpleasant feeling. Also, the less the act is justified by circumstance, the more people feel the need to justify it by bringing their attitude in line with the behavior.

- **Daryl Bem's self-perception theory** offers an alternative explanation to cognitive dissonance. Bem asserted that when people are unsure of their beliefs, they take their cues from their own behavior (rather than actually changing their beliefs to match their actions). For example, if a man demanded $1,000 to work on a Saturday, he would probably realize that he does not like his job all that much.

- **Overjustification effect** follows from self-perception theory. It is the tendency to assume that we must not want to do things that we are paid or compensated to do. A person who loves to sing and is then paid to do so will lose pleasure in singing because the activity is now overjustified.

- **Self-monitoring** is the process by which people pay close attention to their actions. Often, as a result, people change their behaviors to be more favorable.

- **Social comparison** refers to the evaluation of one's own actions, abilities, opinions, and ideas by comparing them to those of others. Because these "others" are generally familiar people from our own social group or strata, social comparison has been used as an argument against **mainstreaming.** When children with difficulties are thrown into classes with children without such difficulties, this comparison may result in lower self-esteem for the children with problems.

- **Objective self-awareness** is achieved through self-perception, high self-monitoring, internality, and self-efficacy. Some experimenters facilitate objective self-awareness by having subjects perform tasks while looking in a mirror. Deindividuation would work against objective self-awareness.

- **Social identity** refers to one's membership in socially defined categories (such as "sister" or "Asian American" or "Christian"). **Personal identity** refers to the all the beliefs one has about oneself that have no objective definitions (such as "smart" or "tall" or "funny"). When people make **intergroup comparisons,** they are comparing themselves to members of other groups. **Intragroup comparisons** refer to comparisons within one's own in-group.

- **Self-promotion** is the presenting of our best selves to others. **Self-verification** involves trying to get others to agree with our views.

- **Ego depletion** refers to a situation in which a person's resources or coping skills have been exhausted, which can make it more difficult for that person to self-regulate.

- **Upward social comparisons** occur when we compare ourselves to those whom we believe are better than we are in some way. **Downward social comparisons** occur when we compare ourselves to those whom we believe are worse off than we are in some way.

- **Stereotype threat** happens when we are at risk for confirming a negative stereotype about our group and causes us to underperform. **Stereotype boost** occurs when we are exposed to positive stereotypes about our group, leading to an improved performance.

INFLUENCE AND PERSUASION

- **M. Fischbein** and **I. Ajzen** are known for their **theory of reasoned action.** This theory states that people's behavior in a given situation is determined by their attitude about the situation and social norms. This was later renamed the **theory of planned behavior.**

- **R. E. Petty** and **J. T. Cacioppo's elaboration likelihood model** of persuasion suggests that people who are very involved in an issue listen to the strength of the arguments in the issue rather than more superficial factors, such as the characteristics of the speaker. The elaboration-likelihood model says that if the audience is interested in the argument and is able to understand it, persuasion is via the central route, and the likelihood of permanent change is high. If an audience is unable or unwilling to listen to an argument, persuasion is best through the peripheral route—make the audience comfortable and happy and hope some of the message sticks.

Study Tip

The best way to learn a task is by practicing or by studying in short, frequent intervals. People learn better if they study for a while, take a break, and then study again. So, just say no to cramming!

- An individual speaker is most likely to change a listener's attitude if:
    o The speaker is an expert and/or trustworthy.
    o The speaker is similar to the listener.
    o The speaker is acceptable to the listener.
    o The speaker is overheard rather than obviously trying to influence.
    o The content is anecdotal, emotional, or shocking.
    o The speaker is part of a two-person debate rather than a one-sided argument.

- **Sleeper effect** explains why persuasive communication from a source of low credibility may become more acceptable after the fact.

- **McGuire's inoculation theory** asserts that people's beliefs are vulnerable if they have never faced a challenge. Once they have experienced a challenge to their opinions, however, they are less vulnerable. A challenge is like a vaccination.

- **Reactance** is the refusal to conform that may occur as a result of a blatant attempt to control. Also, people will often not conform if they are **forewarned** that others will attempt to change them.

ATTRACTION AND CLOSE RELATIONSHIPS

- Humans have a **need for affiliation**—researchers believe this need for love and belonging is vital to our psychological wellbeing.
- In relative order of importance, we are attracted to other people who:
  1. Are near us, because then we get a chance to know them (**proximity**)
  2. Are **physically attractive**
  3. Have attitudes **similar** to our own
  4. Like us back (**reciprocity**)
- **Opposites do not attract.** The old saying is just talk, according to research.
- **Reciprocity of disclosure,** or sharing secrets/feelings, facilitates emotional closeness.
- **Excitation-transfer theory** says that sometimes we attribute our excitement or physiological arousal about one thing to something else. For example, if you go bungee jumping on your first date, you may end up thinking you like your date more than you do because you might think the excitement and physiological arousal is from being around your date instead of from the bungee jumping.
- **Mere-exposure effect** says that simply having some familiarity with something or someone will increase our positive feelings.
- **Repeated exposure effect** is related to proximity and suggests that the more contact we have with something or someone will increase our positive feelings. For example, the more you see your classmates, the more you will feel positively inclined toward them, even if you don't actually talk to them.
- **Elaine Hatfield** and other researchers have looked at different kinds of love. According to Hatfield, the two basic types of love are passionate love and companionate love. **Passionate love** is intense longing for the union with another and a state of profound physiological arousal. **Companionate love** is the affection we feel for those with whom our lives are deeply entwined. Passionate love, which is based on a biophysiological system shared with other primates, is a powerful emotion that can be both positive (when love is reciprocal) and negative (when love is unrequited). Companionate love, on the other hand, is achieved via mutual trust, respect, and commitment and often characterizes later stages of relationships.
- **Sternberg's Triangular model of love** is based on the levels of **intimacy, passion, and commitment.** A person experiencing **romantic** love combines intimacy and passion (e.g., a summer fling). A person experiencing **companionate** love combines intimacy with commitment (e.g., a long-term marriage in which the passion has faded). A person experiencing **fatuous** love combines passion and commitment (e.g., a whirlwind courtship and marriage). The ideal, according to Sternberg, is **consummate** love, which combines all three.

- One's earliest relationships—**attachment styles**—are believed to exert a strong influence on future relationships (see Chapter 10, Developmental Psychology). If a person as a baby develops a secure attachment with the primary caregiver, that person will likely display that attachment in later relationships (high levels of self-esteem and interpersonal trust). If a person develops an avoidant attachment with the primary caregiver, that person will display low levels of self-esteem and interpersonal trust. Other insecure attachments may cause people to display either a low level of self-esteem and high interpersonal trust or high self-esteem and low interpersonal trust.

STEREOTYPES, PREJUDICE, AND DISCRIMINATION

- **Risk aversion** suggests that when making decisions people tend to opt for the choice with less risk, even if the risk is small. The threat of loss is a more powerful motivator than the possibility of gain.

- **Stereotypes** are the preconceived generalized notions people have about particular groups. For example, a person may believe that all librarians are women who wear their hair in a bun and wear cardigan sweaters or that all business people wear suits and carry briefcases. Gender stereotypes refer to specific stereotypes about what a man is or what a woman is in society. Stereotypes can also lead to prejudice and discrimination.

- The **glass ceiling** refers to the way in which women have been limited in how much they can achieve. For example, until a woman is elected President of the United States, women have not broken that glass ceiling. The **glass cliff** refers to putting women in positions of power when that position carries a risk of failure. That way, if the company fails, the blame can be placed on the woman.

- **Tokenism** refers to admitting one or a very few members of a previously excluded group, often to display supposed inclusion and reduce claims of discrimination from minority groups.

- **Prejudice** is having negative beliefs and judgments about a group of people based on a social category, such as race, ethnicity, gender, sexual orientation, or religion.

- **Discrimination** is the negative treatment or behavior based on prejudicial beliefs.

- **Zero-sum outcomes** refer to the belief that if one group gains something, that will necessarily come at the expense of another group.

- **Competition** for scarce resources usually causes conflict in a group. **Muzafer Sherif** showed that win/lose game-type competition can also trigger serious conflict in groups. **Sherif's Robbers Cave Experiment** (a study about prejudice) showed that group conflict is most effectively overcome by the need for cooperative attention to a higher **superordinate** goal. In the Robbers Cave Experiments, in which 2 groups of 12-year-old boys attended a summer camp, Sherif noticed three phases of group dynamics. The first was the in-group phase in which people bonded with their own groups. The second phase was the friction phase in which the 2 groups met and became competitive with one another. The third phase was the integration phase in which the 2 teams had to work together toward a common goal that neither group could accomplish alone. The experiment also revealed a great deal about how easily in-groups and out-groups can form, and it more importantly revealed strategies for conflict resolution.

- **Bona fide pipeline** is a procedure used to determine a person's implicit associations or beliefs about other social groups. Participants have to rate adjectives as positive or negative, but before they rate the adjectives, they are exposed to faces of people from different racial and ethnic backgrounds.

- **Bogus pipeline** is an instrument that measures physiological reactions in order to measure the truthfulness of attitude self-reporting.

- **Ingroup/outgroup bias** refers to a situation in which individuals in one group think their members have more positive qualities and fewer negative qualities than members of the other group even though the qualities are the same in each. This is the basis for **prejudice.**

- **Contact** with the opposing party decreases conflict. We fear what we do not know.

- **Kenneth** and **Mamie Clark** conducted the famous **doll preference studies,** which factored into the 1954 Supreme Court case, *Brown v. Board of Education.* The studies demonstrated the negative effects that group segregation had on African American children's self-esteem. The African American children thought the white dolls were better.

- **M. Rokeach** studied racial bias and the similarity of beliefs. People prefer to be with like-minded people more than with like-skinned people. Also, racial bias decreases as attitude similarity between people increases.

GROUPS AND THE INFLUENCE OF OTHERS

- **Role** is the set of behavior norms that seem suitable for a particular person.
- **Social norms** refer to what is considered normal behavior for a particular society.
- In **collectivist** societies, members are communally oriented and focus on the common good, while members of **individualist** societies care more about personal gain than the welfare of the community as a whole.
- **Hazel Markus** has found that Eastern countries, in contrast to Western, value interdependence over independence. In countries in which interdependence is emphasized (such as Japan), individuals are more likely to demonstrate conformity, modesty, and pessimism. In countries where independence is emphasized (such as the United States), individuals are more likely to show optimism, self-enhancement, and individuality. Some have criticized this research for making generalizations about cultures.

- **Reciprocal interaction,** or the constant exchange of influences between people, is a constant factor in our behavior.
- **Gain-loss theory** suggests that people act in order to obtain gain and avoid loss. People feel most favorably toward situations that start out negatively but end positively (even when compared to completely positive situations).
- **Social exchange theory** suggests that humans interact in ways that maximize reward and minimize costs.
- **Social facilitation** is the tendency for the presence of others to either enhance or hinder performance. **Robert Zajonc** found that the presence of others helps with easy tasks but hinders complex tasks.

- **Conformity** is going along with real or perceived group pressure. People may go along publicly but not privately **(compliance)**, or change actions and beliefs to conform **(acceptance)**. An individual who speaks out against the majority is a **dissenter.** An individual is most likely to conform when:

  o There is a majority opinion.
  o The majority has a unanimous position.
  o The majority has high status, or the individual is concerned with her own status.
  o The situation is in public.
  o The individual was not previously committed to another position.
  o The individual has low self-esteem.
  o The individual scores high on a measure of authoritarianism.

- **Solomon Asch** had participants look at a line on Exhibit A and compare it to three lines on Exhibit B. When the participants did this task alone, they erred less than one percent of the time. Then Asch brought in confederates, who initially chose correctly but then purposely chose incorrect lines. About 33 percent of the participants conformed to the group and chose the incorrect lines. The unanimity of the group seemed to be the influential factor.

- **Stanley Milgram** is known for his very famous study in which participants were given the role of "teacher" and ordered by the experimenter to administer "painful electric shocks" to a "learner" in an adjacent room when the learner provided an incorrect response. However, no one was actually receiving any shocks; the learner was simply a confederate (fakers who were in the experiment). The experiment explored how people responded to the orders of others. Conditions that facilitated conformity were remoteness of the victim, proximity of the experimenter/commander, a legitimate-seeming commander, and the conformity of other subjects. Participants went along through the entire experiment 66 percent of the time. This experiment has been used to explain the actions of Nazi war criminals. It also raised ethical issues in psychological research, as after the conclusion of the experiment, many of the participants were upset that they were willing to deliver such dangerous shocks to someone.

- **Philip Zimbardo** later found that people who were wearing hoods (and so deindividuated) were more willing to administer higher levels of shock than people without hoods. Also, in his classic **prison simulation experiments,** Zimbardo found that normal subjects could easily be transformed into sadistic prison guards. In both cases, Zimbardo showed that people will step into some surprising roles. The BBC attempted in 2006 to replicate Zimbardo's prison experiment for a television special but was unsuccessful. Zimbardo argued that the BBC did not actually replicate the study and that the BBC's research design was problematic.

- **Muzafer Sherif's** classic experiment found that people's descriptions of the autokinetic effect (see Chapter 3, Sensation and Perception) were influenced by others' descriptions.

- **Morton Deutsch** used the **prisoner's dilemma** and the **trucking company game** story to illustrate the struggle between cooperation and competition. The premise of the prisoner's dilemma is that, if two criminal cohorts are detained separately and charged with the crime, the best strategy is for neither to talk. This way, no information will be given. But because a person can never be sure what the other might do (perhaps plea bargain and testify against him), remaining silent is a gamble that requires trust. Therefore, most people spill the beans when they should simply remain silent. The trucking company game describes two companies that can choose to cooperate (and agree on high fixed prices) or compete against each other with lower prices. The best strategy would be to cooperate and agree on high prices, but because one company cannot totally trust the other, they choose to compete. It's the same as the prisoner's dilemma but in economic terms.

- **Compliance** refers to the ways in which a person tries to get another person to do something. Some strategies for compliance include:
    - **Door-in-the-face** is a sales tactic in which people ask for more than they would ever get and then "settle" for less (the realistic amount hoped for).
    - **Foot-in-the-door phenomenon** refers to a situation in which a person who is willing to perform a small favor first is then more willing to do larger ones later.
    - **Low-ball technique** is a method in which a person is offered something at a very low cost (e.g., time or money) and then the cost is raised after they agree.
    - **That's not all technique** involves sweetening a deal before the person has had a chance to say yes or no. This technique has been used on classic television game shows such as *The Price Is Right*.
    - **Deadline technique** occurs when sellers use the threat of a looming deadline to induce compliance. For example, infomercials use this when they say, "If you call in the next 10 minutes, we will double your order free."
    - **Ingratiation** involves using flattery to gain compliance.

- **Deindividuation** occurs in situations in which there is a high degree of arousal and low degree of personal responsibility. In these situations, individual identity or accountability is de-emphasized. This may be the result of mingling in a crowd, wearing uniforms, or otherwise adopting a larger group identity.

- **The Kitty Genovese case** (the murder of a woman witnessed by scores of people) led to the investigation of the **bystander effect,** or why people are less likely to help when others are present.

- **Diffusion of responsibility** is the tendency that the larger the group, the less likely individuals in the group will act or take responsibility. As in the Genovese case, the more bystanders nearby, the less likely anyone will help. Everyone waits for someone else to act.

- **Social loafing** is the tendency to work less hard in a group than one would if working individually. It is guarded against when each individual is closely monitored.

- **Philip Zimbardo** found that antisocial behavior positively correlates with population density. He left broken-down cars in New York City and Palo Alto, California, monitored by hidden cameras. The car in New York City was stripped and destroyed within 10 minutes; the car in Palo Alto was untouched for three days.

- **Group polarization,** studied by **James Stoner,** is the concept that group discussion with like-minded people generally serves to strengthen the already dominant point of view. This explains the **risky shift,** or why groups will take greater risks than individuals.

- **Groupthink,** studied by **Irving Janis,** occurs when the desire for harmony or conformity in a group results in dysfunctional decision making. This is more likely to occur in a group that has unquestioned beliefs, pressure to conform, invulnerability, censors, cohesiveness within, isolation from without, and a strong leader.

- **Pluralistic ignorance** occurs when most of the people in a group privately disagree with something but incorrectly believe that most people in the group agree with it.

EVOLUTIONARY PSYCHOLOGY, PROSOCIAL BEHAVIOR, AND AGGRESSION

- **Empathy** refers to a person's literally feeling what another is feeling, as if they are in another's shoes, as opposed to sympathy, which is feeling bad for another person.

- The **empathy-altruism hypothesis** states that a person will act prosocially simply because they want to help another person in need.

- The **negative state relief model** suggests that people behave prosocially in order to feel better about themselves or their situation.

- The **empathic joy hypothesis** says people behave prosocially specifically to feel good.

- **Kin selection theory,** which comes from evolutionary psychology, states that we are more likely to help members of our own family because we want to make sure our genes survive into the next generation.

- **Social exclusion**—when we are "left out" of a group—diminishes our desire to help others.

- **Drive theories of aggression** refer to early understanding of aggression. Freud suggested that aggression is a result of the Thanatos, or death drive, which underlies the desire to hurt oneself or others. Based on his experiments in ethology, Konrad Lorenz argued that aggression is an inherited instinct to make sure the strongest survive and pass their genes to the next generation.

- The **frustration-aggression hypothesis,** proposed by Dollard and Miller, and researched in depth by **Leonard Berkowitz,** posits that frustration in achieving a goal (no matter how small) leads to the show of aggression.

- The **general aggression model (GAM)** comes from a social learning perspective and suggests that aggression is the result of multiple factors, both situational and personal.

- The **hostile attributional bias** says that when people perceive hostility in others, they are more likely to respond with hostility.

- **Bullying** refers to the acting of aggressive behavior toward another person who is perceived to be of lower status.

- The **catharsis hypothesis** suggests people can redirect aggressive energy by releasing it in other ways. For example, a person might punch a pillow or punching bag, or engage in an exhausting workout at the gym in order to diminish the aggressive impulses.

- **Equity theory** is the idea that people feel most comfortable in situations in which rewards and punishments are equal, fitting, or highly logical.

- **Overbenefited** people tend to feel guilty. Random or illogical punishments make people anxious.

- **Stanley Milgram's stimulus-overload theory** explains why urbanites are less prosocial than country people are; urbanites don't need any more interaction.

OTHER IMPORTANT SOCIAL PSYCHOLOGY IDEAS

- **Richard Lazarus** studied stress and coping. He differentiated between problem-focused coping (which is changing the stressor) and emotion-focused coping (which is changing our response to a stressor).

- **Social support network** effects on mental health have emerged as an area of study that combines social and clinical ideas. Social support has been shown to reduce the effects of stress.

- **J. Rodin** and **E. Langer** showed that nursing home residents who have plants to care for have better health and lower mortality rates.

- **Peter principle** is the concept that people are promoted at work until they reach a position of incompetence, the position in which they remain.

- **Stuart Valins** studied environmental influences on behavior. Architecture matters. Students in long-corridor dorms feel more stressed and withdrawn than students in suite-style dorms.

- **Reciprocal socialization** occurs when two parties (such as parents and children) adapt to or are socialized by each other. For example, we say that parents or adults are socialized by youngsters when parents pick up new lingo, and that children are socialized by parents when children learn to respect rules and traditions.

INDUSTRIAL/ORGANIZATIONAL PSYCHOLOGY

Industrial/organizational psychology (I/O psychology) is the branch of psychology that deals with the workplace. I/O psychologists work to increase an organization's efficiency and functionality by improving the performance and well-being of the people in the organization.

- **Walter Dill Scott** was one of the first people to apply psychology principles to business, by employing psychological principles in advertising. Additionally, he was involved in helping the military to implement psychological testing to aid with personnel selection.

- **Henry Landsberger** coined the term **Hawthorne effect** in 1955 when he was analyzing old data that was collected in the late 1920s in order to increase worker productivity at Hawthorne Works. The researchers reported that anything they did increased productivity, Landsberger postulated that this was because people's performance changes when they are being observed.

- **Sociotechnical systems** are a method of work design that acknowledges the interaction between people and technology in the workplace.

- A **sunk cost** is an expense that has been incurred and cannot be recovered. The best strategy is to ignore these when making decisions, because the money that has already been spent is irrelevant to the future.

Chapter 10
Developmental Psychology

This chapter discusses the fundamental concepts and major theories concerning developmental psychology. It covers animal behavior in terms of ethology and comparative psychology, along with the major tenets of human physical, moral, cognitive, psychosocial, and personality development.

DEFINED: **Developmental psychology is the study of changes and transitions that accompany physical growth or maturation.** It is one of the most heavily tested topics on the exam.

ETHOLOGY

Ethology is the study of animal behaviors, especially innate behaviors that occur in a natural habitat.

Key Contributors

- **Charles Darwin** made the concept of evolution scientifically plausible by asserting that **natural selection** was at its core (more about evolution and natural selection later in this chapter). For this reason, the concept of evolution is most commonly attributed to him, although he was not actually the first to think of it. His ideas about evolution have been applied to and tested in ethology.

- **Konrad Lorenz, Nikolaas Tinbergen,** and **Karl von Frisch,** all major figures in ethology, shared the Nobel Prize in 1973.

- **Konrad Lorenz** was the **founder of ethology** as a distinct research area. He also created well-known terminology and theory in the field. A question about Lorenz appears on virtually every GRE Psychology Test. Other questions about the areas that he pioneered also show up often. Lorenz is best known for work with:

  o **Imprinting.** Through extensive work with animal social relationships, Lorenz discovered the phenomenon of imprinting. He found that in certain species (most often birds), the young attach to or imprint on the first moving object they see after birth. This attachment is most commonly displayed by a "following response" in which the young chicks follow their first contact, whether it be an adult bird or an adult human. Lorenz also found that imprinting was subject to a sensitive learning period, after which imprinting would not occur.

Lorenz and three of his adopted children

○ **Animal aggression.** Lorenz's theory of instinct fueled the fire of ethology's great debate over innate behavior. Most notably, drawing from Darwin's ideas of natural selection, Lorenz argued that certain kinds of aggression were necessary for the survival of species. Contrary to most psychologists, Lorenz argued that aggressive behavior is instinctual rather than learned and that even human intraspecies aggression can be explained through survival needs.

○ **Releasing stimuli.** Lorenz did the earliest work with **releasing stimuli** (also known as **releasers** or **sign stimuli**), which was later continued by Tinbergen. A releasing stimulus in one individual of a species elicits an automatic, instinctual chain of behaviors from another individual in the same species. Lorenz called these elicited chains of behaviors fixed action patterns (examples given below in the description of Tinbergen's research).

• **Fixed action patterns.** As conceived by Lorenz, fixed action patterns are instinctual, complex chains of behaviors triggered by releasing stimuli. They have four defining characteristics: they are **uniform** patterns, they are **performed by most members** of the species, they are more **complex** than simple reflexes, and they **cannot be interrupted** or stopped in the middle. A question about fixed action patterns appears on nearly every GRE Psychology Test.

• **Nikolaas Tinbergen** was one of the founders of modern ethology. Tinbergen is best known for his use of models in naturalistic settings. He continued Lorenz's work with releasing stimuli. Tinbergen's most famous experiments involved stickleback fish and herring gull chicks.

- In the spring, male **stickleback fish** develop red coloration on their belly, and they fight each other. Tinbergen hypothesized that the **red belly** acted as the releasing stimulus for the attacks. To test this, he built various models of stickleback fish, ranging from very crude models (on which the only feature was a red belly) to very detailed models (which lacked only the red belly). The stickleback males attacked the red-bellied models rather than the detailed but non-red models, thus indicating that the red belly was indeed the sign stimulus for fighting.

- Hungry **herring gull chicks** peck at the end of their parents' bills, which have a red spot on the tip. The parent then regurgitates food for the chicks. Tinbergen hypothesized that the **red spot on the bill** is what signals the chick to peck at this particular spot. In testing this, he found that chicks pecked more at a red-tipped model bill than at a plain model bill. Further, he found that the greater the contrast between the bill and the red spot, the more vigorously the chicks would peck, even when the contrast was so strong as to be unnatural. This is the concept of the **supernormal sign stimulus.** Supernormal sign stimuli are artificial stimuli that exaggerate the naturally occurring sign stimulus or releaser. They are more effective than the natural releaser.

- **Karl von Frisch** was a major figure in the study of animal behavior. He is most famous for the discovery that honeybees communicate through a dance that they perform (more on the honeybee dance later in this chapter). Von Frisch also studied the senses of fish.

- **Walter Cannon** coined the term **fight or flight,** referring to the internal physiological changes that occur in an organism in response to a perceived threat (i.e., increase in heart rate or respiration). These changes help to provide the animal with necessary resources to either "fight" or "flee" the threat. Cannon also proposed the idea of **homeostasis,** which is the internal regulation of a body to maintain equilibrium (i.e., decrease the heart rate after the perceived threat is no longer present).

GENETICS

Genetics questions on the GRE Psychology Test mostly pertain to heredity in humans. **Genes** are the basic unit of heredity. Genes are composed of DNA molecules and are organized in chromosomes. The nucleus of human cells contains 23 pairs of chromosomes. Chromosomes in cells act as carriers for genes, and therefore for heredity.

A **gamete,** sperm or ovum in humans, is **haploid** and so contains 23 single chromosomes. (All other human cells are **diploid** and contain 23 pairs of chromosomes.) The individual of any species is the result of equal genetic contributions from the gamete of two individual parents. The genetic material of one parent neither mixes with nor contaminates the genetic material of the other; rather, two separate sets of 23 chromosomes come together in the **zygote** (the fertilized egg cell) to form 23 chromosome pairs. Zygotes are **diploid** because they contain 23 pairs of chromosomes.

The total of all genetic material that an offspring receives (the 23 pairs or 46 total chromosomes) is called the **genotype.** The genotype is an individual's complete genetic makeup, including both **dominant** and **recessive** genes. These possible dominant and recessive gene variations for each characteristic pair up into **alleles.** The two genes that make up the allele occupy the same place on the chromosome. A pair will be constructed as dominant-dominant, recessive-recessive, or dominant-recessive.

Dominant genes always beat out recessive genes. A recessive gene is not manifested unless it is paired with another recessive gene. An individual's combination of dominant and recessive genes determines what he or she looks like on the outside. These external characteristics (eye color, size, etc.) make up the phenotype. Phenotypic expression (how one looks and sometimes acts) is partially determined by heredity or genotype, but can also be influenced by the environment.

EVOLUTION AND NATURAL SELECTION

Darwin asserted that, since there is variation among individuals within one species, and since more animals are born than will survive to maturity, a sort of selection process determines which animals survive and reproduce. Individuals best suited to the environment are most likely to survive, and these individuals will pass on their genes. This process in which only the fit survive is called **natural selection** and is at the heart of evolution. Natural selection explains the evolution or genetic development of various species over time. It also explains the concept of **genetic drift** (the way in which particular genotypes are selected out or eliminated from a population over time).

Fitness

Fitness relates to natural selection's slogan of survival of the fittest. Fitness is the ability to reproduce and pass on genes. Who are the fittest? The fittest animals are sufficiently well suited to the environment to successfully reproduce. This means they have traits that allow them to offset the dangers of competition and predation. This does not mean, however, that individual animals care only about themselves and their own reproduction. In fact, natural selection favors **inclusive fitness** over individual fitness. Inclusive fitness is the concept that animals will be invested in the survival of not only their own genes but also the genes of their kin (since they are carrying the same genes). This **kin selection** creates inclusive fitness. It also explains why parents protect their young and why individual animals may put themselves at risk by sounding alarm calls to warn their siblings of a predator.

INSTINCTUAL BEHAVIOR VERSUS LEARNED BEHAVIOR

Many studies in animal behavior attempt to differentiate between behaviors that are learned and behaviors that are instinctual. **Instinctual** or **innate** behaviors are:

- present in all normal members of a species
- stereotypic in form throughout the members of a species, even when performed for the first time
- independent of learning or experience

Some behaviors have been found to be innate, others learned. Some experiments have shown that there is an interaction between instinct and learning. For example, rodents reared in isolation still perform instinctual nest-building behaviors, but their performance is less efficient and less successful than that of rodents also exposed to learning opportunities. The isolated rodents' nests take longer to build and are of poorer construction.

OTHER THINGS YOU SHOULD KNOW

- **Altruism** is behavior that solely benefits another. While actions of inclusive fitness, such as protecting offspring and siblings are somewhat altruistic, an individual is still aiding in the continuation of its genes through this behavior. Truly altruistic behaviors (those toward non-kin) have somewhat baffled ethologists, because they are incompatible with the idea that individuals do what has the greatest survival value for them. Most likely, altruistic behaviors are similar to a group mentality. Individuals will help others if the benefit outweighs the cost or if they expect to be repaid somehow. In this way, altruism is compatible with natural selection.

- **Courting** refers to behaviors that precede sexual acts that lead to reproduction. Courting serves the purposes of attracting a mate and of isolating a mate of the same species.

- **Estrus** is the period in which a female of the species is sexually receptive (usually used to describe non-human mammals).

- **Inbreeding** is breeding within the same family. Evolutionary controls prevent this. An example of such a mechanism is the facial markings of swans. Swans from the same family have similar markings; swans usually choose mates with dissimilar markings.

- **Mimicry** refers to an evolved form of deception. Some harmless species of snakes, for example, mimic the coloration and patterning of poisonous snakes and escape predation as a result.

- **Instinctual drift** occurs when an animal replaces a trained or forced response with a natural or instinctive response.

- **Pheromones** are chemicals detected by the vomeronasal organ that act as messengers between animals. The exchange of pheromones is thought to be the most primitive form of communication between animals. Pheromones can transmit states such as fear or sexual receptiveness.

- **Reproductive isolating mechanisms** serve to prevent **interbreeding** between two different (but closely related and possibly genetically compatible) species. There are four forms of isolating mechanisms:
    - o **Behavioral isolation** occurs when courtship or display behavior of a particular species allows an individual to identify a mate within its own species—only a member of that species will respond to that particular type of courting.
    - o **Geographic isolation** occurs when different species breed in different areas to prevent confusion or genetic mixing.
    - o **Mechanical isolation** occurs when different species have incompatible genital structures.
    - o **Isolation by season** occurs when potentially compatible species mate during different seasons.
- **Sensitive** or **critical periods in learning** are times when a developing animal is particularly vulnerable to the effects of learning (or to the lack of such learning). For example, certain bird species have a critical period for learning the song of their species. If such birds are reared in isolation during this critical period, they cannot develop a normal song later. Critical periods also factor into imprinting. Some developing animals imprint on the first moving objects they experience. Later, they will follow and attempt to mate with this type of animal no matter what their later experiences are.
- **Sexual dimorphism** refers to the structural differences between the sexes. Sexual dimorphism has arisen through both natural and sexual selections.
- **Sexual selection,** according to Darwin in *The Descent of Man* (1871), is a form of natural selection. In sexual selection, however, it is not the fittest that necessarily win out but rather those with the greatest chance of being chosen as a mate (usually the best fighters, the best courters, and the most attractive individuals).
- **Selective breeding** is contrived breeding. Mates are intentionally paired to increase the chances of producing offspring with particular traits.

COMPARATIVE PSYCHOLOGY

Comparative psychology is closely related to ethology. Through research studies, different species are compared in order to learn about their similarities and differences. Psychology draws from animal studies to gain insight into human functioning.

Important Animal Experiments and Discoveries

Bees, Birds, and Bats

- **Karl von Frisch** discovered the **dance of the honeybees,** which was only one of several important discoveries about the behavior of honeybees.

  o **Communication.** Honeybees communicate by "dancing." Once a scouting bee has located a promising food source, it returns to the hive and conveys the location of food to the rest of the hive through a series of movements. A **round dance** (dancing in circular motion) indicates food that is extremely nearby. A **waggle dance** (dancing with wiggle-type movements) indicates food that is far away. The longer the dance, the farther the food, and the more vigorous the display, the better the food. Most important, the dance is performed on the vertical sheets of the hive. The angle between a perfectly vertical line and the direction the bee orients when dancing is the same angle as between the sun and the food source. The same type of dance is used to communicate potential nesting sites.

  o **Navigation.** Bees are exemplary navigators. Scouting bees do nothing other than look for food and nesting sites and return with the information. While it is known that bees use landmarks as simple location cues, they are also able to use the Sun, polarized light, and magnetic fields as navigational aides.

  o **Hierarchy.** Honeybees form a hierarchy within the hive as only one bee emerges as the queen. Once queen, this bee produces a chemical that suppresses the ovaries in all of the other female bees, so that she is the one reproducer. The **queen bee** is constantly tended to and fed by all of the other bees (the female worker bees), and in the spring, she lays thousands of eggs. As these eggs mature, scouts find a new hive site for the old queen and her workers. When a new queen is ready to emerge in a hive, the old queen and her crew depart for a new site.

  o **Mating.** Very few male bees **(drones)** are produced. They serve only one purpose: to mate with the queen. The same mating areas are used year after year even though no bee survives from one year to the next. No one knows how they know to gather in the nearest mating site.

  o **Flower selection.** Bees can see ultraviolet light, so they see flower coloration in a more complex way than humans do. Von Frisch found that honeybees could see certain markers on flowers **(honeyguides)** that people could not.

- **Navigation** is a broad topic, but certain animals are frequently held to be adept navigators. Some animals use a sort of map-and-compass navigation, with the map being landmarks and the compass being sense of direction from elements like the Sun or stars. Other animals have true navigational abilities in which they can point toward their goal with no landmarks and from any position. For example, if captured and moved around the world during migration, some birds arrive at their usual goal anyway (true navigation) whereas others are not able to correct their "compass" for the displacement. **Birds** and **bees** are commonly cited as expert celestial navigators. Different cues may serve as a compass:

- ○ **Atmospheric pressure.** Pigeons are sensitive to pressure changes in altitude.

- ○ **Infrasound.** Pigeons can hear extremely low-frequency sounds (infrasounds) that humans cannot. These low-frequency sounds, emitted by surf for example, travel great distances and may be used as navigational cues.

- ○ **Magnetic sense.** Pigeons and bees are thought to have magnetic sensitivity, which allows them to use the Earth's magnetic forces as cues.

- ○ **Sun compass.** Both pigeons and bees are known to use the Sun as a compass and to compensate for its daily movements.

- ○ **Star compass.** Many birds use star patterns and movement for navigation.

- ○ **Polarized light.** When the Sun is obscured by clouds, bees can use polarized light to infer the positioning of the Sun.

- **Echolocation** is a most sophisticated type of perception, which generally replaces sight. Marine mammals (like dolphins) use echolocation, but **bats** are probably the most commonly used examples. Bats emit high-frequency bursts of sound and locate nearby objects from the echo that bounces off these objects. Though the description is simple, the accuracy of echolocation is not. Research studies have found that bats with 40 cm wing spans can fly through grids of thin nylon string, that bats can discriminate between edible and inedible objects, and that bats can locate and eat small flying insects at the rate of two per second.

- **Owls,** like bats, must navigate at night, but owls do not use echolocation. Rather, their hearing is similar to that of humans. Like humans, they judge direction and distance by comparing the differing intensities and arrival times at the two ears. Owls are better than humans at determining elevation of the source of sound; however, because their ears are asymmetrical (one higher than the other), sound from above or below will reach the different ears at different times and with different intensities.

- **Harry Harlow** researched development with rhesus monkeys. Of particular significance to developmental psychology were his results with social isolation and maternal stimulation.

- ○ **Social isolation.** Harlow compared monkeys raised in social isolation to monkeys raised with a peer group. With the isolated monkeys, a lack of interaction and socialization with normal, young monkeys hampered their social development. Once brought together with other monkeys, isolated male monkeys did not display normal sexual functioning and isolated female monkeys lacked maternal behaviors.

- ○ **Contact comfort.** Harlow studied the phenomenon of attachment with infant monkeys. Separated at birth from their mothers, infant monkeys were placed in cages with two "surrogate mothers." One surrogate mother was a plain wire dummy monkey equipped with a feeding bottle and the other surrogate mother was a terrycloth dummy mother with no feeding bottle. Surprisingly, the infant spent most of its time with the terrycloth mother and ran to this surrogate when afraid. The infant approached the wire mother only to feed. It seems then that infants attach to their mothers through comforting experience rather than through feeding.

Other Experiments

- **R. C. Tyron** selectively bred "maze bright" and "maze dull" rats to demonstrate the heritability of behavior. Later, **R. M. Cooper** and **John Zubek** demonstrated the interaction between heredity and environment. In the latter experiment, the selectively bred bright rats performed better than the dull rats in maze problem solving only when both sets of rats were raised in normal conditions. Both the bright and dull rats performed well when raised in an enriched environment (with lots of food and available activities, for example); both the bright and dull rats performed poorly when raised in an impoverished environment.

PHYSIOLOGICAL DEVELOPMENT

In humans, fertilization occurs in the fallopian tube of the female when a sperm unites with an egg or ovum and travels to the uterus. The **zygote** (the fertilized ovum) then goes through three stages of **gestation** or prenatal development:

- The **germinal** stage lasts two weeks, during which time the zygote moves down the fallopian tube, grows into 64 cells through cell division, and implants itself into the wall of the uterus.
- The **embryonic** stage lasts until the end of the second month and consists of organ formation.
- The **fetal** stage lasts from the third month until birth. Quantitative growth occurs during this time, as well as movement (called "quickening").

Six weeks after conception, the presence of H-Y antigen causes testes to form, while the absence of H-Y antigen causes ovaries to form. Approximately three months after conception, the testes secrete testosterone, which results in the formation of the rest of the male reproductive system, while the absence of testosterone (generally from ovaries developing instead of testes) results in the formation of the female reproductive system.

A **neonate** is a newborn. The behavior of neonates is reflexive. The best-known reflexes are the **sucking reflex** (elicited by placing an object in the baby's mouth), **head turning reflex** (elicited by stroking the baby's cheek), **Moro reflex** (the throwing out of arms and legs elicited by loud or frightening noises), **Babinski reflex** (the fanning of the toes elicited by touching the bottom of the baby's foot), and **Palmar reflex** (the hand grasping elicited by placing an object in the baby's hand).

The other most commonly addressed developmental stage is **adolescence**. This period spans the teen years (13 to 19) and begins with the onset of puberty. At this point, the adrenal and pituitary glands secrete hormones (**androgen for boys** and **estrogen for girls**) that cause the visible secondary sex characteristics and the growth spurt.

Nature versus nurture is the central debate in psychology. People are constantly trying to determine if things like personality and behavior are the result of genetics (nature) or environment (nurture). **Twin studies** are frequently used to examine nature and nurture combinations. The influence of genetics can be examined by comparing and contrasting the similarities between monozygotic (identical) twins, which have the exact same genetic makeup, and dizygotic (fraternal) twins, which share about half of their genetic makeup (like all siblings). Fraternal siblings are used instead of just siblings because they are believed to have grown up in a more similar environment since they were going through the same stages of development at the same time in the same place. The influence of environment can be examined by comparing identical twins that were separated at birth, having the same genetic makeup but different environments. Most researchers believe that a person's attributes like behavior and personality are the result of both nature and nurture working together.

JEAN PIAGET: COGNITIVE DEVELOPMENT

Piaget is such a major player in developmental psychology and so favored by the GRE Psychology Test that you should expect several questions about him. Piaget is best known for his work in child development, in particular for his theory of child cognitive development. He asserted that humans experience an interaction between internal maturation and external experience that creates qualitative change. This **adaptation** happens through **assimilation** (fitting new information into existing ideas) and **accommodation** (modification of cognitive schemata to incorporate new information). All children go through the following stages during cognitive development, and while the age may vary, the order of the stages does not:

For more on Piaget, see Chapter 8, Thinking.

STAGE	AGE	CHARACTERISTICS
Sensorimotor	0–2 years	First, reflexive behavior cued by sensations; then **circular reactions** (repeated behavior intended to manipulate environment); later, development of **object permanence** (knowing an object exists even when it can no longer be seen); finally, acquiring the use of **representation** (visualizing or putting words to objects)
Preoperational	2–7 years	Egocentric understanding; rapidly acquiring words as symbols for things; inability to perform mental operations, such as causality or true understanding of quantity
Concrete Operational	7–12 years	Understanding of concrete relationships, such as simple math and quantity; development of **conservation** (knowing changes in shape are not changes in volume)
Formal Operational	12+ years	Understanding of abstract relationships, such as logic, ratios, and values

Piaget suggested that the progress of language development was determined by the individual's current cognitive stage.

Rochel Gelman showed that Piaget might have underestimated the cognitive ability of pre-schoolers. Gelman said they can deal with ideas such as quantity in small sets of objects.

Piaget also dabbled with **moral development** in children. In *Moral Judgment of the Child*, he hypothesized three stages:

AGE	CHARACTERISTICS
4–7 years	Imitates rule-following behavior; does not question acceptance of rules
7–11 years	Understands rules and follows them
12+ years	Applies abstract thinking to rules; can change rules if all parties agree

COGNITION AND EMOTION

Various theories address the biological and cognitive components of emotion:

- The **James-Lange Theory of Emotion** claims that bodily reactions to situations cause emotion. First, physiological responses are present in situations (crying, fleeing, trembling); then we feel the emotion that comes with these bodily reactions. We feel scared because we are trembling.

- The **Cannon-Bard Theory of Emotion,** also known as the **emergency theory,** asserts that emotions and bodily reactions occur simultaneously. In emotional situations, our body is cued to react in the brain (emotion) and in the body (biological response). We tremble and feel scared in response to danger.

- **Stanley Schachter** and **Jerome Singer** proposed a **cognitive theory of emotion.** Similar to the James-Lange theory, the **Schachter-Singer theory** asserts that emotions are the product of physiological reactions. But, Schachter and Singer claim that cognitions are the missing link in the chain. A particular bodily state is felt. Since many different situations produce similar bodily reactions, how we interpret the state is key. The cognition we attach to a situation determines which emotion we feel in response to physiological arousal. For example, when a situation causes us to tremble, we feel fear or anger depending on the ideas we have about what emotion fits the situation.

SIGMUND FREUD: PERSONALITY DEVELOPMENT

Freud saw the driving force behind humans (and their development) as sexual. For Freud, this force meant sensual gratification and not just "sex." So his five stages of development deal with how the individual meets these sensual gratification or **biological needs**. Each stage has an **erogenous zone,** which can be thought of as the focal point for the activity of that stage. Advancing through the stages affects personality development. Parental over- or under-indulgence at a particular stage might result in **fixation** (inability to move on to the next stage). Later, life stressors might result in **regression** (a return to an earlier stage).

Stage	Age	Erogenous Zone (Tasks)	Successful Resolution	Fixation
Oral	0–1 years	Mouth (sucking, chewing, eating, biting, vocalizing)	Weaning	Oral aggression (verbally abusive) or oral passivity (smoking, overeating)
Anal	1–3 years	Anus (bowel and bladder control)	Toilet training	Anal retention (overly neat/tidy) or anal expulsion (disorganized)
Phallic	3–6 years	Genitals (presence/absence of penis); Oedipus complex (males); Electra complex (females)	Gender identification	Difficulty with intimate relationships
Latency	6–12 years	N/A (sexual feelings dormant during this stage)	Social interaction	Arrested development
Genital	12+ years	Other people's genitals (reproduction and pleasure)	Intimate relationships	Fixation in prior stage could result in sexual and intimacy issues

LAWRENCE KOHLBERG: MORAL DEVELOPMENT

Kohlberg created the best-known theory of moral development through analyzing responses of children to nine hypothetical moral dilemmas. One example is the **Heinz dilemma,** in which a woman is dying and needs an expensive medication. Because the woman's husband cannot afford the medication, the dilemma is whether he should steal it or let his wife die. Using responses to such dilemmas, Kohlberg discerned the progress of moral understanding.

Stage	Understanding of Morals
Preconventional/Premoral "If I steal the medicine, I'll get in trouble."	Level 1: should avoid punishment Level 2: should gain rewards
Conventional/Morality of Conformity "Stealing is against the law."	Level 3: should gain approval Level 4: should follow law and authority
Postconventional/Morality of Self-Accepted Principles "It is unjust that money is an obstacle to life. It is ethical that I save my wife."	Level 5: beyond the black and white of laws; attentive to rights and social welfare Level 6: makes decisions based on abstract ethical principles

Carol Gilligan asserted that Kohlberg's moral development theory was biased toward males because it was dominated by rules, whereas women's morality focuses more on compassion.

ERIK ERIKSON: LIFE SPAN DEVELOPMENT

Erikson is best known for a development scheme that addresses the entire life span. Erikson viewed each stage of life as having its own unique **psychosocial** conflict to resolve.

Stage	Age	Outcomes
Trust vs. Mistrust	Infancy	Trust: infant's needs are met (optimism) Mistrust: infant's needs are not met
Autonomy vs. Shame	Early childhood	Autonomy: children learn self-control Shame: children remain dependent
Initiative vs. Guilt	Preschool age	Initiative: children achieve purpose Guilt: children are thwarted in efforts
Industry vs. Inferiority	School age	Industry: children gain competence RC: children feel incompetent
Identity vs. Role Confusion	Adolescence	Industry: adolescents learn sense of self RC: adolescents lack own identity
Intimacy vs. Isolation	Young adulthood	Intimacy: YAs develop mature relationships Isolation: YAs are unable to create social ties
Generativity vs. Stagnation	Middle age	Generativity: adults contribute to others/society Stagnation: adults feel that life is meaningless
Integrity vs. Despair	Later life	Integrity: adults develop wisdom re: lifetime Despair: adults feel unaccomplished

BOWLBY AND AINSWORTH: ATTACHMENT THEORY

John Bowlby

John Bowlby theorized that the bonded relationship between the infant and primary caregiver (usually the mother) is the main force that drives the child's development and is also the determining factor in terms of any future maladjustment. Unlike behaviorists, who would argue that the infant is simply conditioned to bond with the mother because she provides food, Bowlby asserts that human beings are genetically wired to form a powerful **attachment** to the primary caregiver for evolutionary advantage. Infants exhibit certain behaviors, such as smiling and crying, that produce nurturant feelings in the mother, which enhances the child's chances of survival. Because the mother-child attachment is so powerful, early separations are the source of subsequent psychopathology and the relationship becomes the prototype for all future meaningful interpersonal interactions.

Mary Ainsworth

Mary Ainsworth, best known for her famous **"Strange Situation"** infant study, expanded on Bowlby's theory of attachment. Ainsworth observed the behavior of several mother-infant dyads in turn, arranging for a stranger to enter the room and for the mother and baby to be briefly separated. Her results revealed three distinct **attachment styles. Secure** infants were largely happy and explorative and appeared emotionally attached to their mothers, were comforted by them in the presence of the stranger, acted distressed when separated from them, and interacted with them when they returned. **Ambivalent/resistant** infants were highly distressed by the presence of the stranger and by the maternal separation, refusing to interact with their mothers when they returned. **Avoidant** infants showed little or no emotion with strangers or with their mothers, did not react negatively to the separation, and did not interact much with their mothers when reunited with them. Ainsworth theorized that the secure infants basically had their needs met, while the ambivalent infants' needs were satisfied only erratically. The mothers of the avoidant infants were largely unresponsive to their needs. **Disorganized attachment** occurs when a toddler does not engage in coherent or consistent behavior during the reunion with the caregivers. These children may freeze or run away from the caregiver. Usually, this results from neglect or abuse from the caregiver.

DIANA BAUMRIND: PARENTING STYLE

Diana Baumrind studied the relationship between parenting style and personality development. **Authoritarian parents** (demanding, unaffectionate, strict) had children who were withdrawn and unhappy. **Permissive parents** (affectionate, not strict) had children who were happy but lacking in self-control and self-reliance. **Authoritative parents** (affectionate, firm but fair) had self-reliant, self-confident, assertive, friendly, happy, high-functioning kids. Authoritative parents help children understand and accept the norms of society so that they function well within it.

JOHN B. WATSON: BEHAVIORIST THEORY

In order to demonstrate that emotions can in fact be conditioned, Watson conducted his infamous "**Little Albert**" experiment on an eleven-month-old boy. Unrestrained by modern ethical rules and standards, Watson classically conditioned the infant to fear a white rat by pairing the rat's presence (which Albert had not previously minded) with an inherently frightening loud noise. Eventually Albert exhibited a fear response to the rat in the absence of the noise.

John B. Watson's approach to understanding child development is consistent with the fundamental principles of behaviorism: all changes and aspects of the development process are conditioned by the environment. Watson greatly downplays any potential effects of genetics or innate mechanisms in favor of explanations based on classical and operant conditioning. At birth the child is essentially a "tabula rasa," or blank slate, and is passively molded by his or her environment, most notably the parents. According to Watson, human beings can be conditioned to adopt all sorts of traits, dispositions, cognitions, and overt behaviors.

ARNOLD GESELL: MATURATIONAL DEVELOPMENTAL THEORY

Arnold Gesell was an early child developmentalist who believed that nature provided a "blueprint for development" through maturation and that environment, or "nurture," filled in the details. Gesell observed that children appear to go through the same predetermined developmental sequences, albeit at their own rates and paces, and that a child's chronological and developmental ages might be significantly different. He identified four areas of growth and development that have normative trends: (1) motor, (2) adaptive (cognitive), (3) language, and (4) personal/social behavior. Many factors, both internal and external, affect these changes, such as genetics, temperament, learning style, physical growth, parental and familial influences, cultural norms, etc. Gesell's multifaceted approach implicating both "nature" and "nurture" in the developmental processes is widely used as a model today.

GENDER DEVELEOPMENT

Study Tip
Make a separate list of the concepts that just won't stick in your memory. Rewriting the information will help.

While **biological sex** is assigned at birth, an individual's **gender identity** (the extent to which a person identifies with different aspects of "maleness" and/or "femaleness") typically develops prior to the age of four, although some individuals experience changes later in life. Gender identity can be influenced by many biological, psychological, and social factors, including genetics, prenatal and postnatal hormones, and socialization processes. Traditionally most children adopt **gender roles** (conventional, often stereotyped attitudes about how to behave based upon biological sex), although in recent years the distinction between typically male and female behavior has been somewhat blurred. The frequency of sex-typed behavior is low during prepubescence, highest in young adulthood, and lower again in later life.

Chapter 11
Personality

This chapter covers the theories of personality, starting with old school type theories. Included are discussions of the famous psychoanalytic theories (Freud, Jung, and Adler), the humanistic perspective, and the behavioral and social cognitive perspectives. Cognitive perspectives discussed include rational emotive behavioral therapy rational emotive behavior therapy as well as Beck's cognitive therapy. Also included are discussions of Gestalt theory, Existential theory, as well as the trait theories. The chapter concludes with information on where personality comes from and gender differences.

> **DEFINED: Personality is the study of why people act the way that they do and why different people act differently.** Various perspectives have emerged to help explain personality, each also offering people a key to how to change.

OLD SCHOOL: TYPE THEORY

Type theory originally dominated personality theory. As far back as Hippocrates, people were placed into personality-type categories often based on physical appearance. In the 1800s, **phrenology** (the practice of examining head and skull shape) was used to discern personality.

Later, **William Sheldon** devised a system based on **somatotypes** (body types). Although the theory has no modern credence, it is an important part of the evolution of the field. Sheldon isolated three physiques and the corresponding personality types:

- **Endomorph**—short, plump body = pleasure-seeking, social behavior.
- **Mesomorph**—muscular, athletic body = energetic, aggressive behavior.
- **Ectomorph**—skinny, fragile body = inhibited, intellectual behavior.

More recently than Sheldon, **Alfred Adler** suggested a personality typology. (For more on Adler, see page 121.)

PSYCHOANALYTIC THEORY

Originator: **Sigmund Freud**

With psychoanalytic theory, Freud contributed the most extensive and complex theory of human nature. For the GRE Psychology Test, you should know psychoanalytic vocabulary and the history and structure of the theory. Applying the theory is complex and takes years of training. It will not be required of you on the GRE Psychology Test.

Psychoanalytic theory views **conflict** as central to human nature. The conflict is that between different **drives** (particularly conscious and unconscious) vying for expression. The individual is motivated by **the need to seek pleasure and avoid pain.** Originally, Freud postulated that an individual's greatest conflict was that between the **libido** (or sexual force) and the **ego.** Later, Freud revised his theory and asserted that the true conflict is that between **Eros** (the life instinct, including sex and love) and **Thanatos** (the death instinct, including self-destructive behavior). This was summed up in Freud's famous quote (via Schopenhauer): "The aim of all life is death."

Another major change in Freud's theory was the way in which he viewed the layout of the mind. Initially, Freud preferred a **topographic** model of mental life in which **conscious** elements were openly acknowledged forces, preconscious forces were just below the surface and accessible if need be, and unconscious elements, such as drives and wishes, were many layers below consciousness. Freud's idea of unconscious mental life was perhaps his greatest contribution to psychology. Later, Freud's revised model of mental life was **structural,** meaning that mental life has particular organization other than layers. He organized the mind into three components:

- **Ego.** The part of the mind that mediates between the environment and the pressures of the id and the superego. The ego operates on the **reality principle** and responds to the demands of the environment by delaying gratification.

- **Id.** The part of the mind that contains the unconscious biological drives and wishes. At birth, mental life is composed solely of the id and its biological drives, such as sex and aggression. With development, the id also includes unconscious wishes. The id operates on the **pleasure principle,** the human motivation to seek pleasure and avoid pain; it's particularly salient in early life.

- **Superego.** The part of the mind that imposes learned or socialized drives. The superego is not something one is born with, but rather develops over time, and therefore is particularly influenced by moral and parental training.

In psychoanalytic theory, an individual's mental life consists of a constant push-pull between the competing forces of the id, superego, and environment. Each of these areas struggles for acknowledgment and expression. How well a person's ego handles this determines his mental health.

Model of psychopathology: Freud often worked with women who were diagnosed as "hysterical" (a pejorative term derived from the word for "uterus") or neurotic. To Freud, neurosis was the result of repressed drives and conflicts, which become manifested in dysfunctional ways. **Pathological behavior, dreams,** and **unconscious behavior** are all symptoms of underlying, unresolved conflict, which are manifested when the ego does not find acceptable ways to express conflict. This is called **psychic determinism.**

Therapy: **Psychoanalysis** or **"analysis"** is the original "talk" therapy. A patient in traditional psychoanalysis is usually seen four to five times per week (as opposed to one to two times per week for most other therapies) and often for many years. Portrayals of classic psychoanalysis (as seen in the movie *Harold and Maude*) often include a reclining patient facing away from a very silent analyst. This is an old stereotype; most modern-day analysts run their sessions much like other therapists, with the therapist and patient seated, facing one another.

Though initially Freud used **hypnosis** (borrowed from **Jean Charcot** and **Pierre Janet**) with patients, he later switched to the technique of **free association** (developed with **Joseph Breuer**). Free association is the central process in which a patient reports thoughts without censure or guidance. According to Freud, because unconscious material is always looking for a way out, the patient can uncover and express repressed material through free association. This discharge of repressed emotion is called **catharsis** or **abreaction.** Freud also used dream analysis, as he believed that dreams were "the royal road to the unconscious." He would analyze both the **manifest content** (the actual content of the dream) and the **latent content** (the unconscious forces the dreams are trying to express).

Another idea central to psychoanalysis is **transference.** Freud postulated that patients would react to the therapist much like they reacted to their parents. The therapist-patient relationship then serves as a metaphor for the patients' repressed emotions about their parents and, thus, as a way of examining those unconscious feelings. **Countertransference** refers to how a therapist feels about his or her patient. **Object relations therapy** is a technique in which the therapist uses the patient's transference to help him or her resolve problems that were the result of previous relationships by correcting the emotional experience in the therapist-patient relationship.

Goal of therapy: Psychoanalysis aims to lessen the unconscious pressures on the individual by making as much of this material conscious as possible. This will allow the ego to be a better mediator of forces.

Criticisms: Freud has been criticized for his methodology. He developed theories from **single case studies** of women in the late 1800s and early 1900s. This is not a "scientific" method (see Chapter 14, Measurement and Methodology).

Defense Mechanisms

Defense mechanism. A way in which the ego protects itself from threatening unconscious material or environmental forces. The following are defense mechanisms:

- **Sublimation**—satisfying a personally or socially unacceptable instinct by substituting a more acceptable, often creative or highly productive behavior than the one that the individual would otherwise engage in to satisfy the impulse (e.g., Carl is physically aggressive, so he becomes a professional boxer instead of beating up strangers who annoy him).

- **Regression**—reverting back to an earlier psychosexual stage of development, often in response to anxiety (e.g., five-year-old Mary becomes ill and starts to suck her thumb like she did as a toddler).

- **Rationalization**—denying the true motivations for one's behavior in favor of false, albeit more acceptable or self-serving ones (e.g., after scoring poorly on a medical school entrance exam, Henry decides that the reason he didn't study adequately for the test is that he knew in his heart that he didn't really want to be a doctor).

- **Projection**—attempting to disown one's own unacceptable feelings or characteristics by falsely attributing them to others (e.g., Jack is mean to Fred because he, Jack, envies him, then dismisses Fred's angry response as simply the result of Fred's envy of Jack).

- **Undoing**—trying to negate or reverse an act that one considers unacceptable by doing its opposite (e.g., Bill drives recklessly and hits a dog with his car, then adopts three new puppies and volunteers at an animal shelter).

- **Reaction formation**—behaving in a manner that is directly opposed to an underlying impulse that the individual considers unacceptable (e.g., Sue deeply resents her new baby sister so she acts overly nice and loving toward her).

- **Displacement**—transferring (often aggressive) impulses or feelings from their original object to one perceived as less threatening (e.g., Joey is humiliated by a bully at school so he comes home and kicks the cat).

- **Denial**—preventing painful or anxiety-producing truths from entering into one's consciousness (e.g., Jane cannot accept the idea that she is seriously ill, so she accuses a multitude of doctors of being incompetent).

- **Repression**—denying painful or anxiety-producing memories, feelings, or thoughts from becoming conscious (e.g., Karl has no recollection of his parents' bitter divorce because that period of his life is too unpleasant for him to remember).

- **Intellectualization**—(e.g., Victor copes with having been the victim of a violent crime by reading books on the subject instead of acknowledging his fear and emotional trauma).

Other Important Ideas in Psychoanalysis

- **Aggression.** A central force in humans that must find a socially acceptable outlet.
- **Screen memory.** Memories that serve as representations of important childhood experiences.
- **Anna Freud** applied Freudian ideas to child psychology and development.
- **Melanie Klein** pioneered **object-relations theory** and psychoanalysis with children.
- **Neo-Freudians** accept some of Freud's ideas and reject others:
    - **Karen Horney** emphasized culture and society over instinct. She suggested that neuroticism is expressed as movement toward, against, and away from people.
    - **Harry Stack Sullivan** emphasized social and interpersonal relationships.
- **Psychodynamic theory** is a general term that refers to theories (such as individual or analytical) that emphasize the role of the unconscious.

INDIVIDUAL THEORY

Originator: **Alfred Adler**

Adler, a contemporary of Freud, broke away to create his own theory. In **individual** or **Adlerian theory,** people are viewed as **creative, social,** and **whole.** Adler described people in the process of realizing themselves or in the process of **"becoming."** During this journey, the individual is motivated by **social needs** and **feelings of inferiority** that arise when the current self does not match the self-ideal. A healthy individual pursues goals in spite of feelings of inferiority; a healthy individual has a **"will to power"** or a quest for feelings of superiority. On this quest, a healthy individual will pursue goals that are outside of himself and **beneficial to society.**

Model of psychopathology: Unhealthy individuals are too much affected by inferior feelings to pursue the will to power. They may make excuses or have a **"yes, but"** mentality. If they do pursue goals, however, these are likely to be **self-serving** and egotistical.

Therapy: Adlerian therapy is a **psychodynamic** approach in which unconscious feelings do play a role. More importantly, however, is the examination of a person's lifestyle and choices. A patient may examine his motivations, perceptions, goals, and resources. Adler is also known for his pioneering work in **family therapy.**

Goal of therapy: Adlerian therapy aims to **reduce feelings of inferiority** and to **foster social interest** and **social contribution** in patients.

Criticisms: Adlerian therapy is best used with "normal" people in search of growth.

Adler's Typology

Adler created a personality typology based on personal activity and social interest:

- **Ruling-dominant type (choleric).** High in activity but low in social contribution; dominant.
- **Getting-leaning type (phlegmatic).** Low in activity and high in social contribution; dependent.
- **Avoiding type (melancholic).** Low in activity and low in social contribution; withdrawn.
- **Socially useful type (sanguine).** High in activity and high in social contribution; healthy.

ANALYTICAL THEORY

Originator: **Carl Gustav Jung**

Carl Jung, Freud's most beloved student, broke from Freud to form his own theory. Jung felt that Freud placed too much emphasis on the libido. Jung's analytical theory postulated that the **psyche** was directed toward **life and awareness** (rather than sex). In each person, the psyche contains conscious and unconscious elements. Most importantly, the unconscious is further divided into two types:

- **Personal unconscious.** Material from an individual's own experiences; this can become conscious.
- **Collective unconscious.** Dynamics of the psyche inherited from ancestors. This is common to all people and contains the archetypes.

The **archetype** is probably Jung's best-known concept. Archetypes are universally meaningful concepts, passed down through the collective unconscious since the beginning of man. Archetypes allow us to organize our experiences with consistent themes and are indicated by cross-cultural similarity in symbols, folklore, and myths. The most commonly cited archetypes are:

- **Persona.** A person's outer mask, the mediator to the external world; this is symbolized in cultures by masks.
- **Shadow.** A person's dark side, often projected onto others; this is symbolized in cultures by devils and evil spirits.
- **Anima.** The female elements that a man possesses; this complements his own maleness.

- **Animus.** The male elements that a female possesses; this complements her own femaleness.
- **Self.** The full individual potential, symbolized in cultures by figures such as Buddha or Jesus; and by the **mandala.**

Model of psychopathology: Psychopathology is a signal that something is wrong in the makeup of the psyche. It provides clues about how one could become more aware.

Therapy: The approach is psychodynamic because unconscious elements are addressed. In order to become more aware, unconscious material is explored through the **analysis of an individual's dreams,** artwork, and personal symbols. These are all unconscious messages expressing themselves.

Goal of therapy: Use unconscious messages in order to become more aware and closer to full potential.

Criticisms: Many scientists view analytical theory as too mystical or spiritual.

HUMANISTIC THEORY
Originator: **Carl Rogers**

Also known as **person-centered** or **Rogerian** theory, client-centered theory is **humanistic** in that it takes the entirety of human experience into account, not simply drives or behaviors. It is also a growth-oriented perspective. Its main tenet is that individuals have an **actualizing tendency** that can direct them out of conflict and toward their full potential. This is best accomplished in an atmosphere that fosters growth, one of **unconditional positive regard,** in which a person knows they are loved unconditionally even if others close to them might disagree with some of their actions. The humanistic perspective is also known as the **"Third Force"** in psychotherapy in reaction to psychoanalysis and behaviorism.

Model of psychopathology: People who **lack congruence** between their real selves and their self-concept develop psychological tension. Incongruence occurs when feelings or experiences are inconsistent with the acknowledged concept of the self. For example, a self-concept that one is perfect will be shaken by experiences of failure.

Therapy: Person-centered therapy is directed by the client, who decides how often to meet and what to discuss in sessions. The therapist is **nondirective,** providing only an atmosphere for the client's self-exploration. The job of the therapist is to provide:

- **Empathy.** The therapist should appreciate rather than just observe the client's world. He or she should attempt to stand in the shoes of the client and take an interest in the client's perspective.
- **Unconditional positive regard.** This facilitates a trusting and safe environment. The therapist maintains positive feelings for the client no matter what choices, feelings, or insights the client explores in therapy.

- **Genuineness/congruence.** The feelings and experiences of the therapist should match, just as those of the client should match. Therapists should not maintain a professional reserve, but instead speak and act genuinely with the client.

Goal of therapy: The aim of client-centered therapy is to **provide a trusting atmosphere** in which the client can engage in self-directed growth and tap his own "vast resources." Evidence of growth includes a **congruent self-concept, positive self-regard,** an **internal locus-of-evaluation,** and **willingness to experience.**

Criticisms: Rogers used no diagnostic tools because he believed that client-centered therapy applied to any psychological problem. Many disagree with this notion.

Other Important Ideas in the Humanistic Perspective

- **Abraham Maslow** was a leader of the humanistic movement in psychology. Maslow is best known not for any contribution to therapy, but for his pyramid-like **hierarchy of needs,** which really pertains to human motivation. Maslow asserted that humans start at the bottom and work their way up the hierarchy toward self-actualization by satisfying the needs at the previous level. Here are the levels from top to bottom:

- **George Kelly** suggested that **personal constructs** (conscious ideas about the self, others, and situations) determine personality and behavior.

BEHAVIOR THEORY

Originators: **B. F. Skinner, Ivan Pavlov, Joseph Wolpe**

Behavior theory is the application of classical and operant conditioning principles to human behavior. It is a model of behavior **based on learning.** Behaviorists change maladaptive behavior through new learning.

Radical behaviorism is associated with Skinner's operant ideas that behavior is related only to its consequences. **Neobehaviorism** incorporates internal events (such as cognition or emotion) into account when understanding behavior.

Model of psychopathology: Maladaptive behavior is simply the **result of learning maladaptive responses.**

Therapy: Behavior therapy is generally **short-term and directed.** Thoughts, feelings, and unconscious motivations are not addressed in behavior therapy. The therapist uses specific **counter-conditioning** techniques to foster the learning of new responses in the client. The most cited techniques are the following:

- **Systematic desensitization,** developed by Joseph Wolpe, applies **classical** conditioning in order to **relieve anxiety.** The patient is exposed to increasingly anxiety-provoking stimuli until the anxiety associated with those stimuli is decreased. For example, someone who has a fear of snakes may first look at pictures of a snake and then over time work up to holding a snake.

- **Flooding** or **implosive therapy** also applies **classical** conditioning in order to **relieve anxiety.** The client is repeatedly exposed to an anxiety-producing stimulus, so that, eventually, the overexposure simply leads to lessened anxiety.

- **Aversion therapy** employs classical conditioning in order to **increase anxiety.** An anxiety-reaction is created where there previously was none. This is generally used to treat addiction.

- **Shaping** uses **operant** conditioning to change behavior. The client is reinforced for behaviors that come closer and closer to the desired action.

- **Modeling** employs **social learning** principles; this method exposes the client to more adaptive behaviors. (See Chapter 5, Learning.)

- **Assertiveness training** provides tools and experience through which the client can become more assertive.

- **Role playing** allows a client to practice new behaviors and responses.

Goal of therapy: To change behavior in the desired or adaptive direction. Behavior therapy has been extremely successful in treating **phobias, obsessive-compulsive disorder,** and **childhood disorders** (particularly nocturnal enuresis, or bed-wetting).

Criticisms: Behavior therapy has been accused of **treating the symptoms** rather than the underlying problem.

Other Important Ideas in the Behaviorist Perspective

- **Neal Miller** proved experimentally that anomalous behavior can be learned.
- Miller, along with his colleague **John Dollard,** integrated the behavioral perspective with psychoanalytic thinking. They examined the Freudian concept of displacement in a learning context where they put two rats in an apparatus and gave them electric shocks until they started fighting. After they learned this response, the researchers put a doll in with them, but the rats still fought each other when the shocks started. But when one animal was removed and the shock started, the animal took out its aggression on the doll. Dollard and Miller also studied fear as an acquired drive and types of conflict, including **approach-avoidance conflict.**

SOCIAL COGNITIVE PERSPECTIVE

Originators: **Albert Bandura and Walter Mischel**

The **social cognitive perspective** of personality suggests that personality is a result of interactions between behaviors, cognitions, and the environment. This relationship is known as **reciprocal determinism.** This perspective incorporates behavioral and cognitive processes learned through not only classical and operant conditioning but also social learning. These include a person's perceived **self-efficacy** beliefs (how good or bad you believe you are at some specific task) and a person's locus of control.

Model of psychopathology: Psychological problems are usually the result of dysfunctional expectancies, in which a person has expectations that either cannot or will not be fulfilled in the way desired.

Therapy: Any type of therapy that will address these faulty expectations serves, but will usually consist of cognitive-behavioral therapy, in which both maladaptive thoughts and behaviors are addressed.

Goal of therapy: The goal is to improve a person's perceived self-efficacy beliefs.

Criticisms: The social cognitive perspective has been criticized for not being a unified, systematic approach to studying personality.

Other Important Ideas in the Social Cognitive Perspective

- **Walter Mischel** spent much of his life studying the idea of **delay of gratification** with his famous **Marshmallow Test** experiment. The experiment looked at whether children would eat one marshmallow now or wait a few minutes and get two later. Mischel's research, a dramatic example of longitudinal research as it has been continuing for 50+ years, showed correlations between a child's ability to wait and future success. Recent research has called into question some of Mischel's findings as the results are different for children of different socioeconomic backgrounds. A particularly confounding variable has been shown to be food insecurity—if a child generally does not have enough to eat, eating the first marshmallow is not about a lack of attention and goal-setting, but rather about fear.

- **External locus of control** is a personality characteristic that causes one to view events as the result of luck or fate. Too much of this breeds helplessness. **Internal locus of control** causes a person to view events as the outcome of her own actions. Too much of this can breed self-blame. These terms were developed by **Julian Rotter.**

- **Learned helplessness,** the brainchild of **Martin Seligman,** demonstrates how experience can change people's personalities. After a series of events in which one may feel helpless or out of control, a negative or pessimistic explanatory style develops. The person basically gives up in general and exhibits a helpless disposition. This can be countered with cognitive training that fosters **learned optimism** for the person.

COGNITIVE THEORY

Originator: **Aaron Beck**

Cognitive theory gives **conscious thought patterns** (as opposed to emotions or behaviors) the starring role in people's lives. The Beck Depression Inventory (BDI) is used most frequently as a research tool to determine the number of depressive symptoms a particular person has, but it is sometimes used in the clinical setting as well. The way a person interprets experience, rather than the experience itself, is what's important.

Model of psychopathology: **Maladaptive cognitions** lead to maladaptive behavior or disturbed affect. Various types of maladaptive cognitions exist:

- **Arbitrary inference.** Drawing a conclusion without solid evidence: "My boss thinks I'm stupid because he never asks me to play golf."

- **Overgeneralization.** Mistaking isolated incidents for the norm: "No one will ever want to be with me."

- **Magnifying/minimizing.** Making too much or little of something: "It was luck that I did well on my exam."

- **Personalizing.** Inappropriately taking responsibility: "Our office's failed project was all my fault."

- **Dichotomous thinking.** Black-and-white thinking: "If I don't score a 750 on the GRE, I'll have no future."

Beck postulated that a **cognitive triad** (negative views about the self, the world, and the future) causes depression. The **Beck Depression Inventory (BDI)** measures such views and is used to gauge the severity of diagnosed depression.

Therapy: **Directed** therapy helps to expose and restructure maladaptive thought and reasoning patterns. This is generally **short-term** therapy in which the therapist focuses on **tangible evidence of the client's logic** (such as what the client says and does).

Goal of therapy: To correct maladaptive cognitions.

Criticisms: Similar to behavior therapy, cognitive therapy addresses how a person thinks, rather than why the thought patterns were initially developed. **Removing the symptoms** (maladaptive cognitions) may not cure the problem.

RATIONAL-EMOTIVE BEHAVIORAL THERAPY

Originator: **Albert Ellis**

Rational-emotive behavioral therapy (REBT) includes elements of cognitive, behavioral, and emotion theory. Ellis believed that intertwined thoughts and feelings produce behavior.

Model of psychopathology: Psychological tension is created when an activating event occurs **(A)**, and a client applies certain beliefs about the event **(B)**, and this leads to the consequence of emotional disruption **(C).**

Therapy: Therapy is highly **directive.** The therapist leads the client to dispute **(D)** the previously applied irrational beliefs.

Goal of therapy: The goal is for effective rational beliefs **(E)** to replace previous self-defeating ones. Then a client's thoughts, feelings, and behaviors can coexist.

Criticisms: Like cognitive and behavior theory, REBT has been called **too sterile** and mechanistic.

GESTALT THEORY

Originators: **Fritz Perls, Max Wertheimer, Kurt Koffka**

Gestalt theory encourages people to stand apart from beliefs, biases, and attitudes derived from the past. The goal is to **fully experience and perceive the present** in order to become a whole and integrated person.

Model of psychopathology: Difficulties arise from **disturbances of awareness.** The client **may not have insight** (the ability to see how all the pieces of experience fit together), or the client **may not fully experience** his present situation (choosing not to acknowledge certain aspects of the situation).

Therapy: The Gestalt therapist engages in a **dialogue** with the client, rather than leading him or her toward any particular goal. The client learns from the shared dialogue. Together they focus on the **here-and-now** experience, rather than talking about the past.

Goal of therapy: The goal is **exploration of awareness and full experiencing of the present.** A successful therapy connects the client and her present existence.

Criticisms: This therapy is not suited for low-functioning or disturbed clients.

EXISTENTIAL THEORY

Originator: **Victor Frankl**

Existential theory revolves around age-old philosophical issues, particularly the issue of meaning. According to existential theory, a person's greatest struggles are those of **being versus non-being** and of **meaningfulness versus meaninglessness.** An individual is constantly striving to rise above a simple behavioral existence and toward a genuine and meaningful existence. Frankl called this **"will to meaning." Rollo May** is a major contributor to existential therapy.

- A **phenomenological view** of personality theory (or of psychotherapy) focuses on the individual's unique **self** and experiences.

Model of psychopathology: The response to perceived meaninglessness in life is neurosis or **neurotic anxiety** (as opposed to normal or justified anxiety).

Therapy: Existential therapy is talking therapy in which deep questions relating to the client's perception and meaning of existence are discussed.

Goal of therapy: The goal is to help clients understand how they create meaning in the world and to help them make different choices based on what gives life meaning.

Criticisms: This therapy has been called too abstract for severely disturbed individuals.

NEW SCHOOL: TRAIT THEORY

Gordon Allport emphasized an **ideographic** approach to personality theory. This approach attempts to capture an individual's unique, defining characteristics, as opposed to a **nomothetic** approach, which uses large numbers of people to study the commonalities of personality. Allport was concerned only with conscious motives governed by the **proprium** or **propriate function** (his version of the ego), and he believed that the proprium acted somewhat consistently based on traits it had developed through experience.

Allport and his students worked to identify all of the possible traits that could go with personality. **Traits** are the relatively stable characteristics of behavior that a person exhibits, such as introversion, politeness, and stinginess. Using a **lexical approach** (meaning picking all of the possible traits out of the dictionary), Allport gathered about 5,000 possible traits. Next, Allport hypothesized that people act differently in different situations because they have a trait hierarchy: at the top are **cardinal** traits, which are rare, usually occur later in life, and so dominate the personality that the person often becomes known for that trait. Next are **central** traits, which are the qualities that one possesses across situations. Last are the **secondary** traits, which are personality traits that appear only in particular situations. (In trait theory, be sure to understand the difference between **traits** and **states.** Traits are relatively enduring characteristics. States are temporary feelings or characteristics. A trait might be "outgoing," whereas a state might be "tired.")

Later, statistical techniques were used to create **taxonomies** (organized categorization systems) for personality. **Raymond Cattell** used factor analysis in data reduction of Allport's 5,000 traits. Eventually, he identified **sixteen bipolar source traits,** such as relaxed-tense, that seemed to underlie all of the 5,000 (often overlapping) traits. These were Cattell's **sixteen personality factors** tested in his 16PF questionnaire. Amazingly, Cattell accomplished this massive factor analysis before the computer age.

Later, using advanced computer statistical programs, modern theorists could not replicate Cattell's findings, but they did generate findings of their own. The hot topic in personality trait theory today is the **"Big Five."** The Big Five are **superfactors,** or five dimensions that seem to encompass all of personality. They are superordinate traits or facets, and exist on a continuum from low to high. Know these Big Five dimensions:

Study Tip
The acronym OCEAN will help you remember the Big Five!

1. **O-dimension** (openness to experience, intellectual curiosity)
2. **C-dimension** (conscientiousness)
3. **E-dimension** (extroversion)
4. **A-dimension** (agreeableness)
5. **N-dimension** (neuroticism, nervousness)

Other Important Ideas in the Trait Perspective

- **Hans Eysenck** used factor analysis to identify the underlying traits of the two personality-type dimensions—**introversion-extraversion** and **stable-unstable (neuroticism).** These two dimensions formed a cross and, therefore, four quadrants: **phlegmatic, melancholic, choleric,** and **sanguine.** He also criticized the effectiveness of psychoanalysis, arguing that Freud's work was not scientific and empirically sound.

- **Meyer Friedman** and **Ray Rosenman** studied Type A personality. **Type A personality** is characterized by drive, competitiveness, aggressiveness, tension, and hostility and is most commonly found in middle- to upper-class men. **Grant Dahlstrom** linked Type A personality to heart disease and other health problems. The connection between personality and health is currently a popular area of study.

- **Authoritarianism** is the disposition to view the world as full of power relationships. Authoritarian individuals are highly domineering (if they are the top dog of the situation) or highly submissive (if they are in the presence of a more powerful figure). These individuals are also likely conventional, aggressive, stereotyping, and anti-introspective. This is measured by the **F-scale** (also known as the Fascism scale).

- **Seymour Epstein** was critical of personality trait theory.
- **Barnum effect** is the tendency to agree with and accept **personality interpretations** that are provided.
- **Costa and McCrae** found that personality changes very little after age **30.**

WHERE DOES PERSONALITY COME FROM?

Originally, personality theory was dominated by **dispositionists** (people who emphasized internal determinants of behavior). Of course, **situationists** (such as behaviorists) have argued that only circumstances determine behavior. Currently, **interactionists** are in the forefront; they assert a combination of stable, internal factors and situations.

Evidence for both disposition and situation exists. Critics such as **Seymour Epstein** and **Walter Mischel** have asserted that trait and type theories have always had a big problem: both theories assume that a person's behavior is stable across situations and that people fail to take circumstances into account. Studies (and real life) show that people often act differently in different situations. The possibility that a person may behave inconsistently—that a respected minister may be a closet adulterer, for example—is called the **consistency paradox** and presents real problems for labeling people as having one internal disposition.

One way of showing that personality traits exist within a person would be to show that the person exhibits those traits in a variety of different situations. Mischel, with **Nancy Cantor**, proposed the **cognitive prototype approach,** in which cognitive behavior (such as the formulation of and attention to prototypes), is examined in social situations. In short, Mischel thought that consistency of behavior is the result of cognitive processes, rather than the result of personality traits per se.

Twin studies have indicated that the heritability of personality is about 40–50 percent. After locating identical twins separated at birth, psychologists have found remarkable similarities in personality and behavior. Most notably, the "Jim" twins had wives with the same name, dogs with the same name, and the same habits. But, of course, they were not exactly the same, and this shows that environment has some impact on personality.

GENDER DIFFERENCES

The **nature-nurture debate** is most alive in the area of gender differences. Some assert that no true gender differences exist—children are simply reinforced for stereotypical behaviors. It is true that after taking into account differential social reinforcement, very few gender differences remain. Still, the prevailing point of view is **interactionist.**

- **Kay Deaux** found that **women's successes** at stereotypical "male" tasks are often attributed to **luck,** while **men's successes** are often attributed to skill. This suggests that gender is a social construct that colors interpretations. Also, studies have found that women themselves attribute their successes to luck more than men, indicating that women have **lower self-esteem** than men.

- **Sandra Bem** studied **androgyny** (possessing both male and female qualities) and created the **Bem Sex Role Inventory.** Androgynous individuals have been found to have higher self-esteem, lower anxiety, and more adaptability than their highly masculine or feminine counterparts.

- **Matina Horner** suggested that females shunned masculine-type successes not because of fear of failure or lack of interest, but because they **feared success** and its negative repercussions, such as resentment and rejection.

- **Alice Eagly** found an interaction between gender and social status with regard to how easily an individual might be influenced or swayed.

- **Eleanor Maccoby** and **Carol Jacklin** scrutinized studies of sex differences and found that relatively few existed that could not be explained away by simple social learning. The most consistent difference that seems independent of social influence is that **females have greater verbal ability** and **males have greater visual/spatial ability.** This has been attributed to internal biological or hormonal differences but is still hotly debated.

OTHER IMPORTANT IDEAS IN PERSONALITY

- People often make assumptions about the dispositions of an individual based on the actions of that person. These are known as **implicit theories** about personality.

- **Self-awareness** is a **state;** it is the temporary condition of being aware of how you are thinking, feeling, or doing. For example, right now you may be aware that you are nervous.

- **Mirrors** generally make people more self-aware. **Small mirrors** tend not to make people highly self-aware because we see ourselves in small mirrors all the time (e.g., in the bathroom). But large mirrors make people very self-aware because we see a view of ourselves as others see us.

- **Self-monitoring** is characterized by scrutiny of one's own behavior, motivation to act appropriately rather than honestly, and ability to mask true feelings.

- **Self-consciousness** is a **trait.** It refers to how often one generally becomes self-aware. If you pay a lot of attention to yourself, then you are highly self-conscious.

- **Self-esteem** is knowing that you are worthwhile and being in touch with your actual strengths. About 50 percent of people perceive themselves accurately and about 35 percent perceive themselves narcissistically.

- **Narcissism** is not the same as self-esteem. Narcissism is believing that you are better than you really are or look better than you really do; it is a sort of unrealistic self-esteem. A narcissistic person might endorse the statement, "The world would be a better place if I were in charge."

- **Self-handicapping** is self-defeating behavior that allows one to dismiss or excuse failure.

- **Stimulus-seeking** individuals have a great need for arousal.

- **Cognitive behavioral therapy (CBT)** employs principles from cognitive and behavioral theory.

- **Play therapy** is used with child clients. During play, a child client may convey emotions, situations, or disturbances that might otherwise go unexpressed.

- **Electroconvulsive shock therapy (ECT)** delivers electric current to the brain and induces convulsions. It is an effective intervention for severely depressed patients.

- **Family therapy** treats a family together and views the whole family as the client.

- **Stress-inoculation training,** developed by **Donald Meichenbaum,** prepares people for foreseeable stressors.

- **Evidence-based treatment** refers to treatment for mental health problems that has been shown to produce results in empirical research studies (for example, studies randomly assigning individuals to types of treatment and following other rules of good research design). Many clinics and researchers argue that only treatment that has been shown to work in research is ethical. Other clinics and researchers argue that controlled experiments are nothing like a real treatment environment and so the results are not as useful (or as widely applicable) as one might suppose.

- Personality tests come in all shapes and sizes. Probably the two best known are the **Minnesota Multiphasic Personality Inventory (MMPI)** and the **California Personality Inventory (CPI).** For more on these tests, see the Measurement chapter.

- **Henry Murray** developed the **Thematic Apperception Test (TAT).** This test consists of ambiguous story cards. Murray asserted that people would project their own "needs" onto these cards, such as the need for achievement.

Chapter 12
Clinical Psychology and Psychological Disorders

This chapter discusses the basic concepts concerning clinical psychology and psychological disorders. It covers the current diagnostic categories and disorders, statistical data regarding mental illness, and psychopharmacological intervention.

DEFINED: Clinical psychology is the study of the theory, assessment, and treatment of mental and emotional disorders. The term "disorder" is used loosely here, referring to anything from minor problems with life adjustments to severe psychopathology. This chapter includes the theories of the major schools of thought, their differing approaches to viewing disordered behavior and treating clients, and descriptions of common psychological disorders. Of course, psychological disorders and psychotherapy are complex topics. The GRE Psychology Test expects you to know only the theoretical and technical basics.

APPLIED PSYCHOLOGY

Applied psychology is the branch of psychology that uses principles or research findings to solve people's problems.

PSYCHOPHARMACOLOGY

Rather than a school of thought, psychopharmacology is the use of medication to treat mental illness. While drugs do not cure mental illness, some are very effective at alleviating symptoms. Sometimes drugs are the only treatment a client needs or receives. In other cases, medication is used in conjunction with therapy.

Model of psychopathology: It is believed that some emotional disturbances are at least partly caused by **biological factors** and, therefore, can be successfully treated with medication.

Therapy: Most "psychopharm" treatments aim to affect **neurotransmitters,** which are the natural chemicals in your brain that transmit impulses from one neuron to another across synapses. The most common neurotransmitters acted upon are **dopamine, serotonin,** and **norepinephrine.** All of these neurotransmitters are in the class of **monoamines.**

- **Antipsychotics** were the first drugs used for psychopathology. They were usually used to treat positive symptoms of schizophrenia, such as delusions and hallucinations, by blocking dopamine receptors and inhibiting dopamine production. Examples include chlorpromazine (Thorazine®) and haloperidol (Haldol®).

- **Mood stabilizers** are the drugs of choice to manage bipolar disorder. Because many psychoactive drugs can have a mood stabilizing effect, this group includes lithium, as well as anti-psychotics and anti-convulsants.

- **Antidepressants** are used to reduce depressive symptoms by increasing the availability of neurotransmitters such as serotonin, norepinephrine, and/or dopamine in the brain. The theory is that abnormally low levels of monoamines cause depression. These drugs act to increase the production and transmission of various monoamines.

- o **Tricyclic antidepressants (TCAs)** have a tricyclic chemical structure—for example, amitriptyline (Elavil®).
- o **Monoamine oxidase inhibitors (MAOIs)** inhibit the activity of monoamine oxidase enzymes—for example, phenelzine (Nardil®).
- o **Selective serotonin reuptake inhibitors (SSRIs)** act only on serotonin (hence the name "selective"). They are the most frequently prescribed antidepressants because they have fewer side effects than TCAs and MAOIs. Examples include fluoxetine (Prozac®), paroxetine (Paxil®), and sertraline (Zoloft®).

- **Anxiolytics** are used to reduce anxiety or to induce sleep, usually by increasing the effectiveness of GABA (since it is an inhibitory neurotransmitter). They also have high potential for causing habituation and addiction. Examples include barbiturates and benzodiazepines such as diazepam (Valium®) and alprazolam (Xanax®).

- **Antabuse®** is a drug that changes the metabolism of alcohol, resulting in severe nausea and vomiting when combined with alcohol; it can be used to countercondition alcoholics.

Goal of therapy: To provide relief from symptoms of psychopathology.

Criticisms: Drugs do not work on everyone, so often psychopharmacologists and patients must experiment to find drugs that are effective. Additionally, research shows that drugs alone are not as effective as drugs in combination with psychotherapy or even psychotherapy alone. Furthermore, drugs often come with a litany of side effects and can also cause withdrawal symptoms after treatment ceases.

Diagnostic and Statistical Manual of Mental Disorders, Fifth Edition (DSM-5)

Diagnostic and Statistical Manual of Mental Disorders, fifth edition (DSM-5) is brought to you by the American Psychiatric Association. It serves as psychology's diagnostic bible. Included in the DSM-5 are various categories of mental disorders, the diagnostic criteria for the various disorders included in each category, and the official numerical codes assigned to each disorder.

First published in 1952, the manual is intended for clinical, research, and educational use. DSM-5 was published in 2013 and is the most current version of the manual. As you expect, the amount of detail in the DSM-5 is quite overwhelming. Simply understand the overall structure of the manual and, if you have time, take a look at a DSM-5 at the library.

PSYCHOLOGICAL DISORDERS

Psychological disorders involve thoughts, feelings, or behaviors not in keeping with social norms, and are severe enough to cause personal distress and/or impairment to functioning. According to the DSM-5, psychological disorders fall into 20 major categories. Probably the best way to understand the relationship between the various disorders is to learn them in the format of the DSM-5. Below, maladaptive behaviors, cognitions, and emotions are described in DSM-5 groupings. As some disorders are cited more often than others on the GRE Psychology Test, the descriptions of the disorders vary in length.

Neurodevelopmental Disorders

- **Intellectual disability** (previously known as "mental retardation"). Unlike earlier versions of the manual, DSM-5 emphasizes adaptive functioning deficits instead of specific IQ scores.
- **Learning disorders:** Indicated by school achievement or standardized scores at least two standard deviations below the mean for the appropriate age and IQ.
- **Autism spectrum disorder:** Indicated by severe problems with social skills, communication, and interests.
- **Attention-deficit/hyperactivity disorder (ADHD)** is indicated by problems with attention, behavior, and impulsivity. ADHD is most frequently treated with stimulants (such as Ritalin® and Adderall®).
- **Tic disorders.** Tourette's syndrome, for example, is indicated by motor and vocal tics.
- **Motor skills disorder:** Indicated by motor coordination below expectations for one's chronological age.
- **Communication disorders:** Indicated by pervasive problems acquiring language across modalities, using language socially, or speaking intelligibly or fluently.

Schizophrenia Spectrum and Other Psychotic Disorders

Each disorder in this category is a psychotic disorder, which means that hallucinations or delusions (erroneous beliefs) are present.

- **Schizophrenia,** formerly known as **dementia praecox,** was renamed by **Eugene Bleuler.** Schizophrenia means "split mind," indicating a mind that has split from reality. Though the community frequently confuses schizophrenia with multiple personality disorder, schizophrenia is not the same as multiple personalities or a split personality. Schizophrenia is a favorite on the GRE Psychology Test.

  Schizophrenic symptoms may be **positive** (not normally present) or **negative** (not normally absent). Positive symptoms include **delusions** (erroneous or distorted thinking); **perceptual hallucinations;** nonsensical or **disorganized speech** (perhaps use of made-up words called **neologisms**); and **disorganized behavior** (inappropriate dress, agitation, shouting). Negative symptoms include **flat affect** (absence of appropriate emotion) or restrictions in thought, speech, avolition, or behavior.

The onset of schizophrenia is generally between late adolescence and the mid-30s. **Process schizophrenia** develops gradually, whereas **reactive schizophrenia** develops suddenly in response to a particular event. Process schizophrenia has a lower rate of recovery than reactive schizophrenia. Generally, an individual with a history of good social and interpersonal skills is more likely to recover from schizophrenia than an antisocial individual.

The cause of schizophrenia is at least partially physiological. According to the **diathesis-stress theory,** schizophrenia results from a physiological predisposition (abnormal brain chemistry) paired with an external stressor. The biochemical factor most associated with schizophrenia is **excessive dopamine** in the brain. Schizophrenia also has a hereditary components. Individuals with a first-degree relative who has the disorder have a 10% chance of developing schizophrenia, compared to 1% in the population at large.

- **Schizoaffective disorder.** Schizophrenic symptoms accompanying a depressive episode.

- **Delusional or manic disorder.** Persistent delusions of various types: **erotomanic** (that another person is in love with the individual); **grandiose** (that one has special talent or status); **jealousy; persecutory; somatic** (bodily, such as believing a part of the body is ugly or misshapen).

- **Brief psychotic disorder** involves a sudden onset of psychotic symptoms lasting less than one month, followed by a remission.

- **Schizophreniform disorder** involves most of the symptoms of schizophrenia but is marked by the duration of symptoms—usually at least one month but less than six months.

Bipolar and Related Disorders

- **Bipolar I disorder** is characterized by cycling from extreme manic episodes to major depressive episodes.

- **Bipolar II disorder** also involves cycling from mania to major depression, but the mania tends to be less severe (hypomania).

- In **cyclothymic disorder**, people experience mood swings similar to the bipolar I and II disorders, but the symptoms are less severe and occur with regularity over a period of at least two years.

Depressive Disorders

- **Major depressive disorder**. A depressive episode evidenced by depressed mood, loss of usual interests, changes in weight or sleep, low energy, feelings of worthlessness, or thoughts of death; the symptoms are present nearly every day for at least two weeks. It is twice as common in females as it is in males.

- **Persistent depressive disorder,** also known as **dysthymia.** Symptoms of major depressive disorder (i.e., lower mood) are present more days than not for more than two years, but there is never an actual depressive episode.

Anxiety Disorders

One component of many different anxiety disorders is the **panic attack.** Such an attack lasts only for a discrete period of time, often under 10 minutes. During a panic attack, an individual has overwhelming feelings of danger or of the need to escape. This is often expressed as an intense fear of spontaneously dying or "going crazy" and is generally accompanied by physical manifestations such as sweating, trembling, pounding heart, and more. While generalized anxiety disorder is frequently treated with anxiolytics, specific anxiety disorders (such as the ones listed below) are usually treated with behavioral therapies that expose the patient to the anxiety-provoking stimulus and change the patient's response to the stimulus (e.g., systematic desensitization and flooding).

- **Panic disorder.** Recurrent panic attacks and persistent worry about another attack; this disorder is often accompanied by a mitral valve heart problem.
- **Agoraphobia.** Fear of a situation in which panic symptoms might arise and escape would be difficult; this usually means fear and avoidance of being outside the home or in crowds.
- **Phobia.** Recognized, unreasonable, intense anxiety symptoms and avoidance anchored to a stimulus. **Specific phobia** is anxiety in response to a stimulus, such as flying, heights, needles, or driving.
- **Social anxiety disorder.** Fear of social situations, usually resulting in avoidance behavior.
- **Generalized anxiety disorder.** Excessive anxiety without a specific cause that occurs on more days than not for a period of at least six months.

Obsessive-Compulsive and Related Disorders

These disorders are characterized by obsessions (persistent thoughts) or compulsions (repetitive behaviors or mental acts) that are time consuming, distressing, and disruptive. Typical obsessions might be uncontrollable thoughts of worrying about locking the door or about becoming contaminated; typical compulsions might be checking behavior, praying, counting, or hand washing.

- **Body dysmorphic disorder** is when a person has an unrealistic sense of their body or perceives flaws or defects that are not actually there. This often accompanies the feeding and eating disorders.
- **Hoarding disorder** occurs when a person excessively saves items other people might see as worthless. This may result in their work or living space becoming uninhabitable.
- **Trichotillomania (hair-pulling disorder)** is when a person twirls or pulls their hair compulsively to the point that they may pull it out.
- **Excoriation disorder (skin-picking disorder)** is similar to Trichotillomania but involves picking off skin.

Trauma- and Stressor-Related Disorders

- **Post-traumatic stress disorder (PTSD):** exposure to trauma that results in decreased ability to function and recurrent thoughts and anxiety about the trauma; this disorder is often linked to war veterans or victims of violence.

- **Acute stress disorder** is similar to PTSD but the symptoms have been presence for less than a month.

- **Adjustment disorder** involves symptoms following a trauma or stressor that have been going on for up to three months from the time of the stressor and involve a greater response than one might normally expect under the circumstances.

Dissociative Disorders

These disorders all involve the disruption of memory or identity. They were formerly known as **psychogenic disorders**.

- **Dissociative amnesia** involves the inability to recall specific biographical information, usually due to a trauma or stressor, that is not related to normal forgetting. This often occurs with the trauma- and stressor-related disorders.

- **Depersonalization/derealization disorder** is an altered sense of oneself or one's surroundings (often a feeling of being detached from one's body or the environment) that is not the result of another disorder (such as schizophrenia).

- **Dissociative identity disorder** (formerly known as **multiple personality disorder**), or the assumption of two or more identities that control behavior in different situations.

Somatic Symptom and Related Disorders

These disorders are manifested by physical or bodily symptoms that cause reduced functioning.

- **Conversion disorder.** Psychological problems are converted to bodily symptoms; the symptoms generally relate to voluntary movement and may be manifested as "paralysis" in part of the body. This disorder was formerly known as "hysteria," from Freud's work.

- **Illness anxiety disorder,** formerly known as hypochondriasis, involves a preoccupation with the possibility of getting sick or having a serious illness despite minimal or no somatic symptoms.

- **Somatic symptom disorder** involves a person focusing on physical symptoms to the point where excessive thoughts, feelings, or behaviors interfere with functioning.

- **Factitious disorder,** formerly known as Munchausen or Munchausen by proxy, involves inducing physical symptoms in oneself or in another for the purpose of garnering attention and being able to play the sick role.

Feeding and Eating Disorders

- **Anorexia nervosa** is refusing to eat enough to maintain a healthy body weight; showing excessive concern about becoming obese.
- **Bulimia nervosa** is binge eating accompanied by harmful ways to prevent weight gain (induced vomiting or laxative).
- **Binge-eating disorder** is indicated by consumption of large amounts of food and a sense of lack of control over this eating behavior.
- **Pica** involves the consumption of non-nutritive, non-food substances.

Elimination Disorders

- **Nocturnal enuresis,** for example, is bed-wetting. These disorders are usually treated with behavior modification.

Sleep-Wake Disorders

- **Dyssomnias** relate to issues involving the quantity or quality of sleep.
  - **Insomnia disorder.** Difficulty falling asleep or staying asleep.
  - **Hypersomnolence disorder.** Excessive sleepiness.
  - **Narcolepsy.** Falling asleep uncontrollably during routine daily activity.
  - **Breathing-related sleep disorders.** Involve problems with breathing during sleep resulting in repeated awakenings throughout the night.
- **Parasomnias** are abnormal behaviors during sleep.
  - **Nightmare disorder.** Frequent disruption of sleep because of nightmares.
  - **Sleep terror.** Frequent disruption of sleep because of screaming or crying.
  - **Sleepwalking.** Involves getting up and walking around while in a state of sleep.

Sexual Dysfunctions

This category includes a variety of diagnoses related to pain during sex, a loss of interest in sex, or an inability to achieve orgasm.

Gender Dysphoria

Previously known as "gender identity disorder," **gender dysphoria** is indicated by a conflict between a person's assigned gender at birth and the gender with which he/she/they/etc. identify. The DSM-5 changed the name in order to emphasize that identifying with another gender is a problem only if the individual experiences persistent and pervasive distress as a result. Treatment generally focuses on coping with the negative feelings involved, not on changing the patient's gender identity.

Disruptive, Impulse-Control, and Conduct Disorders

For each of these, an irresistible urge dictates behavior. Giving in to the impulse usually lessens tension and brings relief, though the behavior is disruptive to overall functioning.

- **Kleptomania.** Irresistible impulse to steal.
- **Pyromania.** Irresistible impulse to set fires.
- **Oppositional defiant disorder** and **conduct disorder** are indicated by patterns of behavior that violate rules, norms, or the rights of others.

Substance-Related and Addictive Disorders

These include disorders that result from the use of any toxin such as cocaine, nicotine, or paint fumes. Diagnoses in this category include the **substance-related disorders,** including alcohol-related disorders, caffeine-related disorders, cannabis-related disorders, hallucinogen-related disorders, opioid-related disorders, tobacco-related disorders, as well as **gambling disorder.**

Neurocognitive Disorders

- **Delirium.** Indicated by disturbed consciousness (awareness, attention, focus) and cognition (memory, disorientation).
- **Major or mild neurocognitive disorders.** Cognitive decline (in memory, spatial tasks, language, executive function, complex attention, learning, perceptual motor or social cognition) from a previous level of functioning; may be the result of the following:
  - **Alzheimer's disease,** also known as major or mild neurocognitive disorder due to Alzheimer's disease.
  - **Parkinson's disease,** also known as major or mild neurocognitive disorder due to Parkinson's disease; characterized by tremors with declining neurological functioning.
  - **Huntington's disease,** also known as major or mild neurocognitive disorder due to Huntington's disease; characterized by genetically progressive degeneration of thought, emotion, and movement.
  - **Major or mild frontotemporal neurocognitive disorder** (formerly known as Pick's disease), a disease of the frontal and temporal lobes of the brain characterized by changes in personality.

Personality Disorders

These disorders are characterized by rigid, pervasive culturally maladaptive personality structures. They are normally not diagnosed in children and are grouped into three clusters:

- **Cluster A** personality disorders are characterized by odd or eccentric behavior.
  - o **Paranoid personality disorder.** Distrust, suspicion.
  - o **Schizoid personality disorder.** Detachment, small range of emotion.
  - o **Schizotypal personality disorder.** Eccentricity, distorted reality.
- **Cluster B** personality disorders are characterized by dramatic or erratic behavior.
  - o **Antisocial personality disorder.** Disregard for the rights of others. Absence of guilt.
  - o **Borderline personality disorder.** Instability in relationships and emotions, impulsivity.
  - o **Histrionic personality disorder.** Excess emotion, attention-seeking.
  - o **Narcissistic personality disorder.** Need for admiration, idea of superiority.
- **Cluster C** personality disorders are characterized by anxious or fearful behavior.
  - o **Avoidant personality disorder.** Social inhibitions, hypersensitivity, perceptions of inadequacy.
  - o **Dependent personality disorder.** Need to be taken care of, clinging.
  - o **Obsessive-compulsive personality disorder.** Excessive orderliness and control, perfectionism.

Paraphilic Disorders

Paraphilic disorders are unusual and troublesome sexual desires.

- **Pedophilic disorder.** Attraction to prepubescent children.
- **Exhibitionistic disorder.** Desire to expose oneself to an unsuspecting person.
- **Sexual sadism disorder.** Sexual gratification derived from the physical pain of another.

Other Mental Disorders

The last psychological disorders category in the DSM-5 is a catch-all category for disorders that do not fit into any of the other 19.

GENDER DIFFERENCES IN PSYCHOPATHOLOGY

Research has shown that males and females differ in terms of the types of mental illnesses they tend to develop. Men are statistically more likely to be diagnosed with substance abuse and disorders involving impulse control and antisocial behavior. In contrast, women are more likely to be diagnosed with depression and anxiety disorders. Psychologists attribute this disparity to a tendency for females to internalize negative emotions while males externalize them. Consequently, women are more likely to withdraw and ruminate over their problems, while men are more apt to act out aggressively in response to stress. Accordingly, therapeutic intervention with males is often geared toward developing an ability to plan responses, as opposed to acting on impulse, and reinforcing non-destructive behavioral patterns. For women, therapy more often centers upon reducing and defeating negative thoughts before depression and anxiety take hold.

PREVALENCE OF SERIOUS MENTAL DISORDERS

Psychological disorders afflict different groups of people at different rates. At any given time, tens of millions of Americans suffer from **serious mental illness (SMI)**. An SMI is essentially a psychological disorder that substantially impairs the individual's functioning and disrupts one or more major life activities.

Race and Ethnicity

Per the most recent data from the National Institute of Mental Health, rates of SMI are highest among individuals who report membership in two or more racial groups. White Americans report the second-highest rates, followed by Native Americans/Alaskan natives, Native Hawaiians, African Americans, and Hispanic/Latino Americans. Asian Americans report one of the lowest rates of serious mental illness in the United States.

Age

Young adults in their late teens and early 20s are more likely to be diagnosed with serious mental illness than are adults in any other age group, followed by adults in their mid-20s to age 50. Adults over 50 are least likely to report a serious mental illness.

Gender

Women are significantly more likely than men to be diagnosed with serious mental illness. However, gender-based stereotypes that encourage males to be self-reliant and stigmatize them for seeking help may cause cases of SMI in men to go unreported.

CULTURAL COMPETENCE

In diagnosing mental illness, clinicians typically evaluate the individual's behavior in terms of the dominant cultural norms of that society. Conduct that conforms to the standards and values of that culture is more likely to be deemed "normal," which presents problems when dealing with those who were reared differently.

For example, a psychologist in the United States might view a woman who rarely smiles as socially awkward, withdrawn, or even hostile, as American women are expected to smile often as a sign of affability. In other parts of the world, however, such as some Asian and European countries, frequent smiling might be viewed as odd. Accordingly, the clinical evaluation of a woman from such a culture might be flawed and she might be wrongly placed into a diagnostic category.

- **Culturally competent** interventions involve treatment or prevention programs that recognize and are tailored to cultural differences. Many therapists are now trained in **cultural competence,** which means that they learn the language, customs, and norms of the various cultures they serve. This minimizes Eurocentric bias and assumptions and prevents individuals from having to constantly explain their respective cultures.

- **Multicultural therapy** can involve any therapeutic approach or methodology but requires that the therapist take into account not only the racial and ethnic background of their clients but also other social categories including gender identity, sexual orientation, religion, ability/disability, immigration status, and social class/socioeconomic status. A multicultural approach looks at a client's issues in the context of these various social identities, as well as understanding the history of oppression and marginalization, and power, or lack thereof, in order to see how the combination of these factors impacts the client's experience.

- **Community psychology** is a model in which psychology is taken into the community via community centers or schools, as opposed to having individuals come to clinics and universities. Community psychology emphasizes respect and also recognizes the logistics that keep the neediest people from seeking help.

HEALTH PSYCHOLOGY

A substantial portion of the changes made in the DSM-5 involve eliminating the distinction between medical and psychological disorders. Increasingly psychologists understand that the mind and body are inextricably linked and that attempts to compartmentalize them are futile. **Health psychology** is a specialty area concerned with how psychological factors affect physical health. Issues of interest include reducing maladaptive behaviors that cause disease (e.g., drinking alcohol or overeating), understanding how certain psychological traits can prevent illness and facilitate recovery, measuring the effects of stress on health, providing coping mechanisms for the terminally ill, understanding and treating the psychological impact of physical ailments, and implementing large-scale improvements to the healthcare system. The current model is **biosocial:** one's health is affected by a combination of biological, psychological, behavioral, and social factors. For example, a patient might have a genetic predisposition toward heart disease (a biological factor), a highly driven and achievement-oriented personality type (a psychological factor), a high-stress career (a behavioral factor), and friends who encourage heavy drinking and drug use (a social factor). The combined effect of these various circumstances might be poor heart health.

American Psychology Association (APA) and Publications

- The **American Psychology Association (APA)** is the governing body of the field of psychology in America. It was founded in 1892 by Stanley Hall. Its purpose is to "promote the advancement, communication, and application of psychological science and knowledge to benefit society and improve lives."

- *American Psychologist* is the official journal of the APA. It is published nine times per year and includes archival, current issue, theoretical, and practical articles from all areas of psychology.

- *Psychological Bulletin* is published monthly by the APA and includes various papers ranging from literature reviews to quantitative reviews.

For more information on the APA and all its print and online resources, go to its website: www.apa.org.

Chapter 13
History

This chapter covers the basics of the history of psychology, featuring many key figures and highlights of their work.

DEFINED: The history of psychology extends from philosophy to current thought. Though psychology is a relatively new science, its roots extend deeply into philosophy. For centuries, debates regarding the nature of existence and the mind entangled philosophers. These cumbersome issues were examined from philosophical and, later, physiological angles until finally a new field emerged to focus exclusively on these questions.

ANCIENT GREEKS AND ROMANS (B.C.E./C.E.)

- **Socrates** was one of the founders of Western philosophy and mentor to Plato. He pondered the abstract ideas of truth, beauty, and justice.

- **Plato** was Socrates's pupil. Plato declared that the physical world was not all that could be known. He asserted the presence of universal forms and innate knowledge. Plato's philosophy was abstract and unsystematic.

- **Aristotle,** Plato's pupil, is recognized as the world's first professor. His studies were based on order and logic. Unlike Plato, Aristotle believed that truth would be found in the physical world.

- **Hippocrates** is considered the father of medicine. He provided one of the earliest theories of personality, suggesting personality, or temperament, was based on the fluids, or humors, in the body. Black bile indicated a melancholic temperament, yellow bile indicated a choleric temperament, red blood from the heart a sanguine temperament, and white phlegm from the lungs a phlegmatic temperament.

- **Galen,** one of the greatest physicians in Ancient Rome, built upon Hippocrates's theory of the humors. He believed that imbalances of these humors led to both physiological and psychological disorders. He also detailed more personality traits associated with the four different types (sanguine types are happy, melancholic types unhappy, phlegmatic types calm, and choleric types angry).

MIDDLE AGES (500–1600)

During the Middle Ages, philosophy changed hands twice. Understanding the mysterious world temporarily became a question for the church. Then, at the brink of the modern world, philosophy was reclaimed by scholars.

THE ENLIGHTENTMENT AND SCIENTIFIC REVOLUTION (1600–1800)

The Enlightenment and Scientific Revolution created the world we know today. Major discoveries shaped the way people viewed existence. First, we figured out that the Earth was not the center of the universe (oops!), and this made man a mere part of the big machine rather than the operator (ouch!). Nothing was the same after that. Meanwhile, philosophy was back in the hands of scholars, and they all had different ideas about the nature of things.

- **René Descartes** said, **"I think, therefore I am."** His focus was figuring out truths through reason and deduction. He pondered dualism or the **mind-body problem,** which posits that the mind is a nonphysical substance that is separate from the body.

- **John Locke** is famous for asserting that, upon entering the world, a person's mind is a tabula rasa, or blank slate. He asserted that what we know and what we are comes from experience. Knowledge was not innate.

- **Thomas Hobbes** asserted that humans and other animals were machines and that sense-perception was all that could be known. From this, he suggested that a science could be formed to explain people just as physics explained the machines of the world.

- **Immanuel Kant** countered Locke's previous claim by asserting that our minds were active, not passive. Kant followed Hippocrates's and Galen's models of the humors but believed there was no overlap between the categories.

THE BRINK OF PSYCHOLOGY (1800–1900)

By the 1800s, psychology (the study of the mind) was the pressing issue for philosophers and physiologists alike. So many professionals were preoccupied with unlocking the secrets of the mind that by the end of the century, psychology emerged as a distinct field.

- **Anton Mesmer (1734–1815)** was the Viennese creator of a kind of popular science. He believed that the healing of physical ailments came from the manipulation of people's bodily fluids, which he believed had magnetic properties. He thought that "animal magnetism" (the force that controls a person's mind and body) was responsible for his patients' recoveries. Mesmer's technique of **mesmerism** began to be used by others under the general term of *hypnotism* (hence, the term *mesmerized*, which means hypnotized).

- **Franz Joseph Gall (1758–1828)** used ideas from physiology and philosophy to create a "science" later termed **phrenology.** Phrenology was the idea that the nature of a person could be known by examining the shape and contours of the skull. Because Gall saw the brain as the seat of the soul, certain features on the head were said to be indicators of particular personality traits. **Johann Gaspar Spurzheim** carried on Gall's work even though other scientists proved the theory incorrect.

- **Charles Darwin (1809–1882)** wrote *On the Origin of Species* (1859) and *The Descent of Man* (1871). Though he did not create the concept of evolution, he made evolution a scientifically sound principle by positing that natural selection was its driving force (see Chapter 10, section on Ethology).

- **Sir Francis Galton (1822–1911)** was an independently wealthy Englishman who traveled extensively and studied various things for fun. As a result, he made important, but random, contributions to psychology. Galton was the first to use statistics in psychology, and he created the correlation coefficient. Most notably, he wrote *Hereditary Genius* (1869) and used Darwinian principles to promote **eugenics.** Eugenics was a plan for selective human breeding in order to strengthen the species. He also proposed the theory that humans have general intelligence that can be scientifically measured. Galton is also credited with being the first to use the phrase "nature versus nurture," the debate about whether psychological phenomena are the result of inborn, genetic factors or the result of cultural and societal influences.

- **Gustav Fechner (1801–1887)** is credited with carrying out the first systematic psychology experiment to result in mathematical conclusions, when he developed the idea of the **just noticeable difference** in sensation and perception. His classic work was *Elements of Psychophysics* (1860).

- **Johannes Müller (1801–1858)** was a German physiologist at the University of Berlin. He wrote *Elements of Physiology* (1842) and postulated the existence of "specific nerve energies." Wilhelm Wundt was a student of Müller.

- **Wilhelm Wundt (1832–1920)** is best known as the **founder of psychology.** He is credited with this title because he founded the first official laboratory for psychology at the University of Leipzig in 1879 and because he began the first psychology journal in 1881. He wrote *Principles of Physiological Psychology* (1873), and created a complicated psychology that attempted to study and analyze consciousness. His ideas were the forerunners of **Edward Titchener's,** but they received even less attention.

- **Herbert Spencer (1820–1903)** wrote *Principles of Psychology* (1855) and became the father of the psychology of adaptation. (He is also a founder of sociology.) Spencer used principles from Lamarckian evolution (the idea that characteristics acquired during lifetime can be passed to future generations), physiology, and associationism to understand people. He asserted that different species or races were elevated because of the greater number of associations that their brains could make.

- **William James (1842–1910)** was busy doing in America what Wundt was doing in Germany: combining the fields of physiology and philosophy into a new field. Though he was informally investigating psychological principles at Harvard University in the late 1870s, he did not officially have a lab or course dedicated to psychology until the 1880s (so Wundt just beat James to the punch as the founder of psychology, but James is known as the father of American psychology). James's *Principles of Psychology* (1890) inspired American psychology in a way that writings from other countries had not. James wrote about the mind's **stream of consciousness** and about **functionalist** ideas that sharply contrasted with structuralist ideas of discrete conscious elements.

- **Hermann von Helmholtz (1821–1894)** was a natural scientist who studied sensation. Much of his work with hearing and color vision is the foundation for modern perception research. Like Wundt, he studied with Müller. (See Chapter 3, Sensation and Perception.)

- **Stanley Hall (1842–1924)** was a student of James and received America's first PhD in psychology from Harvard. He coined the term *adolescence*, started the *American Journal of Psychology* (1887), and was the first president of the **American Psychological Association** (1892).

- **John Dewey (1859–1952)** is recognized as one of America's most influential philosophers. He attempted to synthesize philosophy and psychology and is best known in psychology for his work on the reflex arc. Dewey denied that animals respond to their environment through disjointed stimulus and response chains.

He asserted instead that animals are constantly adapting to their environment rather than processing isolated stimuli. This work was the foundation for **functionalism.** Drawn from Darwinian ideas, functionalism examined the adaptive nature of the mind and body through observational methods.

- **Edward Titchener (1867–1927)** taught at Cornell University and was the founder of **structuralism.** Structuralism focused on the analysis of human consciousness. Through **introspection,** lab assistants attempted to objectively describe the **discrete sensations** and contents of their minds. Titchener was an Englishman who studied with Wundt. The structuralist method dissolved after Titchener's death.

- **James Cattell (1860–1944)** was an American who studied with Hall, Galton, and Wundt. He opened psychology laboratories at the University of Pennsylvania and at Columbia University. He thought that psychology should be more scientific than Wundt did.

- **Dorothea Lynde Dix (1802–1887)** spearheaded the 19th-century movement to provide better care for the mentally ill through hospitalization.

THE SAGA CONTINUES (1900s)

With psychology now a science in its own right, the saga continues. Are we more than what we learn? How can we explain the contents of our minds? What most effectively alters our thoughts and behaviors? Below you will find the most famous figures of the 1900s and the work for which they are best known. With some exceptions, most of these figures are discussed at length in earlier chapters that cover their area of accomplishment.

- **Ivan Pavlov (1849–1936)** acquired fame as the winner of a Nobel Prize for work on digestion. In his later work investigating dogs and digestion, he accidentally uncovered the behavioral concept now called **classical conditioning.** (See Chapter 5, Learning.)

- **John B. Watson (1878–1958)** was an American psychologist who expanded on the ideas of Pavlov and founded the school of **behaviorism.** Watson studied conditioning, stimulus-response chains, and objective, observable behaviors. He saw humans as "squirming bits of flesh" ready to be trained by the environment. (See Chapter 5, Learning.)

- **Edward Thorndike (1874–1949)** was a psychologist at Columbia University. His idea, the **law of effect,** was the precursor of operant conditioning. (See Chapter 5, Learning.)

- **B. F. Skinner (1904–1990)** was a famous behaviorist who studied the ideas of Thorndike and Watson. He is most known for his studies that used the **Skinner box** and that led to the principles of **operant conditioning.** His famous books *Walden Two* (1948) and *Beyond Freedom and Dignity* (1972) philosophically discussed the control of human behavior. (See Chapter 5, Learning.)

> "Give me a dozen healthy infants, well-formed, and my own specified world to bring them up in and I'll guarantee to take any one at random and train him to become any type of specialist I might select...regardless of his talents, penchants, tendencies, abilities, vocations, and race of his ancestors."
>
> —John B. Watson

- **Max Wertheimer (1880–1943), Wolfgang Kohler (1887–1967),** and **Kurt Koffka (1886–1941)** forged the school of **Gestalt psychology** around the early 1900s in reaction to attempts to study the mind and experience in distinct parts. Gestalt psychology, coined from the German word that means "whole" or "form," asserts that in perception the whole is greater than the sum of its parts. (See Chapter 3, Sensation and Perception, and Chapter 12, Clinical Psychology and Psychological Disorders.)

- **Sigmund Freud (1856–1939)** is one of the most influential figures in clinical and personality psychology. He is most famous for his personality theory that advanced a three-part structure of the psyche, known as the **id, ego,** and **superego.** What is most notable about his personality theory is the importance placed on **unconscious drives and conflicts.** Freud also began the form of psychotherapy called **psychoanalysis.** Finally, Freud made significant contributions to the fields of psychology and philosophy through various papers, including *The Interpretation of Dreams* (1900), *Three Essays on the Theory of Sexuality* (1905), *Beyond the Pleasure Principle* (1920), and *Civilization and Its Discontents* (1930). (See Chapter 11, Personality, and Chapter 12, Clinical Psychology and Psychological Disorders.)

- **Alfred Adler (1870–1936),** a colleague of Freud, eventually broke from Freud to create his own **individual psychology.** Adler asserted that people were largely motivated by **feelings of inferiority,** for which people try to compensate. He also created a four-type theory of personality: **ruling-dominant, getting leaning, avoiding,** and **socially useful.** (See Chapter 11, Personality, and Chapter 12, Clinical Psychology and Psychological Disorders.)

- **Carl Gustav Jung (1875–1961),** one of Freud's most beloved disciples, broke from Freud because Jung felt that too much emphasis was placed on the **libido,** or sexual instinct. Jung's own school of thought evolved from his work with Freud and is called **analytic psychology.** Analytic psychology is best known for its metaphysical and mythological components, such as the **collective unconscious** and the unconscious **archetypes.** Jung's autobiography, *Memories, Dreams, Reflections* (1961) is standard required reading in many undergraduate psychology programs. (See Chapter 12, Clinical Psychology and Psychological Disorders.)

- **Jean Piaget (1896–1980),** a Swiss psychologist, is a significant figure in developmental psychology. His most important work concerned cognitive development in children. Piaget's three classic works are *The Language and Thought of the Child* (1926), *The Moral Judgment of the Child* (1933), and *The Origins of Intelligence in Children* (1952). (See Chapter 5, Learning, and Chapter 10, Developmental Psychology.)

- **Clark Hull (1884–1952)** secured a place for himself in the history of psychology with his mechanistic behavioral ideas. Hull used math to explain motivation: **Performance = Drive × Habit**. In other words, we do what we need to do and we do what has worked best in the past. **Kenneth Spence** later modified Hull's theory. (See Chapter 5, Learning.)

- **Edward Tolman (1886–1959)** was a behaviorist who uniquely valued both behavior and cognition. His theory of **purposive behavior** asserted that learning is acquired through meaningful behavior (termed sign learning) and that rats in mazes formed cognitive maps rather than blindly attempting various routes.

Tolman also created the **expectancy-value theory** of motivation in which **Performance = Expectation × Value**. (See Chapter 5, Learning.)

- **Konrad Lorenz (1903–1992),** best known as the founder of ethology, was famous for his work with imprinting in goslings and ducklings. He also wrote *On Aggression* (1966). (See Chapter 10, section on Ethology.)

- **Carl Rogers (1902–1987)** is famous for his creation of **client-centered therapy**. In Rogerian therapy, the **client** (not patient) directs the course of therapy and receives **unconditional positive regard** from the therapist. This therapy is classified as **humanistic** because it focuses on the whole human being, rather than on behaviors or drives or the unconscious. Rogers also made a contribution to research: he was the first to record his sessions for later study and reference. (See Chapter 11, Personality, and Chapter 12, Clinical Psychology and Psychological Disorders.)

- **Abraham Maslow (1908–1970)** was a leading figure in **humanistic** psychology. He examined normal or optimal functioning as opposed to maladaptive functioning. He is best known for his development of the **hierarchy of needs.** Maslow argued that people inherently strive for self-improvement. (See Chapter 11, Personality, and Chapter 12, Clinical Psychology and Psychological Disorders.)

- **Erik Erikson (1902–1994)** postulated eight stages of psychosocial development. His theory has been noted for its completeness, because his stages span development from infancy through old age. Erikson coined the term **identity crisis** in naming the key crisis of adolescence. (See Chapter 10, Developmental Psychology.)

- **Victor Frankl (1905–1997),** a key figure in **existential psychology,** wrote *Man's Search for Meaning* (1963). Existential psychology posits that people innately seek meaningfulness in their lives and that perceived meaninglessness is the root of emotional difficulty. Frankl devised **logotherapy,** a form of therapy that focuses on the person's **will to meaning.** (See Chapter 12, Clinical Psychology and Psychological Disorders.)

- **Aaron Beck (1921–)** is most associated with **cognitive** therapeutic techniques. According to Beck and other cognitive theorists, problems arise from maladaptive ways of thinking about the world. Thus, cognitive therapy involves reformulating illogical cognitions rather than searching for a life-stress cause for these cognitions. Beck also wrote the Beck Depression Inventory (see Chapter 12, Clinical Psychology and Psychological Disorders).

- **Melanie Klein (1882–1969)** was born in Austria and had completed a course of psychoanalysis in Budapest with **Sandor Ferenczi,** who encouraged her to start analyzing her own children. A series of lectures in Britain formed the basis for her first book, *The Psychoanalysis of Children*. She was one of the founders of **object relations** theory, a variation of psychoanalysis in which interpersonal relationships are the primary focus, especially the relationship between child and mother. She developed a technique of **play therapy,** still used for therapeutic work with children.

- **Karen Horney (1885–1952)** was a German-born psychoanalyst who questioned many of the principles of Sigmund Freud, most notably Freud's concept of the Oedipus Complex and penis envy. Horney suggested that many women's issues emerged out of sociocultural gender inequality as opposed to a longing for a physical organ. She emigrated to the United States where she developed her own theory of personality and neurosis, which is based on the nature of the parent-child relationship, particularly a parent's ability and interest in creating a secure environment for the child.

- **Kurt Lewin (1890–1947)** was a German-born psychologist who developed the field theory of behavior, which stated that human behavior is a function of an individual's environment. He is considered one of the founders of social psychology.

- **Anna Freud (1895–1982),** the youngest child of Sigmund Freud, followed in her father's footsteps as a psychoanalyst, working mostly with children. She is considered the founder of child psychoanalysis, but differed in many ways from her contemporary Melanie Klein, especially in thinking that while play was important for children, it was not necessarily able to reveal unconscious conflicts, as Klein believed. She established the Hampstead Child Therapy Course and Clinic, later renamed the Anna Freud Centre, for the research and psychoanalysis of children.

- **Lev Vygotsky (1896–1934)** had a short but very productive life. His research focused on the importance of social interaction in learning and development. His concepts of the **zone of proximal development** and **scaffolding** are still foundational in many schools around the world.

- **Gordon Allport (1897–1967)** is considered one of the founders of the trait perspective of personality. He went through the dictionary, identifying about 4,500 words related to traits and sorted them into three categories: cardinal, central, and secondary. He also conducted groundbreaking research into types of racism and prejudice.

- **Inez Beverly Prosser (1897–1934)** is believed to be America's first African American female psychologist, earning her PhD in 1933 from the University of Cincinnati. Her research into self-esteem and person variables in African American school children led her to the controversial conclusion that Black people fared better in segregated environments.

- **Donald Hebb (1904–1985)** is considered one of the founders of neuropsychology. He described how neural pathways form in the brain—that "what fires together, wires together"—long before the discovery of brain imaging techniques.

- **Raymond Cattell (1905–1998)** further refined Allport's traits, declaring that there were 16 essential personality factors, using a combination of life data and experimental data to determine these factors. Cattell's 16PF was still considered too broad and did not stand up to experimental research. It was replaced with the Five-Factor Model.

- **Harry Harlow (1905–1981)** did the seminal research with primates familiar to most psychology students when he constructed two wire mothers, one with a bottle and one covered in soft cloth, to show the impact of comfort on child development. (See Chapter 10, Developmental Psychology.)

- **John Bowlby (1907–1990)** is best known for his articulation of attachment theory, which states that children will form an attachment to a primary caregiver by the age of about 12 months, and that attachment relationship will impact how the child relates to others generally. (See Chapter 10, Developmental Psychology.)

- **Rollo May (1909–1994)** was a psychologist who introduced European existential philosophical and psychological principles to American audiences. In his books and his psychotherapy practice, he focused on the importance of anxiety as part of the human condition as well as the importance of creating meaning out of experience. (See Chapter 11, Personality.)

- **Mary Ainsworth (1913–1999)** developed the Strange Situation experiment, which operationalized Bowlby's attachment theory. She identified three types of attachments: secure, ambivalent (resistant), and avoidant. (See Chapter 10, Developmental Psychology.)

- **Kenneth Bancroft Clark (1914–2005)** was an African American psychologist who, along with his wife, Mamie (see below) used dolls to study children's views about race. The Clarks also testified in the case of *Brown v. Board of Education* in 1954.

- **Hans Eysenck (1913–1999)** identified personality traits, which he called superfactors, that are then subdivided into the different personality types. He also believed that personality traits were genetically determined and insisted on rigorous experimental method in forming theories of personality.

- **Mamie Phipps Clark (1917–1983)** was one of the first African American women to earn a PhD in psychology at Columbia University. The Clarks' landmark doll study emerged from her master's degree thesis. The research also paved the way for more work in self-esteem and self-concept.

- **Eleanor Maccoby (1917–2018)** was an American social and developmental psychologist known for her work on gender development and sex differences. One of her most famous works is the 1980 book, *The Psychology of Sex Difference*, which she coauthored with Carol Nagy Jacklin. She also did vital research into the effects of divorce on children's development.

- **David McClelland (1917–1998)** developed the need theory (also known as the three needs theory), which described motivation in terms of a need for achievement, power, or affiliation. He also developed a new scoring system for the Thematic Apperception Test, a projective personality measure.

- **Leon Festinger (1919–1989)** developed **social comparison theory** as well as the theory of **cognitive dissonance,** which he showed experimentally with his famous forced compliance experiments where he gave people either $1 or $20 for lying to others about why a boring task was actually interesting.

- **George A. Miller (1920–2012)** was one of the founders of cognitive psychology. He studied short-term memory and linguistics, and is often credited with applying the information processing model to cognitive psychology. His best known paper was "The Magical Number Seven, Plus or Minus Two," written in 1956, in which he discussed the findings that short-term memory can only hold about 5–9 items of information at any given time.

- **Albert Bandura (1925–)** is a Canadian-born psychologist best known for developing the social cognitive perspective of personality, based on the principles of social learning theory. In the Bobo doll experiment, Bandura and his colleagues showed for the first time empirically that people learn through modelling.

- **Walter Mischel (1930–2018)** was an American psychologist who conducted extensive research into the concept of **delayed gratification** with his groundbreaking study the **Marshmallow Test,** a study that ran in various forms for more than 50 years. While more recent research has questioned the universality of the findings, Mischel's work is still a must-read for psychology students.

- **Eleanor Gibson (1932–1979)** was a research psychologist best known for the **visual cliff** experiment, in which she, Richard Walk, and their colleagues showed that depth perception is innate.

- **Carol Gilligan (1936–)** is the author of the classic feminist psychology work, *In a Different Voice*, in which she outlined a theory that women's development happens through relationship and care. Gilligan worked with Erik Erikson and Lawrence Kohlberg, but extended their work by studying girls as well as boys, since most psychological theories up to that time were based on boys and men as subjects.

- **Derald Wing Sue (1942–)** is an American psychologist best known for his work on multiculturalism and cross-cultural counselling. He has extensively researched **microaggressions**, small verbal or behavioral ways in which racism and ethnocentrism are expressed daily, whether intentionally or unintentionally.

- **Martin Seligman (1942–)** is an American psychologist who first gained fame from his research into learned helplessness. He is now best known for his role as founder of the field of positive psychology, a field that looks at a person's character strengths and how those strengths can bring about happiness.

- **Sandra Bem (1944–2014)**, an American psychologist, was best known for her pioneering work in gender studies. She created the Bem Sex Role Inventory, did extensive research on androgyny, and developed the gender schema theory, which described how gender identity is formed.

- **Elizabeth Loftus (1944–)** is an American cognitive psychologist best known for her research into memory, especially in relation to the fallibility of eyewitness testimony.

- **David Buss (1953–)** is an American evolutionary psychologist who is known for his work on mating strategies in women and men, and how jealousy and other challenging experiences may be evolutionarily adaptive.

Chapter 14
Measurement and Methodology

This chapter covers the basics of measurement and research methodology. Included is information about intelligence and intelligence testing, as well as various types of tests (achievement, aptitude, and projective and objective personality testing). The chapter also covers research methodology, including research design, problems in research, and statistics.

DEFINED: Psychological tests are assessments of behavior, attitudes, mental constructs, personality, and mental health. Your best strategy with this section is to learn the basics of the well-known tests and to focus on the intelligence-testing field.

INTELLIGENCE AND INTELLIGENCE TESTING

Intelligence is a cognitive construct that is defined in many ways. In fact, many psychologists have different ideas about what intelligence actually is. The dictionary defines intelligence as the ability to acquire and apply new information. Intelligence is not IQ. IQ is the score one receives on an "intelligence" test. It is unlikely that IQ captures all facets of intelligence.

- **Alfred Binet** developed both the concept of the IQ and the first intelligence test **(Binet scale).** IQ is still most commonly computed by Binet's equation: **(mental age/chronological age) × 100.** Mental age is the age level of a person's functioning according to the IQ test. The highest chronological age used in the computation is 16. After that, intelligence seems to stop developing; therefore, to use adult ages would unnecessarily decrease the IQ ratio.

- The **Mean IQ** of Americans is **100,** with a standard deviation of 15 or 16 depending on the test.

- **Stanford-Binet Intelligence Scale** is the revised version of Alfred Binet's original intelligence test. **Lewis Terman** of Stanford University was the first to revise it, hence the name. The Stanford-Binet is used with children and is organized by age level. Of all of the intelligence Alfred Binet tests, the Stanford-Binet is the best known predictor of future academic achievement. Terman is also famous for his studies with gifted children and for the finding that children with higher IQs are better adjusted.

- **Wechsler Adult Intelligence Scale (WAIS)** is the most commonly used intelligence test for adults. Like all of the Wechsler intelligence tests, it is organized by subtests that provide subscales and identify problem areas. The version in current use is called the WAIS-IV (fourth edition).

- **Wechsler Intelligence Scale for Children (WISC-V)** is for children aged 6 to 16.

- **Wechsler Preschool and Primary Scale of Intelligence (WPPSI)** is for children aged 4 to 6.

- **Goodenough Draw-A-Person Test** for children is notable for its (relatively) cross-cultural application and simple directions: "Make a picture of a man. Make the very best picture that you can." Children are scored based on detail and accuracy, not artistic talent.

- IQ correlates most positively with IQ of biological parents (not adoptive parents) and socioeconomic status of parents (measured by either income or job-type).

- **John Horn** and **Raymond Cattell** found that **fluid intelligence** (knowing how to do something) declines with old age, while **crystallized intelligence** (knowing a fact) does not.

- **Robert Zajonc** studied the relationship between birth order and intelligence. He found that firstborns were slightly more intelligent than secondborns, and so on. He also found that the more children present in a family, the less intelligent they were likely to be. This relationship seems to also be affected by the spacing of the children, with greater spaces between children leading to higher intelligence.

- **Charles Spearman** believed there was a general factor in human intelligence, which he termed "g." For example, someone that is good at logic and reasoning will probably score well on both the math and verbal sections of the SAT (indicative of g), but the person may do better in one than the other. Spearman was influenced heavily by **Sir Francis Galton,** who believed that intelligence was a) quantifiable and normally distributed, and b) influenced by heredity.

- **Howard Gardner** developed a theory of multiple intelligences, in which he outlined eight different types of intelligence, rather than just a single factor. His eight types are Logical/Mathematical, Linguistic, Musical, Spatial, Bodily-Kinesthetic, Naturalist, Interpersonal, and Intrapersonal. Gardner's theory broadened the notion of intelligence beyond cognitive abilities.

- **Robert Sternberg** developed a triarchic theory of intelligence in response to both early theories and Gardner's theory. His theory suggests that only three factors matter in intelligence: 1) analytical ability, 2) practical ability, and 3) creative ability. He believed that intelligence was more about using what you know and have experienced to adapt to the world.

- **Emotional intelligence** refers to the ability to identify and manage one's own emotions as well as those of others. No scientific instrument to measure these constructs has yet been developed, so some believe this is another name for various interpersonal skills.

ACADEMIC TESTS
- **Achievement tests** measure how well you know a particular subject. They measure past learning.
- **Aptitude tests** supposedly measure your innate ability to learn (but this is constantly debated). These tests are intended to predict later performance.

OBJECTIVE PERSONALITY INVENTORIES
Objective tests do not allow subjects to make up their own answers, so these tests are relatively structured. **Structured tests** are often seen as more objectively scored than projective tests (see below). Most objective tests are self-reported—in other words, the subject records her own responses. However, these tests are not completely objective, because any self-report measure allows for the subject to bias her answers.

- **Q-sort** or **Q-measure** technique is the process of sorting cards into a normal distribution. Each card has a different statement on it pertaining to personality. The subject places the cards that he is neutral about at the hump of the curve. Toward one end, he places cards that he deems "very characteristic" of himself, and toward the other end, he places the "not characteristic" cards.

- **Minnesota Multiphasic Personality Inventory (MMPI)** was originally created to look for evidence of psychological disorders, but it is now used as a personality measure. The MMPI consists of 550 "true/false/not sure" questions. Most notably, the MMPI contains items (such as "I would like to ride a horse") that have been found to discriminate between different disorders and that subjects could not "second guess." The test has high validity primarily because it was constructed with highly discriminatory items and because it has three validity scales (questions that assess lying, carelessness, and faking).

- **California Personality Inventory (CPI)** is a personality measure generally used for more "normal" and less clinical groups than the MMPI. It was developed by Harrison Gough at the University of California, Berkeley.

- **Myers-Briggs Type Indicator (MBTI)** is a personality test created by Isabel Briggs Myers and her mother, Kathleen Briggs. It is derived from Carl Jung's personality theory. The MBTI consists of 93 questions, each of which has two answers. When scored, a person is given a four-letter "personality type" with each letter representing one of two possible opposing characteristics: Introverted vs. Extraverted, Sensing vs. Intuition, Feeling vs. Thinking, and Judgment vs. Perception.

- **Julian Rotter** created the **Internal-External Locus of Control Scale** to determine whether a person feels responsible for the things that happen (internal) or that he has no control over the events in life (external).

PROJECTIVE PERSONALITY TESTS

Projective tests allow the subject to create his own answer, thus facilitating the expression of conflicts, needs, and impulses. The content of the response is interpreted by the test administrator. Some projective tests are scored more objectively than others.

- **Rorschach Inkblot Test** requires the subject to describe what he sees in each of ten inkblots. Scoring is complex. The validity of the test is questionable, but its fame is not.

- **Henry Murray** and his colleagues created the **Thematic Apperception Test (TAT),** which is made up of 31 cards (1 blank and 30 with pictures). The pictures show various ambiguous interpersonal scenes (two people interacting). The test taker tells a story about each of the cards, which reveals aspects of their personality. The TAT is often used to measure need for achievement. According to Murray's personality theory, called **personology,** people's **needs** interact with **presses,** which refer to the environmental stimuli impacting the needs.

- **Rosenzweig Picture-Frustration Study (P-F Study)** consists of cartoons in which one person is frustrating another person. The subject is asked to describe how the frustrated person responds.

- **Word Association Test** was originally used in conjunction with free association techniques. A word is called out by a psychologist, and the person says the next word that comes to mind.

- **Rotter Incomplete Sentence Blank** is similar to word association. Subjects finish incomplete sentences.

- **Draw-A-Person Test (see above)** asks the child to draw a person of each sex and to tell a story about them.

OTHER IMPORTANT IDEAS IN TESTING

- **Beck Depression Inventory (BDI)** is not used to diagnose depression. Rather, it is used to assess the severity of depressive symptoms and can be used by a researcher or clinician to track the course of depressive symptoms.

- **Empirical-criterion-keying approach** to constructing assessment instruments involves the selection of items that can discriminate between various groups. Then, the assessment is given to people known to possess those traits. Only the items that apply are kept for the final version of the assessment. An individual's responses to the items determine if he is like a particular group or not. The **Strong Interest Inventory** is an example of an empirically derived test.

- **Vocational tests** assess to what extent an individual's interests and strengths match those already found by professionals in a particular job field.

- **Lie detector tests** measure the arousal of the sympathetic nervous system, which becomes stimulated by lying (and anxiety).

- **Walter Mischel** was extremely critical of personality trait theory and of personality tests in general. He felt that situations (not traits) decide actions.

- **Anne Anastasi** researched intelligence in relation to performance.

- **F-scale**, or **F-ratio**, is a measurement of **fascism** or **authoritarian personality.**

- **Bayley Scales of Infant Development** are not intelligence tests. They measure the cognitive, language, motor, adaptive, and social-emotional development of infants in order to identify developmental issues in children. The Bayley scales are poor predictors of later intelligence.

RESEARCH DESIGN

Research design refers to the way in which a researcher attempts to examine a hypothesis. Different questions call for different approaches, and some approaches are more "scientific" than others.

Big Ideas

- A **scientific approach** to the study of psychology involves:
  - a testable **hypothesis**
  - a reproducible experiment that can be **replicated** by other scientists
  - an **operationalized definition** (observable and measurable) of the concept under study

- A **field study** is an experiment that takes place in a naturalistic setting. Field studies generally have much less control over the environment than laboratory experiments do. For this reason, the field may generate more hypotheses than it is able to prove.

- A study adhering to **experimental design** takes place in a controlled setting (often a lab). In order to draw causal conclusions from an experiment, the researcher must be able to control certain aspects of the environment:
  - **Independent variable.** The researcher is interested in the effect of the independent variable on the dependent variable. The researcher manipulates the independent variable often by applying it in the **experimental** or **treatment condition** and by withholding it from the **control condition.**
  - **Dependent variable.** The researcher does not control the dependent variable but rather examines how the independent variable affects the dependent variable.
  - **Confounding variable.** The researcher attempts to minimize or eliminate confounding variables. These are variables in the environment that might also affect the dependent variable and would blur the effect of the independent variable on the dependent variable.

Example: A researcher is exploring the relationship between eating and sleeping. Specifically, the researcher hypothesizes that eating within an hour before going to bed causes you to sleep unsoundly. The **experimental group** will eat just before bed, but the **control group** will eat four hours before bed. All subjects will eat and sleep in the lab. The independent variable is eating before bed. The dependent variable is quality of sleep. One potential confounding variable is the possibility that simply sleeping in the lab could affect the sleep of some subjects.

Design Considerations

Researchers are generally interested in how an independent variable affects a dependent variable in a **population** (a large group of people, such as women, college students, stockbrokers, or depressed patients). Because it is usually impossible to include all members of a population in a study, a **sample** or **subgroup** is drawn from the population. To make inferences about a population from a sample, the sample must be **representative** of the population and **unbiased.** This is most likely achieved with **random sampling.** (With this sampling procedure, every member of the population has an equal chance of being chosen for the sample.) However, sometimes, random sampling is not feasible, and people use **convenience sampling** (like students in an intro psych course) instead. To make the results more generalizable, though, researchers may use **stratified sampling,** which aims to match the demographic characteristics of the sample to the demographics of the population (i.e., sample that is 50 percent female, like the population).

Other Considerations:

- Particularly in developmental research, psychologists need to study people at different ages. **Longitudinal design** involves studying the same objects at different points in the lifespan and provides better, more valid results than most other methods. However, longitudinal designs are costly and require an enormous time commitment. Another design is **cross-sectional,** in which different subjects of different ages are compared. This is faster and easier than longitudinal design. **Cohort-sequential design** combines longitudinal and cross-sectional approaches.

- A **within-subject** design tests the same person at multiple time points and looks at changes within that person. A **between-subjects** design compares two groups of people at the same time point. For example, if researchers wanted to see if a new drug decreased depressive symptoms, the researchers could use either design. With a within-subjects design, the researchers would measure each person's depression at baseline, administer the drug, and measure depression again. If the participants were less depressed the second time, the researchers would conclude that the drug worked. With a between-subjects design, researchers would give one group of depressed people the drug and one group of depressed people the placebo and then measure depression. If the group that received the drug was less depressed than the group that received the placebo, then the researchers would conclude that the drug was effective.

- **Quasi-experimental** design involves manipulation of the independent variable but no random assignment of participants. Thus, it resembles an experiment, but this design is used when it is not feasible or ethical to use random assignment. For example, it is not ethical to assign one group of people to smoke for 20 years. So, studies that have shown that smoking causes lung cancer are quasi-experimental, since there was no random assignment to determine if people were smokers or not.

- **Double-blind** experiments are those in which neither the subject nor the experimenter knows whether the subject is assigned to the treatment or to the control group. These are considered the "gold standard" for experimental research.

- A **placebo** is an inactive substance or condition disguised as a treatment substance or condition. It is used to form the control group.

- **Predictive value** is the degree to which an independent variable can predict a dependent variable.

- **Generalizability** is the degree to which the results from an experiment can be applied to the population and the real world.

- In **qualitative,** or **nonexperimental,** research, the data collected is descriptive rather than quantitative. Types of qualitative research include case studies, observational studies, ethnographic studies, and phenomenological studies.

- In **mixed methods** research, multiple methodologies, usually a combination of qualitative and quantitative, are used.

Research Problems

- **Acquiescence.** When people tend to respond positively to survey questions more frequently, often without considering the full content of the item in question.

- **Cohort effects.** The effects that might result when a group is born and raised in a particular time period. A cohort is a group of people who share some type of common identity.

- **Demand characteristic.** When subjects act in ways they think the experimenter wants or expects.

- **Experimenter bias.** When researchers see what they want to see. This effect, also known as the **Rosenthal effect,** is minimized in a double-blind experiment.

- **Hawthorne effect.** When subjects alter their behavior because they are being observed. This also applies to workers altering their behavior for the same reason.

- **Nonequivalent control group.** This problematic type of control group is used when an equivalent one cannot be isolated.

- **Placebo effect.** When subjects behave differently just because they think that they have received the treatment substance or condition.

- **Reactance.** An attitude change in response to feeling that options are limited. For example, when subjects react negatively to being in an experiment by intentionally behaving unnaturally or when an individual becomes set on a certain flavor of ice cream as soon as he is told it is sold out.

- **Selective attrition.** When the subjects that drop out of an experiment are different from those that remain. The remaining sample is no longer random.

- **Social desirability.** When subjects do and say what they think puts them in a favorable light (e.g., reporting they are not racist even if they really are).

- **Illusory correlation.** When a relationship is inferred when there actually is none. For example, many people insist a relationship exists between physical and personality characteristics despite evidence that no such relationship exists.

- **Meta-analysis.** A method of study that mathematically combines and summarizes the overall effects or research findings for a particular topic. Best known for consolidating various studies of the effectiveness of psychotherapy, meta-analysis can calculate one overall effect size or conclusion drawn from a collection of different studies. This method is needed when conflicting results are found and when different studies use different methods.

- **Ethical** concerns are extremely important in research, and ethical standards in psychological research are very high. All studies are approved by an Institutional Review Board (IRB), which makes sure that the experiments are safe for participants and do not cause any unnecessary harm. Before participating in a study, all subjects must be provided with information about the risks and benefits of being in the study and then sign a consent form indicating that they are aware of the risks involved. However, these strict ethical guidelines did not always exist. The Milgram experiment was later deemed unethical because of the lasting psychological distress experienced by the participants (see Chapter 9, Social Psychology). The Milgram experiment was the catalyst for higher ethical standards in psychological research.

STATISTICS

Statistics is the process of representing or analyzing numerical data. Descriptive statistics organize data from a sample by showing it in a meaningful way. They do not allow conclusions to be drawn beyond the sample. The five most common forms of descriptive statistics are:

- **Percentiles** are used most commonly on standardized tests. Along with your reported score of 750, you would receive a percentile ranking of 97 percent. This shows your position in the whole group by saying that you scored higher than 97 percent of the group.

- **Frequency distributions** explain how the data in a study looked. The distributions might show how often different variables appeared. Here are some common types of variables:

  - **Nominal variables.** "Nominal" comes from the Latin word for name, so these variables are simply given descriptive names. There is no order or relationship among the variables other than to separate them into groups. Example: male, female, Republican, Democrat.

  - **Ordinal variables.** "Ordinal" implies order. Here, variables need to be arranged by order and that is it. Nothing else can be known because the variables are not necessarily equally spaced. Example: marathon finishers. A different runner comes in first, second, and third, but we do not know how far apart their finishing times were—it may have been seconds or minutes.

  - **Interval variables.** Interval variables are capable of showing order and spacing because equal spaces lie between the values. These variables, however, do not include a real zero. Example: Temperature is ordered, and the values are equally spaced. So 75 degrees is 25 degrees warmer than 50 degrees. Temperature has an arbitrary zero; however, there is no point that signifies the absence of temperature.

  - **Ratio variables.** These variables have order, equal intervals, and a real zero—they can say it all. Example: Age—after an absolute zero of not being born, age increases in equal intervals of years.

- **Graphs** are used to plot data.
  - **Frequency polygon.** This graph has plotted points connected by lines. These are often used to plot variables that are continuous (categories without clear boundaries).

  - **Histogram.** This graph consists of vertical bars in which the sides of the vertical bars touch. Histograms are useful for discrete variables that have clear boundaries and for interval variables in which there is some order. The bars are lined up in order.

  - **Bar graph.** This graph is like a histogram except that the vertical bars do not touch. The various vertical columns are separated by spaces.

- **Measures of central tendency** indicate where on a number line the data set falls in general. Three types of central tendency can be calculated on a set of numbers like this one: {7, 8, 8, 9, 10, 12, 13, 13, 13}.

- o **Mean.** The mean is the same as the **average.** The mean of a set of numbers equals all of the values added together divided by the number of values. Means are highly affected by extreme scores. The mean of the above set is 10.33. **Standard error of the mean** calculates how "off" the mean might be in either direction.

- o **Median.** To find the median of a set of numbers, first line the numbers up in ascending order. Find the value that lies in the center of the row. In the above set, 10 is the number that sits dead center. If there's an even number of values in the set, take the average of the two middle values.

- o **Mode.** The mode is the most frequently occurring value. In the above set, 13 is the mode.

- **Variability** provides additional information to central tendency. It tells you how the scores are spread out overall.

  - o **Range.** This most basic measure of variability simply subtracts the lowest value from the highest value in a data set. This is the overall range or spread.

  - o **Variance** and **standard deviation** tell us how much variation there is among n number of scores in a distribution. To calculate variance, you figure out how much each score differs (or deviates) from the mean by subtracting the mean from each score. Then you must square each of these deviation values (this gets rid of negative values that result when scores fall below the mean). Now you add all these squared deviations to get the sum of the squares. Now divide this sum by the number of scores you had in the first place, by n—this gives you the variance in a sample. But remember that all of these values were squared, so to find the average deviation, or standard deviation, from the mean, you take the square root of the variance. Standard deviation tells you the average extent to which scores were different from the mean. If the average standard deviation is large, then scores were highly dispersed. If the standard deviation is small, then scores were very close together. Different standard deviations make it difficult to compare scores on two different tests.

The Normal Distribution

The **normal distribution,** also known as the **bell curve,** is quite important. In an ideal world, scores such as those for the GRE are intended to look like a bell curve. The larger your sample, the greater your chance of having a normal distribution of values. Here's what you should know about the normal distribution:

- It is **unimodal**—it has only one hump. The majority of scores fall in the middle ranges. There are fewer scores at the extremes. The mean, median, and mode are all equal in normal distribution (at the 50.00 line in the diagram below).

- **Z-scores** refer to the number of standard deviations a score is from the mean. For practical purposes, z-scores of normal distributions range from −3 to +3, because this covers the vast majority of scores on a normal curve.

- **T-scores** are a transformation of a z-score, in which the mean is 50 and the standard deviation is 10. Thus, the formula for calculating T is $T = 10(Z) + 50$.

- To combat problems of comparing scores and distributions of scores with different standard deviations, normal distributions can be standardized. These are known as standard normal distributions. The standard normal distribution is the same thing as a normal distribution, but it has been standardized so that the mean for every such distribution is 0 and the standard deviation is 1. **Standard normal distributions** and z-scores allow you to compare one person's scores on two different distributions. For example, if a person's intelligence matches his or her achievement on the GRE Psychology Test, you would expect someone to receive the same z-score on an IQ test and on the GRE Psychology Test (e.g., a z-score of +2), even though both tests use two different scoring systems. This would mean that the person's score should be 2 standard deviations above the mean in both cases. If we saw that the person's IQ score was 130, or two standard deviations above the mean, giving a z-score of +2, and his or her GRE Psychology Test score was 570, or right at the mean, giving a z-score of 0, we would hypothesize that for some reason this individual was not performing to his or her potential.

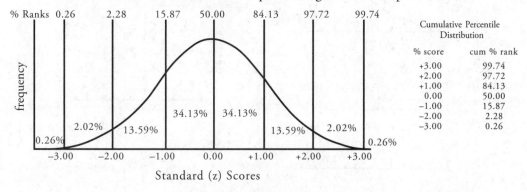

The Standard Normal Distribution

- Know all the numbers on the standard normal distribution and how they map onto a normal distribution. For example, if John scores an 88 in a test in which the mean is 80 and the standard deviation is 4, then on a normal distribution of scores in the class, John's score would lie two standard deviations above the mean. If this normal distribution of scores were then standardized to have a mean of 0 and a standard deviation of 1, then John's score of 88 would now be meaningless— what we would know instead is that he had a z-score of 2. We would also know that John lies in the 97th percentile, meaning that 97 percent of students score lower than he did.

- It is important to be able to reproduce the standard normal distribution and all of the numbers that go with it so that you can evaluate problems similar to the one above. Know what z-scores go with what percentile ranks. And know the percentage of scores that lie in each area; for example, know that 68 percent of scores lie within one standard deviation (in either direction) of the mean. To make this easy, learn this ratio 34:14:2 and know that it applies to both sides of the mean.

Not all distributions are normal. Learn the names of the other types:

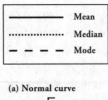

(a) Normal curve

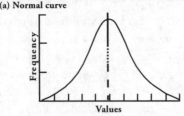

(b) Positively skewed distribution

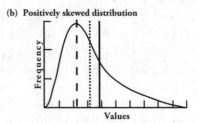

(c) Negatively skewed distribution

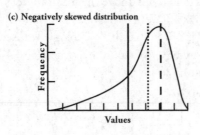

(d) Bimodal distribution

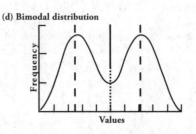

(e) Platykurtic distribution

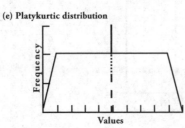

**Examples of frequency distributions found in
behavioral science research**

Correlational Statistics

Correlations are part of statistics but are neither purely descriptive nor purely inferential. Correlations can only show **relationships** (NOT causality) between variables. The different types of correlations or relationships are:

- **Positive.** A positive correlation is simple and linear. As one variable increases, so does the other. Example: Food intake and weight are positively correlated; the more you eat, the more you weigh.

- **Negative.** A negative correlation is simple and linear. As one variable goes up, the other goes down. Example: Exercise and weight. With other factors held constant, as the amount you exercise increases, the amount you weigh decreases.

- **Curvilinear.** A curvilinear relationship is not simple and linear. It looks like a curved line. Example: Arousal and performance. Low arousal and high arousal lead to poor performance, but a medium amount of arousal leads to successful performance.

- **Zero correlation.** There is no relationship between the variables.

The **Pearson *r* correlation coefficient** is a way of numerically calculating and expressing correlation. You don't need to know how to find a Pearson's *r*, but you do need to know what the *r* values mean. The Pearson *r* values range from –1 to +1. A value of –1 indicates a perfect negative correlation. A value of +1 indicates a perfect positive correlation. A value of 0 indicates no relationship. The strength of the relationship is indicated by how far away the value is from zero and how close it is to –1 or +1.

A **Spearman *r* correlation coefficient** is another correlation used only when the data is in the form of ranks. It is the procedure for determining the line that describes a linear relationship. **Regression** is the step beyond simple correlations. A **statistical regression** allows you to not only identify a relationship between two variables but also to make predictions about one variable based on another variable.

Inferential Statistics

Inferential statistics allow you to generalize findings from a sample to a population, which is the larger group from which the sample was drawn. **Statistics** refer to numbers that describe a sample, and **parameters** refer to numbers that describe populations. We use statistics to estimate population parameters. That is, we use statistics to predict or estimate what happens outside the sample.

- When a researcher uses a statistical test (whatever it may be), he or she is usually hoping to find that the sample statistics are **significant**. This means that the numbers that describe the sample (e.g., that men are taller on average than women, or that treatment groups in therapy trials perform better than control groups) are describing a real difference or pattern rather than just random variation. If findings are statistically significant, then researchers can **generalize** these same findings to the population.

- When a researcher uses a **test of significance,** he or she is hoping to **reject the null hypothesis,** which is the hypothesis that no real differences or patterns exist. If a test of significance shows that results were statistically significant (not likely caused by chance), then the null hypothesis is rejected.

- Researchers cannot always know for certain whether their findings are correct, but certain standards are accepted. Most researchers use a significance level, also known as **alpha** level, of <.05 or <.01. This means that the chance that seemingly significant errors are due to random variation rather than to true, systematic variance is less than 5/100 or less than 1/100, respectively.

- **Type I errors** occur when you incorrectly reject the null hypothesis—that is, you thought your findings were significant, but they were really only caused by chance. **Type II errors** occur when you wrongly accept the null hypothesis—in other words, tests showed your findings to be insignificant when in fact they were significant.

Study Tip

Studies have shown that the correlation between GRE scores, interview performance, and success in graduate school is illusory. None exists! So don't let these things intimidate you. Having a difficult time preparing for and applying to school does not mean that psychology grad school is not for you.

Which tests of significance you use depends on the characteristics of your sample and of your dependent variable. The most commonly used tests of significance are the following:

- **T-tests** compare the **means of two different groups** to see if the two groups are truly different. This would mean that the difference between the means is large enough to be considered statistically significant rather than due to chance variation. T-tests analyze differences between means on **continuous data** (anything that is *measured*, such as height or depression score on a depression scale, as opposed to discrete data, which is things that are *counted*: group size, number of hospital visits, number of symptoms, etc.) and are particularly useful with samples that have small "n" (meaning few subjects). T-tests cannot test for differences between more than two groups.

- **Chi-square tests** are used when the *n*-cases in a sample are classified into categories or **cells.** The results of the chi-square test tell us whether the **groups are significantly different in size.** Chi-squares look at patterns or distributions (not differences between means). For example, imagine that 100 members of an Introduction to Psychology class are categorized according to race (Caucasian, African American, Asian American, Hispanic, Native American). Insignificant results of a chi-square test of this data would tell us that no one race tended to be enrolled in Introduction to Psychology significantly more than any other race. Chi-square tests analyze **categorical** or **discrete** data (data that has been counted rather than measured and so is usually limited to positive and whole values) and can be used on small samples. Chi-square tests can also assess the **"goodness of fit"** of distributions or whether the pattern is what would be expected.

- **ANOVA,** or **analysis of variance,** is a highly utilized test because of its flexibility. It is similar to the t-test in that it analyzes the **differences among means** of continuous variables, but it is more flexible than the t-test because it can analyze the difference among more than two groups (even if the groups have different sample sizes). **One-Way ANOVA** simply tests whether the means on one factor or independent variable are significantly different across groups. **Two-Way ANOVA** can test the effects of two independent variables or treatment conditions at once.

- **Factorial analysis of variance** is used when an experiment involves more than one independent variable. This analysis can separate the effects of different levels of different variables. Example: If you were studying the effect of brain lesions on problem solving, you could have two independent variables (lesion and type of problem) and one dependent variable (success with problem). Give each independent variable two levels apiece (with and without lesions, simple and complex tasks). This is a 2 × 2 design, which would yield four different combinations for evaluation. A factor analysis can isolate the **main effects** (the effect of lesions on problem solving and the effect of type of task on problem solving). More importantly, a factor analysis can identify **interaction effects.** Here, you can combine the independent variables. (Do people with lesions do better on simple tasks than people without lesions do on complex tasks?)

- **Analysis of Covariance (ANCOVA)** tests whether at least two groups co-vary. Importantly, the ANCOVA can adjust for preexisting differences between groups.

- **Linear regression** allows you to use correlation coefficients in order to predict one variable y from another variable x. Correlations measure the linear relationship between two variables, but they do not describe the relationship. For example, we might know that the correlation between extraversion and the number of friends you have is 0.73; this does not let us predict from an extraversion score how many friends someone would probably have. Linear regression allows us to define a line on a graph that describes the relationship between x and y. In general, the same data you used to calculate a correlation is now plotted onto a graph. Let's use extraversion score as our x-variable and number of friends as our y-variable. Imagine a graph with extraversion on the x-axis and friends on the y-axis. The dots on the graph are the data from the individual subjects. Linear regression occurs when the least-squares line or regression line is fit to the data. This line would be situated so that the distance between each point of data and the line is as small as possible (this is determined by finding the difference between each data point and the line, squaring these differences to get rid of negative values, and then summing them). Fortunately, computer programs do this for you, and it will not be required on the GRE Psychology Test. Just know that regressions use correlational data to make predictions based on a line fit with the least-squares method.

Creating Measures

Statistics are an important part of creating new tests or measures. They ensure that the measures are on target.

- Tests are **standardized** (or tried out on huge groups of people) in order to create norms.
- **Criterion-referenced tests** measure mastery in a particular area or subject (the final exam of a course, for example).
- **Domain-referenced tests** attempt to measure less-defined properties (like intelligence) and need to be checked for reliability and validity.
- **Reliability** means how stable the measure is:
  - **Test-retest reliability** is measured by the same individual taking the same test more than once. On a test with high test-retest reliability, that person would get approximately the same score each time.
  - **Split-half reliability** is measured by comparing an individual's performance on two halves of the same test (odd versus even questions for example). This reveals the **internal consistency** of a test. Another way to increase internal consistency of a measure is to perform an **item analysis,** analyzing how a large group responded to each item on the measure. This process weeds out dud or problematic questions so they can be replaced with better questions (ones with discriminatory value). This increases internal consistency.

- **Validity** refers to the degree to which a test measures a construct.
  - o **Internal validity** measures the extent to which the different items within a measure "hang together" and test the same thing.
  - o **External validity** is the extent to which a test measures what it intends to measure. There are four aspects of external validity:
    1. **Concurrent validity** refers to how well scores on a new measure positively correlate with other measures known to test the same construct. This process is cross validation.
    2. **Construct validity** refers to the degree to which the test really taps the abstract concept being measured.
    3. **Content validity** refers to the degree to which the content of the test covers a good sample of the construct being measured (not just part of it).
    4. **Face validity** refers to the degree to which a test is effective in its aims.
  - o **Donald Campbell** and **Donald Fiske** created the multitrait-multimethod technique to determine the validity of tests.

Part III
The Princeton Review Practice GRE Psychology Test

Chapter 15
Practice Test 1

PSYCHOLOGY TEST

Time — 170 Minutes

205 Questions

Directions: Each of the questions or incomplete statements below is followed by five suggested answers or completions. In each case, select the one that is best and then completely fill in the corresponding space on the answer sheet.

1. A child with an IQ of 63 would most likely be diagnosed with

   (A) mild intellectual disability
   (B) severe intellectual disability
   (C) profound intellectual disability
   (D) moderate intellectual disability
   (E) borderline intellectual disability

2. A phenomenological view of personality asserts that type theory neglects the

   (A) superego
   (B) self
   (C) supernatural
   (D) proprium
   (E) id

3. Which of the following is one of the personality disorders found in Cluster B?

   (A) Paranoid personality disorder
   (B) Dependent personality disorder
   (C) Schizotypal personality disorder
   (D) Narcissistic personality disorder
   (E) Obsessive-compulsive personality disorder

4. What is the key distinction between classical conditioning and operant conditioning?

   (A) Operant conditioning attempts to pair an unrelated stimulus and response, whereas classical conditioning attempts to extinguish such pairings.
   (B) Operant conditioning focuses on rewards, whereas classical conditioning focuses on punishment.
   (C) Operant conditioning attempts to pair an unrelated stimulus and response, whereas classical conditioning underscores the consequences of behavior.
   (D) Operant conditioning emphasizes the consequences of behavior, whereas classical conditioning emphasizes the association between stimuli.
   (E) Operant conditioning is used in human therapy, whereas classical conditioning is used only with other animals.

5. A child in Piaget's preoperational stage is given a toy and attempts to eat it. This child is demonstrating

   (A) generalization
   (B) accommodation
   (C) assimilation
   (D) transition
   (E) overextension

6. Which of the following is NOT true of systematic desensitization?

   (A) The technique is attributed to Joseph Wolpe.
   (B) It is a highly effective treatment for phobias.
   (C) It employs counterconditioning principles.
   (D) It reduces anxiety.
   (E) It employs operant conditioning.

GO ON TO THE NEXT PAGE.

7. If the GRE Psychology Test had a standard error of zero, then a test taker that took the test two times would necessarily receive

   (A) a score equivalent to a z-score of 1 each time
   (B) the same score on each test
   (C) two scores that correlated perfectly with the test taker's aptitude
   (D) two scores that were above the mean
   (E) two perfect scores

8. Deutsch used the "prisoner's dilemma" to study what social phenomenon?

   (A) Conformity vs. reactance
   (B) Attribution
   (C) Cooperation vs. competition
   (D) Stereotypes
   (E) Bias

9. A brooding herring gull is presented with various eggs of differing size and coloration. She can only incubate one. The egg that she chooses will most likely be

   (A) closest to her nest
   (B) an exact replica of a herring gull egg
   (C) a supernormal sign stimulus
   (D) extremely small in size
   (E) not colored

10. Noam Chomsky posited that humans have a unique, in-born ability to understand the structure of language and to apply this to language learning. Chomsky called this the

    (A) innate surface structure ability
    (B) innate capability index
    (C) prosody index
    (D) language acquisition device
    (E) collective endowment device

11. Two major dimensions of personality hypothesized by Hans Eysenck are

    (A) stability and introversion
    (B) masculinity and femininity
    (C) stability and masculinity
    (D) internal control and external control
    (E) extraversion and repression

12. According to Erik Erikson, a young adult would be most concerned with which of the following issues?

    (A) Identity
    (B) Sex-typed behavior
    (C) Autonomy
    (D) Achievement
    (E) Intimacy

GO ON TO THE NEXT PAGE.

13. The victim of a car accident has no physiological feeling in his body. He can, however, think and speak. The man notices that since the injury, his emotions have been practically nonexistent. This situation supports which theory of emotion?

(A) James-Lange theory
(B) Cannon-Bard theory
(C) Sperry theory
(D) Post-traumatic stress theory
(E) Metacognitive theory

14. When examining the nature-nurture issue, scientists have concluded that

(A) behavior is the product of nature
(B) behavior is the product of nurture
(C) behavior is the product of the interaction of nature and nurture
(D) behavior is half nature and half nurture
(E) behavior is determined by the mind, which is not a physical entity

15. Hazel has experienced feelings of worthlessness, low energy, and a loss of interest in life for most of the days of the past three years. She would most likely be diagnosed with

(A) an external locus of control
(B) persistent depressive disorder
(C) severe melancholia
(D) existential neurosis
(E) bipolar disorder

16. The Strange Situation is used in order to study

(A) infant attachment
(B) Hawthorne effect
(C) groupthink
(D) diffusion of responsibility
(E) Barnum effect

17. Which of the following activities best serves to hold information in short-term memory?

(A) Clustering
(B) Chunking
(C) Rehearsing
(D) Attending
(E) Associating

18. Which of the following is characteristic of stage N1 sleep?

(A) Dreams
(B) REM
(C) Desynchronized EEG patterns
(D) Major muscle twitches
(E) Difficulty being roused

19. The DSM-5 groups psychological disorders into 20 categories of disorders that share similar characteristics, though it is common that a client may be diagnosed with multiple disorders from different categories. Which of the following is NOT a category of diagnoses?

(A) Depersonalization disorders
(B) Neurodevelopmental disorders
(C) Depressive disorders
(D) Feeding and eating disorders
(E) Anxiety disorders

GO ON TO THE NEXT PAGE.

Questions 20–21 apply to the research study described below.

A researcher wants to consider the effects of preparation on standardized test scores. She plans to compare the GRE scores of students who did and did not take a preparation course for the GRE. She also plans to compare the GRE scores of students who took preparation courses through Company X, Company Y, and Company Z.

20. Which of the following statistical tests should the researcher use to analyze her data?

    (A) Pearson's r correlation coefficient
    (B) T-test
    (C) Chi-square test
    (D) $2 \times 2 \times 2$ factor analysis
    (E) 2×3 factor analysis

21. The researcher found that students who took a preparation course with Companies X and Y scored higher on the GRE than students who did not prepare. But students who took a preparation course with Company Z scored no higher on average than students who did not take a preparation course. These results are an example of

    (A) a negative correlation
    (B) a zero correlation
    (C) an interaction effect
    (D) a main effect
    (E) a flat effect

22. With which of the following researchers is androgyny most associated?

    (A) Karen Horney
    (B) Sandra Bem
    (C) Eleanor Maccoby
    (D) Matina Horner
    (E) Diana Baumrind

23. Social comparison theory has been used as an argument against

    (A) deindividuation
    (B) group polarization
    (C) single-sex schools
    (D) segregation
    (E) mainstreaming in schools

24. Which of the following phenomena is minimized by group monitoring?

    (A) Social loafing
    (B) Social comparison
    (C) Ingroup/outgroup bias
    (D) Groupthink
    (E) Group polarization

GO ON TO THE NEXT PAGE.

25. A two-year-old who wants to be handed a ball might simply say "ball." This is an example of

(A) holophrastic speech
(B) telegraphic speech
(C) overregulated speech
(D) overextended speech
(E) neologistic speech

26. After moving into a home very near to a hospital, a young child became frightened and upset each time he heard ambulance sirens racing by. With time, the child seemed less bothered by the sirens. Eventually, the child seemed not to notice the sirens at all. This lessened reaction to the sirens is most likely caused by

(A) chaining
(B) habituation
(C) extinction
(D) sensitization
(E) shaping

27. Which of the following methods is most commonly used to study selective attention?

(A) Shadowing in a dichotic listening task
(B) Presentation of subliminal messages on a screen
(C) Presentation of subliminal messages on an audiotape
(D) Presentation of two stimuli separated by one just noticeable difference
(E) Questionnaires that test the contents of short-term memory

28. Bottom-up information processing is best described as

(A) semantically driven
(B) phonetically driven
(C) schematically driven
(D) morphologically driven
(E) data driven

29. Kohlberg devised his theory of moral development through the use of

(A) observations of individual action in contrived moral dilemmas
(B) naturalistic observations of children
(C) themes in mythology
(D) verbal responses to hypothetical moral dilemmas
(E) objective personality inventories

30. Long-term use of a dopamine-blocking neuroleptic would probably improve the condition of

(A) tardive dyskinesia
(B) Parkinson's disease
(C) schizophrenia
(D) both schizophrenia and Parkinson's disease
(E) Wernicke's syndrome

GO ON TO THE NEXT PAGE.

31. Which of the following figures is credited with founding the first laboratory dedicated to psychology?

    (A) Johannes Müller
    (B) Thomas Harvey
    (C) Sigmund Freud
    (D) Gustav Fechner
    (E) Wilhelm Wundt

32. Which of the following statements is true of maintenance rehearsal?

    (A) Maintenance rehearsal keeps material in short-term memory.
    (B) Maintenance rehearsal keeps material in long-term memory.
    (C) Maintenance rehearsal transfers material to long-term memory.
    (D) Maintenance rehearsal is also called secondary rehearsal.
    (E) Maintenance rehearsal uses elaboration.

33. In many jury trials, defense lawyers use the strategy of blaming the victim, so that the accused perpetrator might be set free. People's tendency to go along with victim blaming can be explained by

    (A) oversimplification
    (B) the representativeness heuristic
    (C) the just world bias
    (D) the illusion of control
    (E) the illusory correlation

34. Which of the following is NOT a morpheme?

    (A) The suffix "-ed"
    (B) The vowel combination "ee"
    (C) The word "cat"
    (D) The suffix "s"
    (E) The prefix "anti-"

35. A neuron in the brain has recently fired. The neuron completes its absolute refractory period and then is in the relative refractory period. At this point, the neuron is stimulated by a stronger stimulus, and it fires again. Which of the following is true of that neuron?

    (A) It is hyperpolarized.
    (B) The action potential will not be completed because of the refractory period.
    (C) The second action potential will be of greater intensity than the first.
    (D) The second action potential will be of the same intensity as the first.
    (E) The second action potential will be of lesser intensity than the first.

36. In the criterion-keying or empirical-keying approach to test construction, the researcher

    (A) must include items that allow for projective answers
    (B) must include items that could produce percentile ranks
    (C) must include items that allow for a range of scores
    (D) must include items that discriminate between groups
    (E) must include items that measure speed

GO ON TO THE NEXT PAGE.

37. According to Piaget, an individual in which of the following stages might demonstrate circular reactions?

(A) Accommodational
(B) Sensorimotor
(C) Preoperational
(D) Concrete operational
(E) Formal operational

38. The theory that a child steals candy because he is a thief is an example of

(A) an availability heuristic
(B) a cognitive bias
(C) a dispositional attribution
(D) a response set
(E) a situational attribution

39. What is an example of conditioned aversion?

(A) No longer wanting to drink alcohol because you had too much and it made you sick
(B) Wanting to eat a lot of asparagus because it is very good for you
(C) Not wanting to eat a cheeseburger because you found out how much saturated fat it contains
(D) No longer wanting to eat spinach because you heard that a lot of people who ate spinach got *E. coli*
(E) Wanting to drink a lot of water after you work out because it keeps you from feeling dehydrated

40. A manager of an advertising company is encouraging her workers to think "outside the box" in order to come up with entirely new angles for advertising. In essence, the manager is asking her employees to think

(A) metacognitively
(B) convergently
(C) fluidly
(D) deductively
(E) divergently

41. A pigeon is placed in a "Skinner box" which is outfitted with a key for pecking and a chute that delivers food. Through shaping, the experimenter plans to condition the bird to peck the key in order to obtain food. The experimenter will need to use

(A) secondary reinforcement
(B) autonomic conditioning
(C) differential reinforcement
(D) autoshaping
(E) trace conditioning

42. Humans see better at night by looking at objects from the side than by looking straight at objects. This is explained by

(A) the opponent-process theory
(B) the way rods are distributed on the retina
(C) the trichromatic theory
(D) lateral geniculate activity
(E) the crossing of the optic nerves in the neural pathway

GO ON TO THE NEXT PAGE.

43. According to Craik and Lockhart, which of the following levels of processing would result in the highest recall of information?

(A) Phonological
(B) Syntactic
(C) Repetitive
(D) Acoustic
(E) Semantic

44. Compared to control rats, rats with a lesion to the amygdala would

(A) be exactly the same as control rats
(B) perform worse at finding food hidden in a maze
(C) exhibit less fear in response to a stimulus that was previously presented with a shock
(D) eat more when given unlimited access to food
(E) have difficulty distinguishing different odors

Questions 45–46 are based on the following experiment.

In a laboratory experiment, subjects wear headphones and are tested individually. Each of 500 subjects is presented first with a light and then possibly with a low-intensity tone in the earphones. Subjects are instructed to push a button if they hear a tone. Subjects are rewarded with $10 for each hit. In 500 trials, 200 times a tone was presented, and 300 times a tone was not presented. One hundred and ninety tones were detected. Also, the button was pressed 270 times in response to no tone.

45. Which of the following describes the subjects' overall performance?

(A) 10 misses and 30 false alarms
(B) 10 misses and 30 correct rejections
(C) 460 hits
(D) 190 hits and 270 misses
(E) 280 misses

46. Which of the following statements about the above experiment is in line with signal detection theory?

(A) The reward offered for hits increased subjects' overall response accuracy.
(B) Subjects were unable to detect at least a few tones because some tones were not a just noticeable difference from the previously presented tones.
(C) The reward for hits probably caused the high number of false alarms.
(D) Some subjects might have been distracted by the experiment design which called on visual and auditory sensory systems.
(E) The tone and the light were probably not effectively paired because the tone only followed the light in 200 of the 500 trials.

GO ON TO THE NEXT PAGE.

47. According to Kohlberg, an individual in a stage of conventional morality would be most concerned with

(A) gaining rewards
(B) gaining approval
(C) avoiding punishment
(D) achieving fairness
(E) adhering to the conservative point of view

48. Which of the following areas in the brain has been shown in experiments to be closely connected to hunger, eating, and satiation?

(A) Medulla oblongata
(B) Hippocampus
(C) Hypothalamus
(D) Thalamus
(E) Corpus callosum

49. Oxytocin has which of the following actions?

(A) Increases blood pressure
(B) Increases pair bonding
(C) Decreases appetite
(D) Decreases libido
(E) Initiates puberty

50. Kenneth and Mamie Clark's doll preference studies were used

(A) to elicit accounts of childhood sexual abuse
(B) to demonstrate regression in adults
(C) to demonstrate gender favoritism in the classroom
(D) as evidence in *Brown v. Board of Education*
(E) as evidence in the Kitty Genovese case

51. To motivate himself to study, a student decides that after learning a chapter of material he will treat himself to a movie. In this situation, seeing a movie is acting as a reinforcement for studying. This situation demonstrates

(A) the Premack principle
(B) a fixed-interval ratio schedule
(C) autoshaping
(D) the Garcia effect
(E) higher-order conditioning

52. The view that the mind is a "tabula rasa" at birth and written on by experience is most commonly associated with

(A) Edward Thorndike
(B) Immanuel Kant
(C) John Locke
(D) René Descartes
(E) Thomas Hobbes

GO ON TO THE NEXT PAGE.

53. An experimenter wants to train a dog to bark at a red light. The dog naturally barks at a mouse when it is presented outside the dog's cage. For countless trials, the experimenter presents the mouse and then the red light. The dog never learns to bark at the red light because

(A) the UCS and the CS are not at all similar
(B) the UCS and the CS are presented in the wrong order
(C) the UCR and the CS are not at all similar
(D) the CS is not salient enough
(E) the CS precedes the UCS

54. According to Roger Brown and other psycholinguistic researchers, children refine the way they apply grammatical rules through

(A) positive reinforcement from caregivers
(B) positive conditioning from caregivers
(C) experience and self-correction
(D) memorization of what others say
(E) structured learning

55. According to Freud's developmental theory, a child who is particularly frustrated during a stage of development is likely to experience

(A) fixation
(B) identification
(C) castration anxiety if a boy
(D) overdevelopment of the superego
(E) ego anxiety

56. Which of the following explains why cartoons are not perceived as a series of still frames?

(A) Autokinetic effect
(B) Motion parallax
(C) The Ponzo illusion
(D) The Müller-Lyer illusion
(E) The Phi phenomenon

57. Mary frequently has people come up and say hi to her on the street, but she does not know who they are even though she has met them many times in the past. She has difficulty recognizing faces and would be diagnosed with

(A) prosopagnosia
(B) social phobia
(C) Tourette disorder
(D) Korsakoff's syndrome
(E) asomatognosia

58. Visual acuity is highest under what circumstances?

(A) When the cones in the periphery of the retina are stimulated
(B) When the rods on the fovea are stimulated
(C) When the rods and the cones are equally stimulated
(D) When the cones on the fovea are stimulated
(E) When the rods in the periphery of the retina are stimulated

GO ON TO THE NEXT PAGE.

59. In research on attachment, Harlow placed infant rhesus monkeys with "surrogate mothers." In this famous experiment, a stimulus that induced fear in the infant would cause the infant to run to

(A) the adult female who most resembled its biological mother
(B) the closest object behind which it could hide
(C) the surrogate with the bottle
(D) the surrogate covered with terrycloth
(E) none of the above, as it knew none were its biological mother

60. A therapist listens to the choices of his client with unconditional positive regard. The goal of this therapy is most likely

(A) a sense of meaningfulness
(B) congruence for the self
(C) complete awareness of the here and now
(D) decreased inferiority
(E) development of effective beliefs

61. Erikson's developmental theory centered on

(A) biological forces
(B) cognitive changes
(C) moral development
(D) psychosocial crises
(E) need development

62. The most common way of studying human cognitive processing is to evaluate

(A) semantic shifts
(B) EEG readings
(C) reaction time
(D) rehearsal time
(E) creativity

63. Because Shay is a good student, her teacher assumes she is also artistic, well behaved, and from a good family. The teacher's assumptions are explained by

(A) the halo effect
(B) oversimplification
(C) good continuation
(D) self-fulfilling prophecy
(E) self-serving bias

64. Trait theory in personality has been most criticized for

(A) having contradictory dimensions
(B) attempting to quantify the impossible
(C) not identifying one agreed-upon dimension of personality
(D) not addressing heredity
(E) assuming that people behave consistently in various situations

GO ON TO THE NEXT PAGE.

65. Which of the following is NOT a maladaptive cognition according to cognitive therapy?

(A) Dichotomous thinking
(B) Personalizing
(C) Denying
(D) Overgeneralizing
(E) Magnifying

66. John was going for a stroll in the woods when he saw a bear in the distance. As the bear started coming toward him, John got scared and started to run in the opposite direction. Which of the following happened when John saw the bear?

(A) His parasympathetic nervous system became activated.
(B) His sympathetic nervous system became activated.
(C) There was an increase in the amount of GABA released into his brain.
(D) There was a decrease in the amount of dopamine released in his brain.
(E) There was a decrease in the amount of cortisol released into his blood stream.

67. Which of the following reflexes might be elicited by stroking the bottom of a baby's foot?

(A) Neo-ped reflex
(B) Moro reflex
(C) Babinski reflex
(D) Palmar reflex
(E) Klinefelter reflex

68. The part of the brain that is connected to the very basic function of simple alertness is the

(A) superior colliculus
(B) inferior colliculus
(C) medulla oblongata
(D) reticular formation
(E) hippocampus

69. Which of the following disorders is the modern name for hypochondriasis?

(A) Munchausen syndrome
(B) Hypersomnolence
(C) Illness anxiety disorder
(D) Somatic symptom disorder
(E) Trichotillomania

Questions 70–71 refer to the following statements.

Tom's favorite hobby has always been skiing. Recently, Tom took a job in which he is paid a large sum of money to patrol the ski slopes daily.

70. According to Daryl Bem, Tom's attitude about skiing

(A) will remain unchanged
(B) will become more negative
(C) will become more positive
(D) will vacillate because of cognitive dissonance
(E) will be negative only on days when he is not paid to ski

71. The change in Tom's attitude, according to self-perception theory, would result from

(A) self-fulfilling prophecy
(B) overjustification
(C) mere-exposure effect
(D) inoculation
(E) gain-loss theory

GO ON TO THE NEXT PAGE.

72. Which of the following would be most inclined toward a situational view of personality?

    (A) Walter Mischel
    (B) Raymond Cattell
    (C) Gordon Allport
    (D) Hans Eysenck
    (E) William Sheldon

73. The APA was founded by

    (A) John Watson
    (B) William James
    (C) Stanley Hall
    (D) Wilhelm Wundt
    (E) B. F. Skinner

74. Prozac, which is frequently used to treat depression, works because it is a

    (A) norepinephrine agonist
    (B) norepinephrine antagonist
    (C) serotonin agonist
    (D) serotonin antagonist
    (E) dopamine agonist

75. Weber's law applies to a specific range of intensities in

    (A) hearing only
    (B) vision only
    (C) hearing and vision only
    (D) all of the senses
    (E) none of the senses because it has been disproved

76. While swimming in the ocean, a woman was stung by several jellyfish. Now the woman refuses to swim at all, even at an indoor pool. Her new fear of swimming can be attributed to

    (A) operant conditioning
    (B) trace conditioning
    (C) delayed conditioning
    (D) second-order conditioning
    (E) classical conditioning

77. Which of the following is true of a variable-ratio schedule of reinforcement as opposed to other schedules of reinforcement?

    (A) It provides a reinforcement for any response.
    (B) Of the various reinforcement schedules, it causes learning to occur the fastest.
    (C) It explains why people wait endlessly for a late bus.
    (D) It is extremely vulnerable to extinction.
    (E) It produces the highest rate of responding.

78. A normal distribution of 2000 scores has a mean of 150 and a standard deviation of 6. Jenny received a 162. Each of the following is true of her score EXCEPT:

    (A) Approximately 68% of students scored lower than she did.
    (B) Approximately 48% of the total scores lie between her score and the mean.
    (C) Her score is two standard deviations from the mean.
    (D) Her score is equivalent to a z-score of +2.
    (E) Her percentile rank is in approximately the 98th percentile.

GO ON TO THE NEXT PAGE.

79. An individual sternly gives orders in his own home and obediently follows orders at work. This person might score particularly high on the

(A) Rotter Locus of Control Scale
(B) TAT
(C) CPI
(D) F-scale
(E) Bem Sex Role Inventory

80. The receptors for hearing are located on which of the following in humans?

(A) Olivary nucleus
(B) Inferior colliculus
(C) Oval window
(D) Tympanic membrane
(E) Basilar membrane

81. According to Piaget, a child who recognizes that a round ball of clay maintains its mass even when flattened into a long thin cylinder must have acquired which cognitive skill?

(A) Object permanence
(B) Transmutation
(C) Generalization
(D) Conservation
(E) Transformation

82. What causes a fetus to develop into a female?

(A) The presence of estrogen
(B) The absence of estrogen
(C) The absence of H-Y antigen
(D) The presence of H-Y antigen
(E) The presence of follicle stimulating hormone

83. Which of the following personality disorders is characterized by excessive emotion and attention seeking?

(A) Histrionic
(B) Antisocial
(C) Dependent
(D) Schizotypal
(E) Borderline

84. An IQ of 146 is approximately how many standard deviations from the mean?

(A) 5
(B) 4
(C) 3
(D) 2
(E) 1

GO ON TO THE NEXT PAGE.

85. The fundamental attribution error is the tendency to

   (A) attribute every behavior to some motive
   (B) personify inanimate objects
   (C) project personal motivations onto the behaviors of others
   (D) attribute one's own mistakes to disposition
   (E) attribute the behaviors of others to disposition

86. On the GRE, a student would answer a question about Erikson more quickly if it were preceded by another question about Erikson than if it were preceded by a question about physiological psychology. This effect is due to

   (A) atmosphere effect
   (B) semantic priming
   (C) chunking
   (D) top-down processing
   (E) acoustic effect

87. An individual with Korsakoff's syndrome might engage in

   (A) neologisms
   (B) echolalia
   (C) echopraxia
   (D) confabulations
   (E) folie a deux

88. Gordon Allport is known for what type of approach to understanding personality?

   (A) Personal construct
   (B) Nomothetic
   (C) Ideographic
   (D) Factor analysis
   (E) Phrenologic

89. According to Piaget, an individual who entertains himself by solving logic puzzles must be in which of the following cognitive stages?

   (A) Accommodational
   (B) Sensorimotor
   (C) Preoperational
   (D) Concrete operational
   (E) Formal operational

90. Which of the following therapies would be most appropriate for an individual who suffered from strong feelings of meaninglessness and who hoped to find more meaning in life?

   (A) Client-centered therapy
   (B) Psychoanalytic therapy
   (C) Existential therapy
   (D) Individual therapy
   (E) Gestalt therapy

GO ON TO THE NEXT PAGE.

91. Which of the following brain areas is important for speech?

   (A) Right cerebral hemisphere
   (B) Cerebellum
   (C) Thalamus
   (D) Hippocampus
   (E) Wernicke's area

92. E. L. Thorndike is known for each of the following EXCEPT

   (A) the law of effect
   (B) the concept of instrumental learning
   (C) the discovery of state-dependent learning
   (D) learning experiments using cats in puzzle boxes
   (E) asserting that individuals repeat behaviors that lead to positive consequences

93. In a territory that is inhabited by many similar looking and closely related bird species, a male bird performs an elaborate display prior to mating. The display ensures that the female partner will be of the same species as the male. This is an example of

   (A) a behavioral isolating mechanism
   (B) a fixed action pattern
   (C) paternal behavior
   (D) habituation
   (E) exploratory behavior

94. Which of the following theorists has been recognized for creating a developmental theory that covers the entire life span?

   (A) Abraham Maslow
   (B) Lawrence Kohlberg
   (C) Erik Erikson
   (D) Jean Piaget
   (E) Sigmund Freud

95. The Kitty Genovese case sparked research into

   (A) vicarious behavior
   (B) the glass ceiling
   (C) racial segregation
   (D) the bystander effect
   (E) violence against women

96. In research on social learning theory, Bandura conducted the famous Bobo doll experiment. Based on this experiment, what did Bandura conclude was important to social learning in children?

   (A) Observational learning
   (B) Primary reinforcement
   (C) Rewards
   (D) Concept learning
   (E) Shaping

GO ON TO THE NEXT PAGE.

97. Watson would expect which of the following factors to most influence child behavioral development?

    (A) Morality
    (B) Imitation
    (C) Psychodynamic influences
    (D) Psychosocial factors
    (E) Exploration needs

98. According to Collins and Quillian, to which of the following statements would subjects take the longer amount of time to answer "true"?

    (A) A shoe is a piece of clothing.
    (B) A ballet slipper is a shoe.
    (C) A boot is a shoe.
    (D) A sandal is a piece of clothing.
    (E) A sandal is a shoe.

99. Which is true of the ossicles in the auditory system?

    (A) The stapes taps against the oval window.
    (B) The stapes taps against the tympanic membrane.
    (C) Their movement is known as the traveling wave.
    (D) They are located in the inner ear.
    (E) They are located in the outer ear.

100. Which of the following types of tests is paired correctly with its form of memory testing?

    (A) Essay test . . cued recall
    (B) Language test . . recognition
    (C) Fill-in-the-blank test . . cued recall
    (D) Multiple-choice test . . cued recall
    (E) Sentence completion test . . recognition

101. Upon spotting a predator, a hidden bird makes a call of alarm. This display of altruism now places the hidden bird at increased risk while placing its nearby siblings at decreased risk. Such an act is best explained by the concept of

    (A) contact comfort behavior
    (B) operant behavior
    (C) natural selection
    (D) irrelevant behavior
    (E) inclusive fitness

102. Benzodiazepines work to relieve anxiety by enhancing the effects of

    (A) GABA
    (B) glutamate
    (C) serotonin
    (D) endorphins
    (E) dopamine

GO ON TO THE NEXT PAGE.

103. The idea that people will alter their actions or beliefs so that their actions and beliefs are in agreement with one another is the theory of

(A) risky shift
(B) cognitive dissonance
(C) Purkinje shift
(D) self-serving bias
(E) acceptance

104. Henry Landsberger discovered that

(A) people behave differently when observed (Hawthorne effect)
(B) people remember uncompleted tasks better than ones they completed (Zeigarnik effect)
(C) conclusions are influenced by the way information is phrased (atmosphere effect)
(D) a single point of light will appear to move in the darkness (autokinetic effect)
(E) people spend a larger percentage of sleep in REM after they have been deprived of it (Rebound effect)

105. Which of the following argued that Kohlberg's moral stages were not directly applicable to females?

(A) Carol Gilligan
(B) Diana Baumrind
(C) Matina Horner
(D) Eleanor Maccoby
(E) Jenny Field

106. Which of the following personality types is NOT associated with Alfred Adler's theory of personality?

(A) Sanguine
(B) Choleric
(C) Melancholic
(D) Ectomorphic
(E) Phlegmatic

107. A woman attempts to sell a car for $10,000 and then settles for $8,000. Because the seller only hoped to collect $8,000 in the first place, she was employing which of the following tactics in social psychology?

(A) Reactance
(B) Foot-in-the-door
(C) Door-in-the-face
(D) Guilt bias
(E) False cooperation

108. Which of the following is the path of a received "message" through a single neuron?

(A) Presynaptic cell, cell body, axon, post-synaptic cell
(B) Postsynaptic cell, cell body, axon, terminal buttons
(C) Presynaptic cell, cell body, axon, dendrites
(D) Dendrites, axon, cell body, terminal buttons
(E) Dendrites, axon, axon hillock, terminal buttons

GO ON TO THE NEXT PAGE.

Questions 109–110 refer to the following study.

A researcher is studying the effect of diet on depression. The hypothesis is that a diet high in carbohydrates will help to alleviate the symptoms of depression. The group being studied is a random group of depressed inpatients. Every other day the subjects fill out a depression symptom inventory.

109. In the above study, the symptom inventory provides information about the

    (A) interaction effect
    (B) confounding variable
    (C) independent variable
    (D) dependent variable
    (E) control variable

110. Which of the following is the most serious confounding variable?

    (A) Some subjects are male and others are female.
    (B) Some subjects are teenagers and other subjects are in their twenties.
    (C) Some subjects have been in the hospital longer than others.
    (D) Some subjects are on antidepressants and others are not.
    (E) Some subjects have been depressed before and others have not.

111. Which of the following is NOT a dissociative disorder?

    (A) Amnesia
    (B) Multiple personality disorder
    (C) Identity disorder
    (D) Depersonalization disorder
    (E) Derealization disorder

112. Behavior therapy would be most useful in treating

    (A) a childhood disorder
    (B) paranoid schizophrenia
    (C) depression
    (D) tardive dyskinesia
    (E) a conversion disorder

113. According to Piaget, a child who looks under a pillow for a lost toy is able to appreciate

    (A) conservation
    (B) concrete operations
    (C) object permanence
    (D) exploration needs
    (E) determination

GO ON TO THE NEXT PAGE.

114. A subject is presented with two tones of differing intensities. The subject, however, states that the tones seem to be of the same intensity. According to Weber, this is probably because

   (A) the tones were not separated by at least one just noticeable difference
   (B) the tones were presented too closely together
   (C) the tones were of varying pitches
   (D) the subject was not motivated to pay attention
   (E) response bias affected the subject

115. Hermann von Helmholtz is, in part, famous for his theory of

   (A) retinal disparity
   (B) color vision
   (C) lateral inhibition
   (D) sensory transduction
   (E) tone deafness

116. The structuralist school of psychology viewed consciousness as

   (A) divided into three separate layers
   (B) a flow of ideas without clear boundaries
   (C) a collective unit passed down genetically
   (D) a set of discrete sensations
   (E) a blank slate waiting for experience

117. The Whorfian hypothesis posits that

   (A) two closely related species will develop different breeding seasons
   (B) a diagnostic label influences how others interpret an individual's behavior
   (C) the way an eyewitness is questioned may affect his memory of events
   (D) excessive dopamine activity is a factor in schizophrenia
   (E) a culture's language structure influences how the speakers perceive reality

118. According to Freud, the Oedipus complex in boys and the Electra complex in girls are resolved through

   (A) moving into the latency stage
   (B) identification with the opposite-sex parent
   (C) identification with the same-sex parent
   (D) the emergence of death instinct
   (E) the strengthening of the ego

119. When reciting the alphabet, children often recall A, B, C, D and X, Y, Z more readily than the letters in between. This is the result of

   (A) retroactive inhibition
   (B) retroactive interference
   (C) proactive interference
   (D) primary and secondary rehearsal
   (E) primacy and recency effects

GO ON TO THE NEXT PAGE.

120. According to Schachter and Singer, an emotional response would involve which of the following factors in order of appearance?

(A) Physiological reaction, cognition, emotion
(B) Cognition, physiological reaction, emotion
(C) Physiological reaction, emotion, cognition
(D) Emotion, physiological reaction, cognition
(E) Cognition, emotion, physiological reaction

121. Which classic experiment indicated that behavioral traits could be at least partly determined by heredity?

(A) Tyron's experiment with maze-bright and maze-dull rats
(B) Garcia's experiment with food aversion
(C) Thorndike's experiment with cats in puzzle boxes
(D) Von Frisch's experiment with honeybees
(E) Tinbergen's experiment with stickleback fish

122. As opposed to longitudinal design, a cross-sectional study is able to control for

(A) cohort effects
(B) demand characteristics
(C) experimenter bias
(D) the Hawthorne effect
(E) reactance

123. Which of the following tests includes items that discriminate between groups but that seem lacking in face validity?

(A) Thematic Apperception Test (TAT)
(B) Minnesota Multiphasic Personality Inventory (MMPI)
(C) California Personality Inventory (CPI)
(D) Q-sort
(E) Rotter's Incomplete Sentence Blank

124. Wearing uniforms has been found to promote

(A) depressive affect
(B) authoritarianism
(C) deindividuation
(D) objective self-awareness
(E) mental creativity

125. Word order in a sentence is determined by which of the following types of rules?

(A) Phonological
(B) Morphological
(C) Prosody
(D) Syntax
(E) Semantic

GO ON TO THE NEXT PAGE.

126. A binocular cue used in depth perception is

(A) good continuation
(B) interposition
(C) motion parallax
(D) disparity
(E) linear perspective

127. Which of the following groups of theorists offers stage models of development?

(A) Piaget, Freud, and Erikson
(B) Piaget, Freud, and Kohlberg
(C) Freud, Maslow, and Watson
(D) Freud, Erikson, and Kohlberg
(E) Freud, Adler, and Piaget

128. Which of the following areas in the brain is the "master" of the endocrine system?

(A) Thyroid
(B) Amygdala
(C) Limbic system
(D) Thalamus
(E) Pituitary gland

129. The Acme Scale of Aggression has a +0.10 correlation with four other standardized aggression scales. Also, a correlation of +1.00 exists between the scores of any student who takes the Acme Scale of Aggression twice. This indicates that the Acme Scale of Aggression has

(A) low internal validity but high external validity
(B) low concurrent validity but high reliability
(C) low face validity but high reliability
(D) moderate external validity and moderate reliability
(E) high content validity but low reliability

130. According to Ebbinghaus's forgetting curve, which pattern of forgetting is likely to take place after learning new material?

(A) Forgetting happens gradually and consistently.
(B) Forgetting happens gradually for 24 hours and then more rapidly.
(C) Forgetting happens quickly and is then offset by spontaneous recovery.
(D) Forgetting happens rapidly at first and then gradually.
(E) Forgetting happens in an all-or-none fashion.

131. Which of the following pairs of items is incorrectly associated?

(A) Dewey: functionalism
(B) Frankl: cognitive psychology
(C) Adler: individual psychology
(D) Titchener: structuralism
(E) James: stream of consciousness

GO ON TO THE NEXT PAGE.

132. Research has proven that holding and interacting with infants enhances

    (A) motor development
    (B) physical development
    (C) emotional development
    (D) intellectual development
    (E) all of the above

133. Which of the following children would probably acquire language the slowest?

    (A) A girl exposed to only one language
    (B) A boy exposed to only one language
    (C) A girl exposed to two languages
    (D) A boy exposed to two languages
    (E) Because of the LAD, all children acquire language at precisely the same rate.

134. According to Piaget's cognitive stages, an individual who has just learned that water poured from a tube into a bowl maintains the same volume must have recently entered which of the following stages?

    (A) Accommodational
    (B) Sensorimotor
    (C) Preoperational
    (D) Concrete operational
    (E) Formal operational

135. Andrea does not like to go to parties because she knows how people will conduct themselves. She has likely developed which of the following about parties?

    (A) A script
    (B) A deduction
    (C) A prototype
    (D) A heuristic
    (E) A convergence

136. Which of the following is a result of diffusion of responsibility?

    (A) Cooperation in a group task
    (B) Two-person theory of psychotherapy
    (C) Shyness of individuals in a large group
    (D) Blaming the group for individual failures
    (E) Tendency for individuals in a large group not to help others

137. In an attempt to separate the effects of heredity and learning, an experimenter takes a litter of cats and places each one with a different parent for rearing. This way, because the litter inherited very similar genes, the observed differences between the cats could more easily be attributed to experience. This experimental technique is called

    (A) hybrid design
    (B) cross fostering
    (C) surrogate parenting
    (D) intentional design
    (E) selective breeding

GO ON TO THE NEXT PAGE.

138. Martin Seligman maintains that cognitive training can offset

(A) low self-esteem
(B) cognitive bias
(C) self-handicapping
(D) internal locus of control
(E) learned helplessness

139. Which of the following sensory systems involves the ganglion cells and the ciliary muscles?

(A) Cutaneous
(B) Auditory
(C) Visual
(D) Olfactory
(E) Gustatory

140. Which of the following individuals pioneered object-relations theory?

(A) Melanie Klein
(B) Carol Gilligan
(C) Andrea Raring
(D) Mary Ainsworth
(E) Karen Horney

141. Which of the following factors has the greatest influence on interpersonal attraction?

(A) Similarity of needs
(B) Similarity of background
(C) Polarity
(D) Proximity
(E) Emotional balance

142. According to Collins and Quillian, individuals decide on the relationship between words by assessing the

(A) personal experience they have with the words
(B) acoustic similarity of the words
(C) words' respective locations in semantic hierarchies
(D) common characteristics between the words
(E) parts of speech of the words

143. The idea that over-benefited people tend to feel guilty is explained through

(A) equity theory
(B) social exchange theory
(C) gain-loss theory
(D) reciprocal interaction
(E) diffusion of responsibility

GO ON TO THE NEXT PAGE.

144. Each of the following figures performed famous experiments in the area of conformity EXCEPT

(A) Stanley Milgram
(B) Philip Zimbardo
(C) Leon Festinger
(D) Solomon Asch
(E) Muzafer Sherif

145. A double-blind experimental design is used to minimize

(A) cohort effects
(B) experimenter bias
(C) the halo effect
(D) reactance
(E) the Hawthorne effect

146. Drugs that attempt to impact behavior generally try to

(A) hinder or facilitate the transmission of "messages" at the synaptic junction
(B) speed up the action potential
(C) increase the number of neurons present in the brain
(D) stimulate the axon hillock
(E) stimulate the nodes of Ranvier

147. An individual with fluent aphasia would have difficulty

(A) understanding what is said to him
(B) uttering words
(C) creating a logical sentence
(D) spelling
(E) remembering recent events

148. Learned helplessness is associated with

(A) neuroticism
(B) introversion
(C) androgyny
(D) extreme femininity scores
(E) an external locus of control

149. Each of the following factors facilitates accurate recall of a list of words from short-term memory EXCEPT

(A) acoustic similarity among the items
(B) meaningful items
(C) concrete items
(D) lack of similarity between items
(E) subject's investment in the task

GO ON TO THE NEXT PAGE.

150. Mr. C is passed over for a promotion at work for the fifth year. Instead of showing his anger and frustration, Mr. C responds by being the first to congratulate the promoted worker. This gracious behavior would most likely be interpreted by a psychoanalyst as

(A) repression
(B) undoing
(C) reaction formation
(D) sublimation
(E) denial

151. Which of the following individuals is associated with the discovery of secure versus insecure infant attachment?

(A) Matina Horner
(B) Anna Freud
(C) Karen Horney
(D) Diana Baumrind
(E) Mary Ainsworth

152. Which of the following is a negative symptom of schizophrenia?

(A) Delusions
(B) Flat affect
(C) Hallucinations
(D) Neologisms
(E) Disorganized behavior

Questions 153–154 each refer to the following sentence.

Two bears and a donkey lived happily ever after.

153. Which of the following is true of the sentence above?

(A) "Two cats and a dog lived happily ever after" shares the same deep structure.
(B) The word "bears" is made up of two morphemes.
(C) Only the word "lived" has any semantic meaning.
(D) The sentence is structured by phonological rules.
(E) Syntax is not employed in this sentence.

154. According to Chomsky's work, this sentence has its own unique

(A) surface structure
(B) deep structure
(C) semantic differential
(D) morphemes
(E) phonemes

155. Bartlett found that memory is largely

(A) procedural
(B) episodic
(C) declarative
(D) reconstructive
(E) sensory

GO ON TO THE NEXT PAGE.

156. Which of the following figures is known for developing field theory?

(A) Festinger
(B) Asch
(C) Heider
(D) Triplett
(E) Lewin

157. Which of the following brain areas would most likely be used for complex problem-solving?

(A) Occipital lobe
(B) Frontal lobe
(C) Cerebellum
(D) Hypothalamus
(E) Hippocampus

158. Group polarization is the tendency

(A) for a group to identify a common enemy
(B) for a group to break into two opposing sides
(C) for a group to feel strongly about the dominant viewpoint
(D) for an ingroup to identify an outgroup
(E) for a group to become deadlocked during decision making

159. A researcher has performed an experiment with a random sample. He wants to test his results for statistical significance and then draw conclusions about his population. He should use which of the following type of statistics?

(A) Correlations
(B) Frequency distributions
(C) Descriptive statistics
(D) Inferential statistics
(E) Referential statistics

160. Edward Tolman's theory of motivation postulated that

(A) Performance = Expectancy × Value
(B) Motivation = Need − Fear
(C) Success = Practice × Drive
(D) Performance = Drive × Habit
(E) Performance = Ability × Practice

161. Billy is a two-year-old. He is most likely bothered by

(A) an Oedipus complex
(B) separation anxiety and stranger anxiety
(C) castration anxiety
(D) separation anxiety and trust anxiety
(E) expression anxiety and mobility anxiety

GO ON TO THE NEXT PAGE.

162. According to Matina Horner, a woman might choose not to work because of

(A) fear of success
(B) fear of failure
(C) insecurity that success is dependent on luck
(D) self-handicapping
(E) low self-esteem

163. Which of the following is true of schizophrenia?

(A) It is more common in the upper class.
(B) It has been proven to be entirely biological.
(C) An individual with a strong social history will likely not recover.
(D) There is a lower recovery rate for process than for reactive schizophrenia.
(E) There is a lower recovery rate for reactive than for process schizophrenia.

164. According to Piaget, most five-year-old children should be in which of the following cognitive stages?

(A) Accommodational
(B) Sensorimotor
(C) Preoperational
(D) Concrete operational
(E) Formal operational

165. Which of the following is referred to as white matter in the brain and spine?

(A) Nerve fibers made of axons
(B) Nerve fibers made of cell bodies
(C) Gyri
(D) Sulci
(E) Bone matter

166. A random sample of students in a lecture hall could be obtained by selecting

(A) the students who raise their hands first
(B) the students with blonde hair
(C) the students with credit card numbers ending in 5
(D) every seventh student who volunteers
(E) every fifth student seated throughout the room

167. In general, people attach concepts and attributes to items and events. This knowledge is used to categorize and understand new stimuli and is best known as a person's

(A) algorithm
(B) heuristic
(C) schema
(D) mental set
(E) metacognition

GO ON TO THE NEXT PAGE.

168. A sign stimulus serves to trigger

   (A) a homing mechanism
   (B) a variable-interval ratio
   (C) a simple reflex
   (D) a fixed action pattern
   (E) a pheromone reaction

169. Which of the following exemplifies the illusion of control?

   (A) A teacher who believes she influences her students
   (B) A woman who practices superstitious behavior
   (C) A boy who practices positive imagery to help calm his stage fright
   (D) A girl who ties a string around her finger to remember to do something
   (E) A parent who believes that punishment is a deterrent

170. Which of the following statements about sensation is false?

   (A) Meissner's corpuscles detect temperature changes.
   (B) The organ of corti is the technical name for the ear.
   (C) Papillae are taste buds.
   (D) The tympanic membrane is the eardrum.
   (E) The olfactory bulb is located at the base of the brain.

171. Which of the following most effectively lessens group conflict?

   (A) High individual scores on the F-scale
   (B) Groupthink
   (C) A charismatic leader
   (D) A superordinate goal
   (E) Similarity of individuals in the group

172. In a series of learning experiments with monkeys, Harlow asserted that monkeys gained a sort of cumulative knowledge about solving problems. He came to this conclusion because with every novel problem it took the monkeys less time to learn how to solve it. Harlow called this

   (A) higher-order conditioning
   (B) simultaneous conditioning
   (C) learning to learn
   (D) trained anticipation
   (E) instinct-learning interaction

173. A city has different-sounding sirens for police, fire, and hospital vehicles. In addition, each of these vehicles can emit varying patterns of the sirens. Regardless of the type of siren heard by a line of traffic, however, the cars all know to pull to the right and clear the way. This is an example of

   (A) stimulus-response theory
   (B) stimulus discrimination
   (C) stimulus generalization
   (D) forward conditioning
   (E) operant conditioning

GO ON TO THE NEXT PAGE.

174. Which of the following concepts is NOT central to psychoanalytic theory?

(A) Aggression
(B) Libido
(C) Free association
(D) Transference
(E) Animus

175. The vestibular sacs in the inner ear are essential for

(A) sensory transduction in audition
(B) detecting low frequencies
(C) detecting high frequencies
(D) physical balance
(E) proprioception

176. Robin made a grocery list of items in no particular order. She later lost the list and attempted to retrieve it from memory. When recalling items, she successfully remembered all of the frozen foods, and then all of the snack foods. This is an example of

(A) clustering
(B) chunking
(C) mnemonics
(D) imagery
(E) mediation

177. According to Vygotsky, what happens to the meaning that a child initially gives to a word?

(A) It creates a bias about how that child will later perceive reality.
(B) It undergoes change as the child gains experience.
(C) It consistently mirrors that of the parents.
(D) It facilitates the memorization of language.
(E) It remains stable throughout life.

178. The Bayley Scales of Infant Development do which of the following?

(A) Help to identify cognitive developmental delays in infants
(B) Measure intelligence in preschoolers
(C) Measure IQ in preschoolers
(D) Guide parents in school placement
(E) Measure cognition in infants

179. Which of the following is an obsessive-compulsive disorder that involves pulling out one's own hair?

(A) Pick's disease
(B) Dysthymia
(C) Trichotillomania
(D) Conversion disorder
(E) Follicle phobia

GO ON TO THE NEXT PAGE.

180. Maccoby and Jacklin found that one of the few true gender differences seems to be

(A) better visual ability in girls
(B) better spatial ability in boys
(C) more compassion in girls
(D) better science skills in boys
(E) better mathematical skills in boys

181. The limbic system is crucial in the regulation of

(A) the autonomic nervous system
(B) the somatic nervous system
(C) hormone activity
(D) the heart and lungs
(E) emotion

182. Rochel Gelman criticized Piaget's cognitive stages for

(A) ending at adolescence
(B) using unnatural testing instruments
(C) creating gender-biased stages
(D) underestimating preschoolers' ability
(E) overestimating adolescents' ability

183. According to feature detection theory, a subject would most quickly find the letter "C" if it were placed

(A) somewhere on a page among rows of "O's" and "Q's"
(B) somewhere on a page among rows of "T's" and "M's"
(C) near the top of a page among rows of "Q's"
(D) near the center of a page among rows of "O's"
(E) near the bottom of a page among rows of "O's"

184. Which of the following figures introduced the logic theorist, the first computer model of human problem solving?

(A) Collins and Quillian
(B) Newell and Simon
(C) Collins and Loftus
(D) Pearson
(E) Einstein

185. Which of the following tests allows unconscious motivation, particularly the need for achievement, to be expressed?

(A) Minnesota Multiphasic Personality Inventory (MMPI)
(B) Goodenough Draw-A-Person Test
(C) Thematic Apperception Test (TAT)
(D) California Personality Inventory (CPI)
(E) Q-sort

GO ON TO THE NEXT PAGE.

186. Milgram used which theory to explain urbanites' tendency to be less social than country dwellers?

    (A) Social loafing
    (B) Inoculation
    (C) Social facilitation
    (D) Stimulus-overload
    (E) Self-monitoring

187. Abraham Maslow is well known as

    (A) a forerunner of the humanistic movement in psychology
    (B) the creator of cognitive-behavioral therapy
    (C) the creator of client-centered therapy
    (D) a forerunner of object-relations theory
    (E) the creator of the archetype concept

188. Diana Baumrind found that which parenting style produces the most well-adjusted children?

    (A) Authoritative
    (B) Authoritarian
    (C) Permissive
    (D) Attached
    (E) All parenting styles were equally effective.

189. Which of the following sensory system components is said to "accommodate"?

    (A) Cornea
    (B) Lens
    (C) Retina
    (D) Tympanic membrane
    (E) Basilar membrane

190. Activity in which of the following areas is analyzed by lie detector tests?

    (A) Central nervous system
    (B) Somatic nervous system
    (C) Sympathetic nervous system
    (D) Parasympathetic nervous system
    (E) EEG patterns

191. Subjects in a psychology experiment attempt to remember the social security number of the person sitting next to them. Half of the subjects are told to put their heads down on their desks for 3 minutes. The other half are told to solve math problems for 3 minutes. If the group that solved math problems recalled the numbers as accurately as the other group did, this would support which theory of forgetting?

    (A) Interference theory
    (B) Trace theory
    (C) Proactive inhibition theory
    (D) Proactive interference theory
    (E) Association theory

192. Harlow, in experiments with social isolation in monkeys, found each of the following EXCEPT that

    (A) socially isolated adult females did not exhibit normal maternal behavior
    (B) socially isolated adult males did not exhibit normal sexual behavior
    (C) exposure to a peer group is an important factor in developing mature behavior
    (D) being reared with other young monkeys provides positive socialization
    (E) for normal development, monkeys must be exposed to their biological parents

GO ON TO THE NEXT PAGE.

193. Five hundred undergraduates were asked to report their favorite television show from a list of 100 different shows. What kind of scale can best organize the data?

(A) Ordinal
(B) Interval
(C) F-scale
(D) Ratio
(E) Nominal

194. If during a chess game a player were to write down all of the possible moves she could make, this set of moves would be an example of

(A) functional fixedness
(B) a heuristic
(C) a mental set
(D) a problem space
(E) inductive reasoning

Questions 195–196 refer to the following statements.

A speaker is attempting to convince an audience of listeners that a particular theory of evolution is correct. The audience consists of 500 adult men and women.

195. Which of the following factors would NOT increase the likelihood that the speaker will convince the audience?

(A) The speaker confidently tells the audience it will be convinced.
(B) The speaker engages in a debate with an opponent.
(C) The speaker is similar to the audience.
(D) The speaker is perceived as an expert.
(E) The speaker uses anecdotal information.

196. According to the sleeper effect, which of the following would be true?

(A) Individuals in the audience who do not pay close attention will be convinced.
(B) The message of a speaker with low credibility might be believed later.
(C) Individuals who cannot make up their minds will follow the majority opinion.
(D) Individuals who previously had no opinion on the topic will be convinced.
(E) The message will seem less convincing with the passage of time.

197. A rat is conditioned to press a lever to receive food. In the beginning, the rat is rewarded with food every time it presses the lever. Then, the experimenter stops rewarding the rat for this behavior and eventually the rat stops pressing the bar altogether. Three days later the rat tries pressing the bar again. This is an example of

(A) incidental learning
(B) latent responding
(C) positive transfer
(D) spontaneous recovery
(E) systematic desensitization

198. An individual is likely to display the most stereotypical sex-typed behavior during which of the following periods?

(A) Adolescence
(B) Young adulthood
(C) Middle adulthood
(D) Old age
(E) Middle childhood

GO ON TO THE NEXT PAGE.

199. Which of the following is associated with Jung's analytical therapy?

(A) Dream analysis
(B) Transference
(C) Focus on libido
(D) Hypnosis
(E) Defense mechanisms

200. Which of the following figures pioneered the concept of the inferiority complex?

(A) Harry Stack Sullivan
(B) Carl Rogers
(C) Abraham Maslow
(D) Alfred Adler
(E) Hans Eysenck

201. A study requires that a group of college undergraduates be present for a problem-solving workshop every other Saturday. Eventually, a number of students who want to attend fall football games drop out of the study. This is an example of

(A) cohort effects
(B) social desirability bias
(C) selective attrition
(D) nonrandom sampling
(E) reactance

202. A married couple disagrees about why the husband rarely cleans up the house. He says that he forgets. She says that he intentionally leaves the work for her. Their disagreement over the cause of his behavior is an example of

(A) false consensus bias
(B) base-rate fallacy
(C) reciprocal interaction
(D) fundamental attribution error
(E) actor-observer attributional divergence

203. After a serious head injury, Vicky could not remember the events that led up to the accident. Vicky is likely suffering from

(A) dissociation
(B) denial
(C) depression
(D) anterograde amnesia
(E) retrograde amnesia

204. In his revised psychoanalytic theory, Freud named which of the following as the central source of conflict?

(A) Libido
(B) Superego
(C) Secondary process
(D) Eros and Thanatos
(E) Pleasure principle

205. Which of the following personality characteristics has been most closely linked to heart disease?

(A) Internal locus of control
(B) Authoritarianism
(C) Chronic stress
(D) Introversion
(E) Conscientiousness

STOP

If you finish before time is called, you may check your work on this test.

Chapter 16
Practice Test 1:
Answers and
Explanations

ANSWER KEY

To help you zero in on any trouble areas you may have, we have provided the relevant content category next to each answer. Following this, we've also grouped the answers by category. For any answers you missed, be sure to go back and carefully review those sections.

1.	A	Clinical/Psychological Disorders	40.	E	Thinking
2.	B	Personality	41.	C	Learning
3.	D	Clinical/Psychological Disorders	42.	B	Sensation and Perception
4.	D	Learning	43.	E	Memory
5.	C	Developmental Psychology	44.	C	Physiological/Behavioral Neuroscience
6.	E	Clinical/Psychological Disorders	45.	B	Sensation and Perception
7.	B	Measurement and Methodology	46.	C	Sensation and Perception
8.	C	Social Psychology	47.	B	Developmental Psychology
9.	C	Physiological/Behavioral Neuroscience	48.	C	Physiological/Behavioral Neuroscience
10.	D	Language	49.	B	Physiological/Behavioral Neuroscience
11.	A	Personality	50.	D	Social Psychology
12.	E	Developmental Psychology	51.	A	Learning
13.	A	Thinking	52.	C	History
14.	C	Developmental Psychology	53.	B	Learning
15.	B	Clinical/Psychological Disorders	54.	C	Language
16.	A	Developmental Psychology	55.	A	Developmental Psychology
17.	C	Memory	56.	E	Sensation and Perception
18.	D	Physiological/Behavioral Neuroscience	57.	A	Sensation and Perception
19.	A	Clinical/Psychological Disorders	58.	D	Sensation and Perception
20.	E	Measurement and Methodology	59.	D	Physiological/Behavioral Neuroscience
21.	C	Measurement and Methodology	60.	B	Clinical/Psychological Disorders
22.	B	Personality	61.	D	Developmental Psychology
23.	E	Social Psychology	62.	C	Thinking
24.	A	Social Psychology	63.	A	Social Psychology
25.	A	Language	64.	E	Personality
26.	B	Learning	65.	C	Clinical/Psychological Disorders
27.	A	Sensation and Perception	66.	B	Physiological/Behavioral Neuroscience
28.	E	Thinking	67.	C	Developmental Psychology
29.	D	Developmental Psychology	68.	D	Physiological/Behavioral Neuroscience
30.	C	Clinical/Psychological Disorders	69.	C	Clinical/Psychological Disorders
31.	E	History	70.	B	Social Psychology
32.	A	Memory	71.	B	Social Psychology
33.	C	Social Psychology	72.	A	Personality
34.	B	Language	73.	C	Clinical/Psychological Disorders
35.	D	Physiological/Behavioral Neuroscience	74.	C	Physiological/Behavioral Neuroscience
36.	D	Measurement and Methodology	75.	D	Sensation and Perception
37.	B	Developmental Psychology	76.	E	Learning
38.	C	Personality	77.	E	Learning
39.	A	Learning	78.	A	Measurement and Methodology

79.	D	Personality
80.	E	Sensation and Perception
81.	D	Developmental Psychology
82.	C	Physiological/Behavioral Neuroscience
83.	A	Clinical/Psychological Disorders
84.	C	Measurement and Methodology
85.	E	Social Psychology
86.	B	Thinking
87.	D	Clinical/Psychological Disorders
88.	C	Personality
89.	E	Developmental Psychology
90.	C	Clinical/Psychological Disorders
91.	E	Physiological/Behavioral Neuroscience
92.	C	Learning
93.	A	Physiological/Behavioral Neuroscience
94.	C	Developmental Psychology
95.	D	Social Psychology
96.	A	Learning
97.	B	Developmental Psychology
98.	D	Thinking
99.	A	Sensation and Perception
100.	C	Memory
101.	E	Physiological/Behavioral Neuroscience
102.	A	Clinical/Psychological Disorders
103.	B	Social Psychology
104.	A	Social Psychology
105.	A	Developmental Psychology
106.	D	Personality
107.	C	Social Psychology
108.	B	Physiological/Behavioral Neuroscience
109.	D	Measurement and Methodology
110.	D	Measurement and Methodology
111.	B	Clinical/Psychological Disorders
112.	A	Clinical/Psychological Disorders
113.	C	Developmental Psychology
114.	A	Sensation and Perception
115.	B	Sensation and Perception
116.	D	History
117.	E	Language
118.	C	Developmental Psychology
119.	E	Memory
120.	A	Thinking
121.	A	Physiological/Behavioral Neuroscience
122.	A	Measurement and Methodology
123.	B	Measurement and Methodology
124.	C	Social Psychology
125.	D	Language
126.	D	Sensation and Perception
127.	A	Developmental Psychology
128.	E	Physiological/Behavioral Neuroscience
129.	B	Measurement and Methodology
130.	D	Memory
131.	B	History
132.	E	Developmental Psychology
133.	D	Language
134.	D	Developmental Psychology
135.	A	Thinking
136.	E	Social Psychology
137.	B	Physiological/Behavioral Neuroscience
138.	E	Personality
139.	C	Sensation and Perception
140.	A	Clinical/Psychological Disorders
141.	D	Social Psychology
142.	C	Thinking
143.	A	Social Psychology
144.	C	Social Psychology
145.	B	Measurement and Methodology
146.	A	Physiological/Behavioral Neuroscience
147.	C	Language
148.	E	Personality
149.	A	Memory
150.	C	Clinical/Psychological Disorders
151.	E	Developmental Psychology
152.	B	Clinical/Psychological Disorders
153.	B	Language
154.	A	Language
155.	D	Memory
156.	E	Social Psychology
157.	B	Physiological/Behavioral Neuroscience
158.	C	Social Psychology
159.	D	Measurement and Methodology
160.	A	History
161.	B	Developmental Psychology
162.	A	Personality
163.	D	Clinical/Psychological Disorders
164.	C	Developmental Psychology
165.	A	Physiological/Behavioral Neuroscience
166.	E	Measurement and Methodology

167.	C	Thinking
168.	D	Physiological/Behavioral Neuroscience
169.	B	Social Psychology
170.	A	Sensation and Perception
171.	D	Social Psychology
172.	C	Physiological/Behavioral Neuroscience
173.	C	Learning
174.	E	Clinical/Psychological Disorders
175.	D	Sensation and Perception
176.	A	Memory
177.	B	Language
178.	A	Measurement and Methodology
179.	C	Clinical/Psychological Disorders
180.	B	Personality
181.	E	Physiological/Behavioral Neuroscience
182.	D	Developmental Psychology
183.	B	Sensation and Perception
184.	B	Thinking
185.	C	Measurement and Methodology
186.	D	Social Psychology
187.	A	Clinical/Psychological Disorders
188.	A	Developmental Psychology
189.	B	Sensation and Perception
190.	C	Physiological/Behavioral Neuroscience
191.	B	Memory
192.	E	Physiological/Behavioral Neuroscience
193.	E	Measurement and Methodology
194.	D	Thinking
195.	A	Social Psychology
196.	B	Social Psychology
197.	D	Learning
198.	B	Developmental Psychology
199.	A	Clinical/Psychological Disorders
200.	D	Clinical/Psychological Disorders
201.	C	Measurement and Methodology
202.	E	Social Psychology
203.	E	Clinical/Psychological Disorders
204.	D	Clinical/Psychological Disorders
205.	C	Personality

Answer Key by Category

This breakdown groups questions by content category to help you identify your areas of strength and weakness as you study. If you find that certain categories contain higher amounts of wrong answers, focus on the corresponding chapters.

Clinical Psychology and Psychological Disorders

1. A
3. D
6. E
15. B
19. A
30. C
60. B
65. C
69. C
73. C
83. A
87. D
90. C
102. A
111. B
112. A
140. A
150. C
152. B
163. D
174. E
179. C
187. A
199. A
200. D
203. E
204. D

Personality

2. B
11. A
22. B
38. C
64. E
72. A
79. D

88. C
106. D
138. E
148. E
162. A
180. B
205. C

Learning

4. D
26. B
39. A
41. C
51. A
53. B
76. E
77. E
92. C
96. A
173. C
197. D

Developmental Psychology

5. C
12. E
14. C
16. A
29. D
37. B
47. B
55. A
61. D
67. C
81. D
89. E
94. C
97. B

105. A
113. C
118. C
127. A
132. E
134. D
151. E
161. B
164. C
182. D
188. A
198. B

Measurement and Methodology

7. B
20. E
21. C
36. D
78. A
84. C
109. D
110. D
122. A
123. B
129. B
145. B
159. D
166. E
178. A
185. C
193. E
201. C

Social Psychology

8.	C
23.	E
24.	A
33.	C
50.	D
63.	A
70.	B
71.	B
85.	E
95.	D
103.	B
104.	A
107.	C
124.	C
136.	E
141.	D
143.	A
144.	C
156.	E
158.	C
169.	B
171.	D
186.	D
195.	A
196.	B
202.	E

Psychological/Behavioral Neuroscience

9.	C
18.	D
35.	D
44.	C
48.	C
49.	B
59.	D
66.	B
68.	D
74.	C
82.	C
91.	E
93.	A

101.	E
108.	B
121.	A
128.	E
137.	B
146.	A
157.	B
165.	A
168.	D
172.	C
181.	E
190.	C
192.	E

Language

10.	D
25.	A
34.	B
54.	C
117.	E
125.	D
133.	D
147.	C
153.	B
154.	A
177.	B

Thinking

13.	A
28.	E
40.	E
62.	C
86.	B
98.	D
120.	A
135.	A
142.	C
167.	C
184.	B
194.	D

Memory

17.	C
32.	A
43.	E
100.	C
119.	E
130.	D
149.	A
155.	D
176.	A
191.	B

Sensation and Perception

27.	A
42.	B
45.	B
46.	C
56.	E
57.	A
58.	D
75.	D
80.	E
99.	A
114.	A
115.	B
126.	D
139.	C
170.	A
175.	D
183.	B
189.	B

History

31.	E
52.	C
116.	D
131.	B
160.	A

PRACTICE TEST 1 EXPLANATIONS

1. **A**   The question asks what a child with an IQ of 63 would most likely be diagnosed with. The average IQ scores range from 90–109, and the categories range on either side in 10-point increments from 40 to 160. The 80–89 range is considered to be low average IQ. The 70–79 range is considered borderline impaired or delayed, so eliminate (E). The 55–69 range is considered to be mild impairment of delay. Eliminate (B), (C), and (D). The correct answer is (A).

2. **B**   The question asks what the phenomenological view of personality asserts that type theory neglects. The phenomenological viewpoint of personality emphasizes personal experience and subjectivity as a factor of personality, whereas trait theory tries to distill personality into a few salient characteristics. Use Process of Elimination to evaluate the answer choices. Eliminate (A) and (E) since the *superego* and *id* are Freudian concepts. Keep (B) since the *self* pertains directly to the phenomenological theory of personality with regard to the human experience and self-concept. Eliminate (C) because the *supernatural* has nothing to do with either theory. Eliminate (D) because while *proprium* has to do with the self-concept, it is not associated with the phenomenological viewpoint, but rather that of Gordon Allport. The correct answer is (B).

3. **D**   The question asks which of the following is one of the personality disorders found in Cluster B. Use Process of Elimination to evaluate the answer choices. Eliminate (A) and (C) because *paranoid personality disorder* and *schizotypal personality disorder* are from Cluster A, which focuses on odd or eccentric thinking or behavior. Eliminate (B) and (E) because *dependent personality disorder* and *obsessive-compulsive personality disorder* are from Cluster C, which is characterized by anxious or fearful thinking or behavior. Keep (D) because *narcissistic personality disorder* falls under Cluster B, which is characterized by dramatic, emotional, and unpredictable thinking or behavior. The correct answer is (D).

4. **D**   The question asks for the key distinction between classical conditioning and operant conditioning. Since this question has two parts to it, evaluate the first part of the statement using Process of Elimination to save time. Eliminate (A) because operant conditioning does not attempt *to pair an unrelated stimulus and response.* Eliminate (B) because operant conditioning does not focus on *rewards,* and classical conditioning does not focus on *punishment.* Eliminate (C) for the same reason as (A). Keep (D) because *consequences of behavior* are rewards and punishment. Read further at this point for classical conditioning. It is also true that classical conditioning is *the association between stimuli.* Eliminate (E) because while operant conditioning is used in *human therapy,* classical conditioning is not *only* used with *other animals.* The correct answer is (D).

5. **C**   The question asks what a child is demonstrating in Piaget's preoperational stage who is given a toy and attempts to eat it. Use Process of Elimination to evaluate the answer choices. Eliminate (A), because *generalization* is a term connected with classical conditioning, less so with Piaget's development. Eliminate (B) because *accommodation* would be changing a thought to allow understanding of a seemingly contradictory thought. Keep (C) because by the child placing the toy in its mouth, it is gaining information to organize the new information in preexisting schema, thus *assimilating* the information. Eliminate (D) because *transition* refers to moving from one stage to the next. Finally, eliminate (E), as the child is not speaking in this scenario. *Overextension* refers to word usage errors made by children to label multiple things with the same word that adults would otherwise distinguish between. The correct answer is (C).

6. **E**   The question asks which of the following is NOT true of systematic desensitization. With NOT questions, eliminate what IS true. Eliminate (A) because it is a technique attributed to *Joseph Wolpe.* Eliminate (B) because it is *highly effective* at treating *phobias,* where it is frequently used. Eliminate (C) because systematic desensitization relies on *counterconditioning* individuals to have different reactions

rather than their previous reactions to a given stimulus. Keep (E) because systematic desensitization is not an *operant* form of conditioning with reward and punishment, but rather an associative form of learning. The correct answer is (E).

7. **B**   The question asks if the GRE Psychology Test had a standard error of zero, what would happen if a test taker took the test two times. The standard error measures how far the sample mean is likely to be from the true population mean. To find the standard error, divide the standard deviation by the number of samples. Use Process of Elimination to evaluate the answer choices. Eliminate (A) because a *z-score of 1* is one standard deviation above the mean. While this *may* be true, it is not necessarily true. Keep (B) because a test taker should receive the *same score* on the test each time. Eliminate (C) because the test does not necessarily correlate *perfectly* with aptitude. Eliminate (D) because the two scores were not necessarily *above the mean*, though they *may* have been. Eliminate (E) because it is not necessary that the test taker got *perfect scores*. The correct answer is (B).

8. **C**   The question asks what social phenomenon Deutsch's "prisoner's dilemma" studied. The prisoner's dilemma is the paradox in which two people acting in their own self-interests do not necessarily produce the optimal outcome because they often are undermining each other. Use Process of Elimination to evaluate the answer choices. Eliminate (A) because it would suggest that the individuals would conform to each other to gain the desired reaction. Eliminate (B) because attribution theory attributes behaviors to traits, and there is not as much discussion of individuals' traits in the prisoner's dilemma. Keep (C) because oftentimes the individuals compete against one another instead of cooperating with each other in the prisoner's dilemma. Eliminate (D) because stereotypes are perceived truths about others or oneself. Eliminate (E) because biases are prejudices for or against something, which are not part of the prisoner's dilemma. The correct answer is (C).

9. **C**   The question asks which egg a brooding herring gull will likely chose to incubate if she can incubate only one. Use Process of Elimination to evaluate the answer choices. Eliminate (A) because location does not matter to the signification of the sign. Eliminate (B) because an exact replica is not a super sign. Keep (C) because a supernormal sign stimulus is like an exaggerated version of a normal stimulus, and it is highly likely that the super sign stimulus may elicit an exaggerated reaction as well. For instance, a bird may feed fake birds with wider and more open mouths than real baby birds. The same could be true about whichever egg is the most exaggerated version of an object that is "egg-like." Eliminate (D) because an extremely small egg would most likely be the opposite of a super sign. Eliminate (E) because shape is likely more important to making something look "egg-like" than color. The correct answer is (C).

10. **D**   The question asks what Chomsky calls the inborn ability humans have to understand the structure of language and apply it to language learning. Chomsky is a nativist who believes in an innate ability in all healthy individuals to comprehend and structure language. Use Process of Elimination to evaluate the answer choices. Eliminate (A) because the *surface structure* refers only to the phonological form of a sentence. Eliminate (B) because, while it initially sounds tempting, it is not a real term. Eliminate (C) because *prosody* has to do with syllables and larger units of speech, such as tone, intonation, and stress. This does not address humans' innate ability to *acquire* language. Keep (D) because the *language acquisition device (LAD)* refers to the instinctive capacity for language acquisition. Eliminate (E) because it is not a real term. The correct answer is (D).

11. **A**   The question asks about two major dimensions of personality hypothesized by Hans Eysenck. Eysenck's theory of personality is on gradation of introversion to extroversion as well as from high to low neuroticism. Use Process of Elimination to evaluate the answer choices. Keep (A) since *stability and introversion* are both in line with these concepts. Eliminate (B) because *masculinity and femininity* are not part of Eysenck's theory. Eliminate (C) for this same reason, that *masculinity* is not one of

Eysenck's theory. Eliminate (D), which refers instead to the locus of control theory. Eliminate (E) because *repression* is a Freudian term. The correct answer is (A).

12. **E**   The question asks what a young adult would be most concerned with, according to Erik Erikson. Review Erikson's stages of psychosocial development. Use Process of Elimination to evaluate the answer choices. Eliminate (A) because Identity vs. Role Confusion happens during adolescence. Eliminate (B) because *sex-typed behavior* is not a part of Erikson's stages. Remember, Erikson was concerned with psycho*social* development, whereas Freud was concerned with psycho*sexual* development. Eliminate (C) because Autonomy vs. Shame occurs in early childhood. Eliminate (D) because *Achievement* is not really a term used in Erikson's stages, though it could be associated with Generativity vs. Stagnation or Integrity vs. Despair, both of which happen in adulthood or late adulthood, not in *young adults*. Keep (E) because Intimacy vs. Isolation is the stage of psychosocial development associated with young adulthood. The correct answer is (E).

13. **A**   The question asks which theory of emotion supports the situation described in the question. The question states that the victim of a car accident *has no physiological feeling in his body. He can, however think and speak. The man notices that since the injury, his emotions have been practically nonexistent.* Use Process of Elimination to evaluate the answer choices. First of all, eliminate all answer choices that are not theories of emotions: (C), (D), and (E). Keep (A) because the *James-Lange theory* asserts that physiological arousal has a direct correlation to emotion, which fits the scenario since the victim's physiological and emotional feelings are both nonexistent. Eliminate (B) because according to the *Cannon-Bard theory*, the man should be able to feel emotion regardless of physiological arousal. The correct answer is (A).

14. **C**   The question asks what scientists have concluded when examining the nature-nurture issue. The answer to this question is not an easy one, and is a conglomeration of biological and social factors. Use Process of Elimination to evaluate the answer choices. Eliminate (A), which concludes that behavior is only *the product of nature*. Eliminate (B) because behavior is not only *the product of nurture*. Keep (C), since *the interaction of nature and nurture* matches the idea of a conglomeration of biological and social factors. Eliminate (D) because there is no way to know that behavior is *half nature and half nurture*. Eliminate (E), which is introducing cognition *(the mind)*, deviating from the nature-nurture issue. The correct answer is (C).

15. **B**   The question asks which disorder Hazel would most likely be diagnosed with, given the description in the question. The question states that she has *experienced feelings of worthlessness, low energy, and a loss of interest in life for most of the days of the past three years.* Use Process of Elimination to evaluate the answer choices. Eliminate (A) because while it may seem that Hazel has an *external locus of control* by feeling *worthless*, this is not actually a diagnosable disorder, but rather a concept of social psychology. Keep (B), since *persistent depressive disorder* is characterized by at least two years of the symptoms Hazel has experienced, and she has experienced them for three years. Eliminate (C) because *melancholia* is a specifier for major depressive disorder, not a diagnosis in and of itself. Eliminate (D) because *existential neurosis* is primarily an anxiety-related disorder, and there is no evidence of such anxiety in Hazel's description. Eliminate (E) because *bipolar disorder* is characterized by alternating periods of mania and depression, and there is no evidence of mania in Hazel's description. The correct answer is (B).

16. **A**   The question asks what the Strange Situation is used to study. This study was done by Mary Ainsworth with toddlers and their attachment to parental figures. Use Process of Elimination to evaluate the answer choices. Keep (A) since *infant attachment* matches the study. Eliminate (B), since the *Hawthorne effect* is the altered behavior of subjects who know they are being observed, and that is not the point of the Strange Situation study. Eliminate (C) because *groupthink* has to do with extreme and irrational group decision-making. Eliminate (E) because the *Barnum effect* is the tendency to accept information as true, even if it is vague, such as horoscopes or character assessments. The correct answer is (A).

17. **C** The question asks which of the following activities best serves to hold information in short-term memory. Use Process of Elimination to evaluate the answer choices. While all of these terms are related to attenuation and working memory, only *rehearsing* actively keeps information in short-term memory. The correct answer is (C).

18. **D** The question asks which of the following is characteristic of stage N1 sleep. Stage N1 sleep is characterized by fleeting thoughts, slowed EEG, moderate body movement, and light sleep. Use Process of Elimination to evaluate the answer choices. Eliminate (A) and (B) because *dreams* occur during the *REM* phases of sleep, and therefore not in stage N1. Eliminate (C) because *EEG patterns* begin to slow in stage N1, but they are not desynchronized. Keep (D) because *major muscle twitches* may occur at stage N1. Eliminate (E) because *difficulty being roused* is mostly associated with stage N3 of sleep. The correct answer is (D).

19. **A** The question asks which of the following is NOT one of the DSM-5 categories of psychological disorders. With NOT questions, eliminate what IS true. Keep (A) because *depersonalization disorder* is a specific diagnosis under dissociative disorders. Eliminate (B), (C), (D), and (E) because *neurodevelopmental disorders, depressive disorders, feeding and eating disorders,* and *anxiety disorders* are all categories of disorders in the DSM-5. The correct answer is (A).

20. **E** The question asks which of the following statistical tests the researcher should use to analyze her data based on the information in the paragraph. The paragraph states that the researcher plans to *compare the GRE scores of students who did and did not take a preparation course.* It continues to state that *she also plans to compare the GRE scores of students who took preparation courses through Company X, Company Y, and Company Z.* It would be best to see the results through a way that allows multiple factors to be expressed. Use Process of Elimination to evaluate the answer choices. Eliminate (A) because an *r*-correlation would be helpful between only two variables, and there are multiple layers in this study. Eliminate (B) because a *T-test* also is a statistical piece of inference that works between two groups, and there are more than two groups here. Eliminate (C) because Pearson's *chi-square test* shows the difference between expected and observed frequencies of various categories. Since the question does not show expected results, this test is not helpful. Eliminate (D) because a *2 × 2 × 2 factor analysis* would mean there are three independent variables, whereas here there are two. Keep (E) because the *2 × 3 factor analysis* would help to show the two different scenarios against each other described in this question. The correct answer is (E).

21. **C** The question asks what the results of the question are an example of. The question states that *students who took a preparation course with Companies X and Y scored higher…than students who did not prepare.* The question continues that *students who took a preparation course with Company Z score no higher on average than students who did not take a preparation course.* Use Process of Elimination to evaluate the answer choices. Eliminate (A) because *a negative correlation* means that as one variable increases, the other decreases, which is not the case here. Eliminate (B) because *a zero correlation* indicates there is not a relationship between variables, though the question suggests otherwise. Keep (C) because *an interaction effect* is the interaction of two or more independent variables and at least one dependent variable. Eliminate (D) because *a main effect* is the effect of an independent variable averaged across other independent variables against a dependent variable. Eliminate (E) because *a flat effect* is not a real term. A flat *affect* is a negative symptom of schizophrenia. The correct answer is (C).

22. **B** The question asks which researcher androgyny is most associated with. Sandra Bem is most associated with research into androgyny. The correct answer is (B).

23. **E** The question asks which of the following arguments social comparison theory has been used against. Social comparison theory has to do with individuals measuring their ability and self-worth through

comparing themselves to others they view as peers. Use Process of Elimination to evaluate the answer choices. Eliminate (A) because *deindividuation* is the concept of individuals becoming less socially inhibited in large, emotionally charged group settings. Eliminate (B) because *group polarization* has nothing to do with comparing oneself to others, but rather becoming more extreme in a viewpoint when surrounded by like-minded group members. Eliminate (C) because *single-sex schools* actually eliminate part of a population against which to compare oneself. Eliminate (D) because *segregation* also eliminates part of a population against which to compare oneself. Only *mainstreaming* in schools adds more people with which individuals may compare themselves against, and those with intellectual or physical disabilities might see themselves as less able or inferior to those without a disability. The correct answer is (E).

24. **A** The question asks which of the following phenomena is minimized by group monitoring. Group monitoring has to do with checking in with accountability. Use Process of Elimination to evaluate the answer choices. Keep (A) since *social loafing* is a phenomenon that occurs when individuals feel less personally accountable and therefore do less work in a group setting. Eliminate (B) because while *social comparison* happens in a group setting, it has nothing to do with accountability. Eliminate (C) because biases of any kind do not have to do with accountability. Eliminate (D) because *groupthink* has to do with decision making of the whole group, not members within the group. Eliminate (E) because *group polarization* also does not have to do with accountability of individuals within the group. The correct answer is (A).

25. **A** The question asks what a two-year old saying "ball" is an example of when handed a ball. Use Process of Elimination to evaluate the answer choices. Keep (A) because *holophrastic speech* is a term that describes a child's single word taking the place of an adult's entire sentence, which the child is doing here. Eliminate (B) because *telegraphic speech* is in the two-word stage of language acquisition, such as "me ball," but the example here consists of only one word. Eliminate (C) because *overregulated speech* is the concept of transferring grammatical rules to where they do not apply, such as adding the suffix "-es" to mouse to create *mouses* instead of *mice*. Eliminate (D) because *overextended speech* occurs when a child uses a term to apply to more categories than it does. For instance, a child might say "dog" when it sees a dog, a bear, or a wolf because the child does not yet distinguish between different animals that are furry and have four legs. Eliminate (E) because *neologistic speech* contains made-up words, coined terms or new uses of preexisting words, which is not applicable in this example. The correct answer is (A).

26. **B** The question asks what the likely cause of the child's lessened reaction to sirens. The question states that the child moved *into a home very near to a hospital*, and the sirens initially *frightened and upset [him] each time*. However, *with time, the child seemed less bothered* until the child *seemed not to notice the sirens at all*. Over time, the reaction lessened to the stimulus because the child grew accustomed to the sirens. Use Process of Elimination to evaluate the answer choices. Eliminate (A) because *chaining* is a sequence of behaviors that results in a terminal behavior. There are no such behaviors except for the child's reaction to the sirens. Keep (B) because *habituation* fits with the child becoming accustomed to the sirens and therefore a diminished reaction to the stimulus. While (C) may be tempting, *extinction* involves the absence of a stimulus leading to a diminished reaction or behavior; eliminate (C). Eliminate (D) because *sensitization* would mean the child would become more reactive to the sirens, not less. Eliminate (E), since *shaping* is a form of operant conditioning that teaches behavior in progressive stages. The correct answer is (B).

27. **A** The question asks which of the following methods is most commonly used to study selective attention. Use Process of Elimination to evaluate the answer choices. Keep (A) because *shadowing* is a cognitive test in which the participant reads aloud the message being presented, often while other distractors are

in the background. This would keep the individual concentrating on the central messages as opposed to the distractions, which would demonstrate selective attention. Eliminate (B) and (C) because *subliminal messages* are meant to infiltrate the subconscious, whereas selective attention involves the conscious mind. Eliminate (D) because the *just noticeable difference* would be testing Weber's law, not selective attention. Eliminate (E) because *questionnaires* testing short-term memory may require selective attention, but they do not necessarily do. The correct answer is (A).

28. **E**   The question asks how bottom-up processing is best described. Bottom-up processing takes small pieces of information to construct a more global understanding of the concept. Use Process of Elimination to evaluate the answer choices. Eliminate (A) because *semantics* is meaning-based, and this would be more of a top-down way of processing information. Eliminate (B) because *phonetics* refers to the way language sounds, not what it means. Eliminate (C) because *schematically* refers to an individual's *schema,* which would also be a top-down process. Eliminate (D) because *morphologically* refers to words, not necessarily the meaning of the words. Keep (E) because data is then conglomerated to create understanding. The correct answer is (E).

29. **D**   The question asks what Kohlberg used to devise his theory of moral development. Kohlberg told children moral dilemma stories and asked them questions to reason through it. Use Process of Elimination to evaluate the answer choices. Eliminate (A) because these children were questioned about hypotheticals, not asked to *act* on any moral dilemmas. Eliminate (B) because Kohlberg's work was not only *naturalistic observations* because he also questioned the children. Eliminate (C) because Kohlberg's research had nothing to do with *mythology.* Keep (D) because *verbal responses to hypothetical moral dilemmas* accurately describes his research. Eliminate (E) because *personality* has nothing to do with Kohlberg's conclusions. The correct answer is (D).

30. **C**   The question asks which condition would most likely be improved through long-term use of a dopamine-blocking neuroleptic. Think about what this treatment would do: keep dopamine levels lower. Use Process of Elimination to evaluate the answer choices. Eliminate (A) because *tardive dyskinesia* is a syndrome that causes involuntary movement due to blocked dopamine receptors, so blocking dopamine would not be a helpful treatment. Eliminate (B) and (D) because *Parkinson's disease* is correlated with depleted dopamine levels, so further lowering dopamine levels would not be helpful. Keep (C) because *schizophrenia* is thought to be correlated with overactive dopamine levels. The correct answer is (C).

31. **E**   The question asks which of the following figures is credited with founding the first laboratory dedicated to psychology. The first person to do this was Wilhelm Wundt. The correct answer is (E).

32. **A**   The question asks which of the following statements is true of maintenance rehearsal. Maintenance rehearsal is a process of repeating information to keep it in short-term memory. Use Process of Elimination to evaluate the answer choices. Keep (A) since this matches the definition of maintenance rehearsal. Eliminate (B) because maintenance rehearsal does not have to do with *long-term* memory. Eliminate (C) because maintenance rehearsal is not about *transferal* to long-term memory. Eliminate (D) because maintenance rehearsal is not *secondary rehearsal.* Eliminate (E) because *elaboration* refers to making information meaningful, thus transferring it to long-term memory. The correct answer is (A).

33. **C**   The question asks how to explain people's tendency to go along with victim blaming based on details in the description. The question states that *defense lawyers use the strategy of blaming the victim, so that the accused perpetrator might be set free.* Use Process of Elimination to evaluate the answer choices. Eliminate (A) because *oversimplification* does not necessarily mean guilt for the victim. Eliminate (B) because a *heuristic* is a rule-of-thumb in someone's mind, and there is nothing in the description to suggest that the lawyers are drawing upon people's recent experiences and prior knowledge. Keep (C) because the *just world bias* relies upon people getting "what they deserved," which is consistent with

blaming the victim for what happened to them. Eliminate (D) because the *illusion of control* refers to humans believing that they are in control of a situation when they, in fact, may not be. This has nothing to do with the victim in this case. Eliminate (E) because the *illusory correlation* has to do with people correlating variables that may not be related. This does not have anything to do with lawyers *blaming the victim* since there is nothing to correlate with. The correct answer is (C).

34. **B**   The question asks which of the following is NOT a morpheme. Morphemes are the smallest units of meaningful language. With NOT questions, eliminate what IS true. Eliminate (A) because *"-ed"* is meaningful in that it indicates past tense. Keep (B) because the vowel combination *"ee"* does not impart *meaning*. Eliminate (C) because *"cat"* is an entire word that has a meaning. Eliminate (D) because the suffix *"s"* indicates plurality. Eliminate (E) because the prefix *"anti-"* means against something. The correct answer is (B).

35. **D**   The question asks what is true of the neuron described in the question stem. The question states that the neuron is *in the brain* and that it has *recently fired*. It *completes its absolute refractory period and then is in a relative refractory period*. This means that it needs to be stimulated by something stronger to achieve the same action potential, and that is what happens next, and the neuron *fires again*. Use Process of Elimination to evaluate the answer choices. Eliminate (A) because *hyperpolarization* occurs after the neuron fires, but it does not refer to the repeated firing. Eliminate (B) because the *refractory period* covers the action potential being reached. Now look at the remaining answers and notice the difference of only one word: *greater, same,* and *lesser*. The second action potential should be of the *same* intensity as the first. The correct answer is (D).

36. **D**   The question asks what the researcher must include in the criterion-keying or empirical-keying approach to test construction. A criterion- or empirical-keying approach to a test seeks to show differences in responses from groups already known to differ. Use Process of Elimination to evaluate the answer choices. Eliminate (A) because *projective answers* would not be empirical enough to show differences between groups. Eliminate (B) because *percentile ranks* are not necessarily the information needed for these types of tests because this could show differences within the *same* group instead of different groups. Eliminate (C) because *a range of scores* could be also used within the same group. Keep (D) because *discriminating between groups* is the key piece of information that would require the empirical-keying approach toward a test. Eliminate (E) because *speed* is irrelevant if it is not distinguishing between groups. The correct answer is (D).

37. **B**   The question asks which of the following stages might demonstrate circular reactions, according to Piaget. According to Piaget, circular reactions are repeated pleasurable actions that babies and infants do, such as sucking one's thumb and then repeating the action at a later time. Babies and infants fall into the sensorimotor stage of development. The correct answer is (B).

38. **C**   The question asks which concept the theory that a child steals candy because he is a thief is an example of. Use Process of Elimination to evaluate the answer choices. Eliminate (A) because an *availability heuristic* is a rule-of-thumb concept based on easily accessible pieces of related material in an individual's working memory. Since it is unlikely that there are many preexisting pieces of information that children are thieves in an individual's mind, this concept does not apply. Eliminate (B) because *cognitive bias* is the systemic pattern of behavior or thought that individuals create for themselves that deviate from the norm. Keep (C) because *dispositional attribution* generalizes a person's behavior to their personality, or disposition, rather than the situation they are in. This could fit, since the child might steal candy, but might not steal something more significant or sinister. Eliminate (D) because a *response set* is a person's tendency to answer in a way that is most flattering to themselves, which does not apply here. Eliminate (E) because *situational attribution* refers to a person behaving a certain way because of the specific situation he or she is in, and there is no information as to the child's situation here. The correct answer is (C).

39. **A**   The question asks for an example of conditioned aversion. *Conditioned aversion* is an aversion to a taste associated with toxic or spoiled substances. This usually happens through consuming food or drink that results in vomiting or sickness. Use Process of Elimination to evaluate the answer choices. Keep (A) because *too much* alcohol *made you sick* before, causing you to not want to drink alcohol. Eliminate (B) because there is not *aversion* described in wanting to *eat a lot of asparagus*. Eliminate (C) because while *not wanting to eat a cheeseburger* is aversive, it is because of knowledge instead of aversion. Eliminate (D) because this is something *you heard,* not something you experienced and developed an *aversion* for. Eliminate (E) because there is no *aversion* described. The correct answer is (A).

40. **E**   The question asks about the type of thinking the manager asks of her employees. She asks them to *think "outside the box" in order to come up with entirely new angles for advertising.* Use Process of Elimination to evaluate the answer choices. Eliminate (A) because thinking *metacognitively* is to think about thought processes. Eliminate (B) because to think *convergently* is to bring their ideas together to agreement, which is not what she asks of them. Eliminate (C) because using *fluid* intelligence is to use logic and other abilities to problem solve, which is not necessarily thinking "outside the box." Eliminate (D) because thinking *deductively* is to use logical reasoning to eliminate possibilities. Keep (E) because thinking *divergently* is to think in a diverse way, or "outside the box." The correct answer is (E).

41. **C**   The question asks what the experimenter will need to get the pigeon to peck a key in order to obtain food through shaping. Use Process of Elimination to evaluate the answer choices. Eliminate (A) because the food is already a primary reinforcer, so a *secondary reinforcer* is unnecessary. Eliminate (B) because *autonomic conditioning* is a form of classical conditioning, not operant conditioning. Keep (C) because *differential reinforcement* is key to the process of *shaping*, that is changing the behavior until the final desired behavior is achieved. Eliminate (D) because *autoshaping* requires not reinforcing by reward or punishment, and the pigeon clearly would be rewarded by food in this example. Eliminate (E) because *trace conditioning* is a type of classical conditioning, not operant conditioning. The correct answer is (C).

42. **B**   The question asks which theory explains the fact that humans see better at night by looking at objects from the side than by looking straight at objects. This happens because rods are most densely present at the retina, while cones are less dense through the retina. Use Process of Elimination to evaluate the answer choices. Eliminate (A) because the *opponent-process theory* has to do with opposite colors, and rods are meant for grayscale. Keep (B) because this matches the information necessary to understand this phenomenon. Eliminate (C) because color is not applicable to this scenario. Eliminate (D) because the *lateral geniculate* nucleus is a relay center of visual information in the thalamus, but not what is allowing humans to absorb the visual stimulus to begin with. Eliminate (E) because *the crossing of the optic nerves in the neural pathway* relays information, but is not the receptor itself. The correct answer is (B).

43. **E**   The question asks which of the following levels of processing would result in the highest recall of information according to Craik and Lockhart. Craik and Lockhart posited shallow processing as structural processing (what something looks like), to phonetic processing, to semantic processing, the deepest level. The correct answer is (E).

44. **C**   The question asks, compared to control rats, what rats with a lesion on the amygdala would do. The amygdala is responsible primarily for fear and anxiety responses, along with other emotional responses with the limbic system. Use Process of Elimination to evaluate the answer choices. Eliminate (A) because they would not act the same way as *control* rats. Eliminate (B) because fear and anxiety are not factors in *finding food hidden in a maze*. Keep (C) because *exhibiting less fear* directly relates to an altered fear or anxiety response. Eliminate (D) because *eating more* would have to do with homeostasis, which the hypothalamus is responsible for instead. Eliminate (D) because the amygdala is not responsible for *distinguishing different odors*. The correct answer is (C).

45. **B** The question asks which of the following describes the subjects' overall performance in the experiment described in the paragraph. In the experiment, subjects were presented with first a light stimulus, and then possibly a *low-intensity tone in the earphones* afterwards. They were instructed to *push a button if they hear a tone* and were rewarded *$10 for each hit*. The results were that in 500 trials, *200 times a tone was presented and 300 times a tone was not presented*. The question also states that *190 tones were detected, and the button was pressed 270 times in response to no tone*. This means that 190 of the 200 present tones were hits with 10 misses, and 270 of the 300 times were false alarms with 30 correct rejections. Use Process of Elimination to evaluate the answer choices. Eliminate (A) because there were 30 correct rejections, not *30 false alarms*. Keep (B) because it is consistent with *10 misses and 30 correct rejections*. Eliminate (C) because there were 190 hits, not *460 hits*. Eliminate (D) because while there were 190 hits, there were 270 false alarms, not 270 misses. Remember that a miss is not recognizing something that is there, whereas a false alarm is identifying a stimulus that is in fact not present. Eliminate (E) because it is not possible to add 270 false alarms and 10 misses to call them all misses. The correct answer is (B).

46. **C** The question asks which of the following statements is in line with signal detection theory about the experiment described in the paragraph. Signal detection theory deals with the absolute threshold of detecting a stimulus as well as the just noticeable difference which detects differences between like stimuli. Here the *low-intensity tone* would likely be testing the absolute threshold. Use Process of Elimination to evaluate the answer choices. Eliminate (A) because clearly the *response accuracy* was not very good, given the high number of false alarms. To the contrary, the reward probably even increased the rate of false alarms. Eliminate (B) because the test is not asking subjects to distinguish between *a few tones*, rather to identify if a tone is present or not. Keep (C) because the reward would increase the number of times a subject is inclined to push the button, accounting for the high number of hits and false alarms. Eliminate (D) because there is nothing to suggest that the subjects were *distracted*. Eliminate (E) because the test is not testing for classical conditioning, rather for signal detection. The correct answer is (C).

47. **B** The question asks which an individual in a stage of conventional morality would be most concerned with, according to Kohlberg. Remember that Kohlberg divides moral development into preconventional, conventional, and postconventional. The conventional stage has to do with following rules to maintain social order or to gain approval from others. Use Process of Elimination to evaluate the answer choices. Eliminate (A) because *gaining rewards* is a preconventional concept. Keep (B), because *gaining approval* is stage 3, the first part of conventional moral development. Eliminate (C) because this is also part of the preconventional stage. Eliminate (D) because *achieving fairness* is a postconventional morality. Finally, eliminate (E) because while *adhering to the conservative point of view* may be considered conventional for gaining the approval of others, it is unclear why the individual is doing so. They may genuinely believe in that point of view, which might make it postconventional. The correct answer is (B).

48. **C** The question asks which of the following areas of the brain has been shown to be closely connected with hunger, eating, and satiation. Use Process of Elimination to evaluate the answer choices. Eliminate (A) because the *medulla oblongata* is responsible for transmitting signals from the spine to the brain such as heartbeat and respiration. Eliminate (B) because the *hippocampus* has to do with learning and memory. Keep (C) because the *hypothalamus* is responsible for homeostasis, so hunger, eating, and satiation would be controlled here. Eliminate (D) because the *thalamus* is a relay center. Eliminate (E) because the *corpus callosum* is a dense band of nerves that connects the two hemispheres of the brain. The correct answer is (C).

49. **B**   The question asks what oxytocin does in the body. Oxytocin is released by the pituitary gland and is responsible for emotions of love and human bonding. The correct answer is (B).

50. **D**   The question asks why Kenneth and Mamie Clark's doll preference studies were used. These studies helped to show the effects of segregation on African American children by showing four dolls that were identical except for skin tone. When asked, children of all races tended to prefer the white dolls over the darker-skinned dolls and more readily attributed positive qualities to the white dolls. This proved to be critical evidence in *Brown v. Board of Education*, citing that segregation made African American children feel inferior to white children and that they had lower self-esteem as a result. Use Process of Elimination to evaluate the answer choices. Eliminate (A) because the study did not elicit accounts of *childhood sexual abuse*. Eliminate (B) because the study did not test *adults* nor did it test *regression*. Eliminate (C) because the study did not bring *gender favoritism* into play. All the dolls were identical save for race. Keep (D) as it is correct. Eliminate (E) because the *Kitty Genovese* case is often used to explain the bystander effect. The correct answer is (D).

51. **A**   The question asks what the situation demonstrates given the details in the question stem. The question states that *a student decides that after learning a chapter of material he will treat himself to a movie,* and the movie is *reinforcement.* The statement implies that every time he completes a chapter, he will then treat himself to a movie. Use Process of Elimination to evaluate the answer choices. Keep (A) because the *Premack principle* is the idea that more probable behaviors, such as going to a movie, will reinforce less probable behaviors, such as studying when the student may not want to. Eliminate (B) because there is nothing in the question to indicate a time interval needed for a *fixed-interval ratio schedule.* Eliminate (C) because *autoshaping* as a method of conditioning does not have a reinforcement or punishment, and the movie is explicitly called a reinforcement in the question stem. Eliminate (D) because the *Garcia effect* is an aversion for a taste or smell due to previous conditioning. Eliminate (E) because *higher-order conditioning* has to do with classical conditioning, not operant conditioning. The correct answer is (A).

52. **C**   The question asks who was most commonly associated with the view that the mind is a "tabula rasa" at birth and written on by experience. The person who first posited this idea was John Locke. The correct answer is (C).

53. **B**   The question asks why the dog never learns to bark at the red light based on other details in the question stem. The question states that the dog *naturally barks at a mouse when it is presented,* meaning that the response to the mouse is the UCR. The experimenter *presents the mouse and then the red light.* Use Process of Elimination to evaluate the answer choices. It should not matter if the UCS and the CS are not *similar,* so eliminate (A). Keep (B) because the mouse should be presented first or the two presented simultaneously. Eliminate (C) because, again, similarity should not play a factor. Eliminate (D) because the question does not mention the CS as faint or unnoticeable. Eliminate (E) because this is the opposite that happens, that the CS (the red light) comes after the UCS (the mouse). The correct answer is (B).

54. **C**   The question asks how children refine the way they apply grammatical rules, according to Roger Brown and other psycholinguistic researchers. Brown's theory is that children learn in stages of complexity and self-correct along the way. Use Process of Elimination to evaluate the answer choices. Eliminate (A) and (B) because *positive reinforcement* and *positive conditioning* are forms of operant conditioning, which would imply that children apply grammatical rules only through reward and punishment. Keep (C) because *experience* and *self-correction* are consistent with the theory of the children gaining experience and accuracy over time as they practice. Eliminate (D) because *memorization of what others say* would only allow children to parrot back preexisting sentences rather than form

original thoughts. Eliminate (E) because while *structured learning* can help the process, trial and error in real life conversation is what Brown posited. The correct answer is (C).

55. **A** The question asks what a child is likely to experience if particularly frustrated during a stage of development, according to Freud. Remember that Freud created the stages of psychosexual development. Use Process of Elimination to evaluate the answer choices. Keep (A) because frustration along the way of development would certainly lead to a *fixation* at that stage. Eliminate (B) because *identification* is more of an idea related to Erikson's Identity vs. Role Confusion. Eliminate (C) because *castration anxiety* is an anxiety that is experienced during the Phallic stage if the Oedipus complex is not properly resolved, though the question is asking for a broader sense of frustration during any stage of development. Eliminate (D) and (E) because the *superego* and *ego* are not really integral parts of the psychosexual *developmental* stages, but rather comprise an overarching idea of the psyche. The correct answer is (A).

56. **E** The question asks which effect explains why cartoons are not perceived as a series of still frames. Use Process of Elimination to evaluate the answer choices. Eliminate (A) because the *autokinetic effect* occurs when a single, stationary light appears to move in an otherwise dark or blank surface. Eliminate (B) because *motion parallax* is a monocular cue that allows an individual to perceive change in position. Eliminate (C) because the *Ponzo illusion* is one that shows that humans perceive size based on depth and an object's background. Eliminate (D) because the *Müller-Lyer illusion* suggests that humans often misjudge the midpoint of arrows depending on the direction of their pointing. Keep (E) because the *Phi phenomenon* refers to a situation in which stationary objects appear to be moving when they are placed side by side, such as with blinking lights or still shots of a cartoon. The correct answer is (E).

57. **A** The question asks what Mary would likely be diagnosed with given the details in the question stem. The question states that *Mary frequently has people come up and say hi to her on the street but she does not know who they are even though she has met them many times in the past.* Use Process of Elimination to evaluate the answer choices. Keep (A) because *prosopagnosia* is a syndrome that keeps individuals from recognizing faces. Eliminate (B) because there is no evidence of a *phobia* in the text. Eliminate (C) because *Tourette disorder* is a neurodevelopmental disorder and involves involuntary tics and vocalizations. Eliminate (D) because *Korsakoff's syndrome* is a chronic memory disorder caused by alcohol abuse or deficiency in vitamin B. There is no evidence for this in the question stem, and this would encompass memory troubles beyond facial recognition. Eliminate (E) because *asomatognosia* is the loss of recognition or awareness of part of one's body. The correct answer is (A).

58. **D** The question asks under what circumstances is visual acuity the highest. Vision is strongest in lit conditions, meaning that cones would be stimulated to perceive color. Use Process of Elimination to evaluate the answer choices. Eliminate (B), (C), and (E), which all talk about rods. Now, use opposites in the answer choices. Eliminate (A) because rods, not cones, are denser along the periphery of the retina. Keep (D) because cones on the fovea would be readily reactive. The correct answer is (D).

59. **D** The question asks where the infant monkeys would run when frightened by a fear-inducing stimulus. The monkeys preferred the "cloth" mothers that were snuggly and soft during the experiment and only went to the other "wire" surrogate mother which had a bottle when they were hungry and needed food. Use Process of Elimination to evaluate the answer choices. Eliminate (A) because there were no *adult* monkeys in the experiment. Eliminate (B) because the infant monkeys wanted the cloth mothers for comfort. Eliminate (C) because the *surrogate with the bottle* was preferable only when they were hungry. Keep (D) because the terrycloth surrogate would be much more comforting to them. Eliminate (E) because even though the cloth mother was not a real monkey, the infants still gravitated toward it for comfort in the experiment. The correct answer is (D).

60. **B**   The question asks for the goal of therapy in which the therapist listens to the choices of his client with unconditional positive regard. This contains key words that point to Carl Rogers and the humanistic perspective. Use Process of Elimination to evaluate the answer choices. Eliminate (A) because the therapist is not going to try to assign *meaning* to everything, rather to help the client toward self-actualization. Keep (B) because this matches the ideals of the humanistic approach. Eliminate (C) because this more likely describes *mindfulness* than self-actualization. Eliminate (D) because *inferiority* and *superiority* are words connoting judgement, and the humanistic approach actively avoids judging a client's thoughts or behavior. Eliminate (E) because while this is partially true, it is not the primary goal, rather that the client discovers a fuller sense of self, and their *beliefs* are only one component of this process. The correct answer is (B).

61. **D**   The question asks on which concept Erikson's developmental theory centers. Remember that Erikson posited the stages of psychosocial development. The correct answer is (D).

62. **C**   The question asks for the most common way of studying human cognitive processing. Use Process of Elimination to evaluate the answer choices. Eliminate (A) because *semantic shifts* are a slow process that take place over time in a culture with regard to word usage and language. Eliminate (B) because *EEG readings* will give information over a continuum including the times before and after a process, so it will not be the easiest to decipher when processing began or ended. Keep (C) because *reaction times* are standard ways of showing cognitive processing, i.e., braking in a car. Eliminate (D) because *rehearsal time* is a longer form of processing, engaging the working memory and potentially the long-term memory. Eliminate (E) because *creativity* is very difficult to quantify and study in an evaluative manner. The correct answer is (C).

63. **A**   The question asks which concept best explains the teacher's assumptions. The question states that *Because Shay is a good student, her teacher assumes she is also artistic, well-behaved, and from a good family.* The teacher is assuming other positive attributes to Shay because of one positive. Use Process of Elimination to evaluate the answer choices. Keep (A) because the *halo effect* describes these assumptions. Eliminate (B) because *oversimplification* ignores the details and complexities of an issue. Eliminate (C) because *good continuation* is a Gestalt principle of visual perception, not of character perception. Eliminate (D) because a *self-fulfilling prophecy* is one that a person fulfills reflexively based on beliefs they have about themselves. Eliminate (E) because the *self-serving bias* is putting oneself first, not making assumptions about another person. The correct answer is (A).

64. **E**   The question asks what trait theory has been most criticized for. Trait theory distills personality types into overarching, salient characteristics that are always present. Use Process of Elimination to evaluate the answer choices. Eliminate (A) because while *having contradictory dimensions* can be problematic, the traits are not that contradictory in the different types of personality. Eliminate (B) because while it is impossible to fully quantify personality, this could be said for any of the theories of personality. Eliminate (C) because trait theory does have *agreed-upon dimensions of personality*. Eliminate (D) because *heredity* is not addressed in many theories of personality, not just trait theory. Keep (E) because *various situations* can certainly cause people to behave differently than they normally would. For instance, someone who is normally less anxious could behave in an anxious manner when placed in an anxiety-inducing situation. The correct answer is (E).

65. **C**   The question asks which of the following types of thinking is NOT a maladaptive cognition according to cognitive therapy. With NOT questions, eliminate what IS true. Eliminate (A) because *dichotomous thinking* is a maladaptive cognition in which individuals think in terms of polar opposites instead of along a continuum. Eliminate (B) because *personalizing* can make the individual believe that others' statements are directly about them when in fact they are not. Keep (C) because while *denying*

something is a maladaptive behavior, it is not a *cognition*. Eliminate (D) because *overgeneralizing* causes individuals to attribute thoughts from one experience to a wide variety of different experiences when they likely do not apply to all those experiences. Eliminate (E) because *magnifying* can make a thought or experience grow greatly out of proportion and perspective. The correct answer is (C).

66. **B**   The question asks what happened to John when he saw the bear, based on details in the question stem. The question states that first *John…saw a bear in the distance*. Then, *As the bear started coming toward him, John got scared*. Lastly, he *started to run in the opposite direction*. Use Process of Elimination to evaluate the answer choices. Eliminate (A) because the *parasympathetic nervous system* is responsible for rest and digestion. Keep (B) because the *sympathetic nervous system* is the neurological component of the "fight or flight" response. Eliminate (C) because *GABA* is responsible for motor control and vision among other things, not stress responses, though it does regulate anxiety. Eliminate (D) and (E) because they are the opposite of what would likely happen. The "fight or flight" response would likely release increased dopamine, epinephrine, and norepinephrine. Eventually, the increased stress would increase cortisone levels. The correct answer is (B).

67. **C**   The question asks which of the following reflexes might be elicited by stroking the bottom of a baby's foot. Use Process of Elimination to evaluate the answer choices. Eliminate (A) because this is not a real term, even though it might sound tempting with the root "ped." Eliminate (B) because the *Moro reflex* is the "startle" reflex in which a baby throws back its head when startled. Keep (C), as the reflex elicited when stroking the bottom of a baby's foot is the *Babinski reflex*. Eliminate (D) because the *Palmar reflex* is the "grasping" reflex. Eliminate (E) because the *Klinefelter reflex* is not real, but rather Klinefelter syndrome is diagnosed through checking reflexes. The correct answer is (C).

68. **D**   The question asks which part of the brain is connected to the very basic function of simple alertness. The *reticular formation* is responsible for simple alertness. The correct answer is (D).

69. **C**   The question asks which of the following disorders is the modern name for hypochondriasis. In popular culture, the term still exists to describe someone with a fear of getting sick, but this term does not exist anymore in the DSM-5. Use Process of Elimination to evaluate the answer choices. Eliminate (A) because *Munchausen syndrome* is another outdated term for a factitious disorder. Eliminate (B) because *hypersomnolence* is a sleep disorder. Keep (C) because *illness anxiety disorder* is the modern term for the disorder of someone with a fear of getting sick. Eliminate (D) because *somatic symptom disorder* has to do with physical symptoms with no physical cause. Finally, eliminate (E) because *trichotillomania* is hair-pulling disorder. The correct answer is (C).

70. **B**   The question asks about Tom's attitude about skiing, according to Daryl Bem. Daryl Bem is the originator of the self-perception theory, and posited that people develop attitudes by observing their own behaviors and attributing those behaviors to attitudes that must have caused them. Use Process of Elimination to evaluate the answer choices. Eliminate (A) because it is unlikely that his attitude will *remain unchanged* since he is now getting paid a large sum of money to patrol the ski slopes. Keep (B) because getting paid to patrol the ski slopes will likely make his attitude toward skiing *become more negative* since it is now not just a hobby but also a job. Eliminate (C), as it is the opposite of (B). Eliminate (D) because there is no mention of conflicting thoughts or beliefs to suggest *cognitive dissonance*. Eliminate (E) because attitudes generally are more stable over time through an aggregate than from day to day. The correct answer is (B).

71. **B**   The question asks what would result from the change in Tom's attitude, according to self-perception theory. Self-perception theory is an analysis of attitudes that arise from observing one's own behavior. Use Process of Elimination to evaluate the answer choices. Eliminate (A) because the *self-fulfilling*

prophecy would mean that Tom would have some preconceived notion that would become fulfilled over time, but there is no evidence of such a thought in the question stem. Keep (B) because the *over-justification* effect results when one often finds reduced intrinsic motivation to do a behavior when an external reward is introduced. Eliminate (C) because the mere exposure effect has to do with a preference for things that are familiar, which would make Tom's attitude more positive toward skiing, which is familiar to him. Eliminate (D) because inoculation is a protection against persuasion, and there is no persuasion happening here. Eliminate (E) because the gain-loss theory is used in the context of interpersonal attraction, which is not part of the scenario. The correct answer is (B).

72. **A** The question asks which of the following would be most inclined toward a situational view of personality. Use Process of Elimination to evaluate the answer choices. Keep (A) because *Walter Mischel* posited an individual's behavior is largely based on situational cues, which matches the question. Eliminate (B) because *Raymond Cattell's* theory of personality, though wider than Eysenck's, asserted that behavior was based largely on traits rather than situations. Eliminate (C) because *Gordon Allport* made a hierarchy of traits, but that behavior still largely relied on traits, such as cardinal traits and central traits. Eliminate (D) because *Hans Eysenck* believed behavior stemmed from a couple salient personality traits. Eliminate (E) because *William Sheldon* created somatotype and constitutional psychology, which correlates body types to temperament. The correct answer is (A).

73. **C** The question asks who the APA was founded by. Stanley Hall founded the APA in 1892 at Clark University. The correct answer is (C).

74. **C** The question asks how Prozac works, as it is frequently used to treat depression. Prozac is a *serotonin agonist*, meaning that it prevents the brain from reabsorbing naturally occurring serotonin, which is involved in mood regulation. The correct answer is (C).

75. **D** The question asks in which of the senses Weber's law applies to a specific range of intensities. It applies to all senses, though there is a different scale with which humans detect differences in stimuli, depending on the type of stimulus. For instance, changes in weight are detected on a different scale than intensity of light, yet they are all governed under Weber's law. The correct answer is (D).

76. **E** The question asks what a woman's new fear of swimming can be attributed to based on the details of the question stem. The question states that *While swimming in the ocean, she is stung by several jelly-fish. Now the woman refuses to swim at all, even in an indoor pool.* This indicates that the woman has created an association between swimming and getting stung by jellyfish. Use Process of Elimination to evaluate the answer choices. Eliminate (A) because associations are classical conditioning, not *operant conditioning*. This reasoning instead leads to (E), *classical conditioning*. Eliminate (B) because the CS and UCS would have to be presented separately with a time interval in between, and that is not the case in this scenario. Eliminate (C) because *delayed conditioning* would also indicate that there is a delay in presenting the CS, but there is not enough evidence in the question to support this. Eliminate (D) because *second-order conditioning* would involve another stimulus, but there are only two mentioned here, creating a first-order conditioning. The correct answer is (E).

77. **E** The question asks which of the following statements is true of a variable-ratio schedule of reinforcement as opposed to other schedules of reinforcement. Variable-ratio means that the subject receives randomized reinforcement for completing a task. Use Process of Elimination to evaluate the answer choices. Eliminate (A) because providing reinforcement for *any response* describes *continuous* reinforcement. Eliminate (B) because learning occurs quickly in other forms as well, though that learning might be easier to extinguish with those other methods. Eliminate (C) because this is describing a time *interval*. Eliminate (D) because variable-ratio is the least vulnerable to extinction, as seen in gambling addictions. Keep (E) because it produces the highest response rate, such as gambling. The correct answer is (E).

78. **A**   The question asks which of the following is true about Jenny's score EXCEPT. With EXCEPT questions, eliminate what IS true. The question states that the *normal distribution of 2000 scores has a mean of 150 and a standard deviation of 6*. If Jenny scored a 162, that means she is 2 standard deviations above the mean: 150 + 6 = 156, and 156 + 6 = 162. This would place Jenny at the 98th percentile. Use Process of Elimination to evaluate the answer choices. Keep (A) because more than 68% of students scored lower than she did, making this a candidate for an exception. Eliminate (B) because it is true that *48% of the total scores lie between the mean and her score*, two standard deviations away. Eliminate (C) because it is true that *her score is two standard deviations from the mean*. Eliminate (D) because it is true that her score is can be expressed as *a z-score of +2*. Eliminate (E) because it is true that she is in the *98th percentile*. The correct answer is (A).

79. **D**   The question asks which test the individual who gives stern orders in his own home and obediently follows orders at work might score high on. Use Process of Elimination to evaluate the answer choices. Eliminate (A) because it is one of the most generalized representations of a person's locus of control, and it would not make sense that this person's locus of control would be so disparate in the context of these interpersonal interactions. Eliminate (B) because the *TAT* tests are projection tests to help show an individual's perception of interpersonal relationships. There is not enough information to support this test from the question stem. Eliminate (C) because the *CPI* tests an individual's interpersonal behavior in social contexts. This again would indicate that the individual should not have a great disparity in these two settings. Keep (D) because the F in an *F-scale* test stands for fascist, and it measures the authoritarian personality in a variety of different dimensions of personality. Therefore, different situations could elicit different dimensions of personality. Eliminate (E) because the *Bem Sex Role Inventory* test focuses on gender roles, but there is not enough information about the individual's work environment to know the gender of his workmates. The correct answer is (D).

80. **E**   The question asks where the receptors for hearing are located in humans. Use Process of Elimination to evaluate the answer choices. Eliminate (A) because the *olivary nucleus* is located in the medulla oblongata, not the ears. Eliminate (B) because the *inferior colliculus* is part of the midbrain and while it is an integral part of audition in humans, it is not where the *receptors* are located. Eliminate (C) because the *oval window* leads from the middle ear to the inner ear. Eliminate (D) because the *tympanic membrane* receives vibrations from the outer air, but it does not contain receptors for hearing. Keep (E) because the *basilar membrane* is found in the cochlea and contains the sensory receptors for hearing. The correct answer is (E).

81. **D**   The question asks about the cognitive skill that a child possesses who understands that a round ball of clay maintains its mass even when flattened into a long thin cylinder. The concept that objects maintain their mass even in different shapes is the concept of conservation. The correct answer is (D).

82. **C**   The question asks what causes a fetus to develop into a female. Use Process of Elimination to evaluate the answer choices. Eliminate (A) and (B) because both males and females have the hormone *estrogen*, so the presence or absence is not indicative of sex development in the fetus. Keep (C) because the *H-Y antigen* is a protein that is involved in the formation of testes, so the absence of this protein would result in formation of a female. Eliminate (D) because the presence of such a protein would indicate the fetus would develop into a male. Eliminate (E) because the follicle stimulating hormone is involved in development of women's ovaries and men's testes during puberty as well as ovulation. The correct answer is (C).

83. **A**   The question asks which of the following personality disorders is characterized by excessive emotion and attention seeking. Excessive emotion is indicative of a Cluster B disorder. Use Process of Elimination to evaluate the answer choices. Eliminate (C) and (D), which are not included in Cluster B personality disorders. Keep (A) because *histrionic* personality disorder is characterized by excessive

emotion. Eliminate (B) because *antisocial* personality disorder is characterized by a disregard for others and lack of remorse. Eliminate (E) because *borderline* personality disorder is characterized by risky or impulsive behavior as well as instability in interpersonal relationships and self-concept. The correct answer is (A).

84. C   The question asks how many standard deviations from the mean is an IQ of 146. The mean is around 100, and the standard deviation is roughly 15. Therefore, 100 + 15 + 15 + 15 = 145. Thus, an IQ of 146 would be about 3 standard deviations from the mean. The correct answer is (C).

85. E   The question asks what the fundamental attribution error is. The fundamental attribution error is the tendency for individuals to attribute behaviors to personality instead of to situations. Use Process of Elimination to evaluate the answer choices. Eliminate (A) because disposition, not *motive*, is the reason for the fundamental attribution error. Eliminate (B) because the tendency to *personify inanimate objects* has nothing to do with the fundamental attribution theory. Eliminate (C) for the same reason that disposition, not motivation, is the reason for the fundamental attribution error. Eliminate (D) because the fundamental attribution error refers to attributing others' behavior, not one's own. Keep (E) for this same reason, that the fundamental attribution error is the idea that individuals *attribute the behaviors of others to disposition* rather than situation. The correct answer is (E).

86. B   The question asks about the effect that would result if a student were to answer a question about Erikson more quickly if it were preceded by another question about Erikson than a question about something else. This effect is called *priming*, in which information is more readily available based on a prior experience. The correct answer is (B).

87. D   The question asks what an individual with Korsakoff's syndrome might engage in. An individual with Korsakoff's syndrome would exhibit memory deficiency. Use Process of Elimination to evaluate the answer choices. Eliminate (A), (B), and (C), none of which have to do with memory. Keep (D) because *confabulation* is a symptom of memory disorders in which individuals make up stories to fill in memory gaps. Eliminate (E) because *folie a deux* involves delusions, not false memories. The correct answer is (D).

88. C   The question asks for which type of approach to understanding personality Gordon Allport is known for. Allport classified traits into three levels: cardinal, central, and secondary traits. Use Process of Elimination to evaluate the answer choices. Eliminate (A) because *personal constructs* are unrelated to trait characteristics. Eliminate (B) because a *nomothetic* approach seeks to point out what is shared among the collective instead of what differentiates people. Keep (C) because an *ideographic* approach seeks to emphasize what is unique to individuals, similar to how Allport coined cardinal traits such as "Quixotic" or being a "Mother Theresa," terms that are descriptive of unique people's characters. Eliminate (D) because *factor analysis* is a term used in statistical analysis, not for understanding qualities of personality. Eliminate (E) because a *phrenologic* approach has to do with the size and shape of the human cranium. The correct answer is (C).

89. E   The question asks which of Piaget's cognitive stages an individual is who entertains himself by solving logic puzzles. Use Process of Elimination to evaluate the answer choices. Eliminate (A) because *accommodation* is not a stage of development. Eliminate (B) because the *sensorimotor* stage of development happens during infancy. Eliminate (C) because the *preoperational* stage has not yet developed much logic. Eliminate (D) because while the *concrete operational* stage is characterized by simple manipulations and increased logic, it is not enough to solve complex logic puzzles. Only someone at the *formal operational* stage has the capability for higher reasoning and logic. The correct answer is (E).

90. **C** The question asks which of the following therapies would be most appropriate for an individual who suffered from strong feelings of meaninglessness and who hope to find more meaning in life. Use Process of Elimination to evaluate the answer choices. Eliminate (A) because while *client-centered therapy* might be helpful to this person, a person looking to find *meaningfulness* might be better served looking at the self in the dimension of finding their place within the greater world. Eliminate (B) because *psychoanalytic therapy* might find meaning in the subconscious, but it sounds as though the individual wants to find meaning in their conscious life. Keep (C) because *existential therapy* not only focuses on the self, it focuses on the meaning of the self and the world in which the self exists. Eliminate (D) because *individual therapy* does not indicate a therapeutic approach. Eliminate (E) because *Gestalt* theory is not often used for therapy, but rather as guidelines for rules of perception. The correct answer is (C).

91. **E** The question asks which of the following brain areas is important for speech. The two areas that should come to mind are Wernicke's area and Broca's area, which are involved in processing, understanding, and production of language. Only Wernicke's area is available here. The correct answer is (E).

92. **C** The question asks what E. L. Thorndike is known for EXCEPT. With EXCEPT questions, eliminate what IS true. Eliminate (A) because it is true that Thorndike is known for *the law of effect*. Eliminate (B) because it is true that Thorndike is known for *instrumental learning*, a precursor to Skinner and behaviorism. Keep (C) because *state-dependent learning* is a concept developed by Godden and Baddeley at a much later time. Eliminate (D) because the experiments *using hats in puzzle boxes* was the means for positing the law of effect. Eliminate (E) because *repeat behaviors that lead to positive consequences* is the definition of the law of effect. The correct answer is (C).

93. **A** The question asks what the bird's behavior is an example of. The question states that the territory *is inhabited by many similar looking and closely related birds,* but the male bird *performs an elaborate display prior to mating* which *ensures that the female partner will be of the same species.* Use Process of Elimination to evaluate the answer choices. Keep (A) because a *behavioral isolating mechanism* is one that leads to speciation. Eliminate (B) because a *fixed action pattern* is an action that an animal is "hard-wired" to do, which may not be specific to its species. Eliminate (C) because *paternal behavior* would be a behavior that happens after the bird has already mated. Eliminate (D) because *habituation* is a passive desensitization to an environment, unrelated to mating. Eliminate (E) because *exploratory behavior* is the natural tendency to explore and be curious about a new environment, which is not specific to any species. The correct answer is (A).

94. **C** The question asks which of the following theorists has been recognized for creating a development theory that covers the entire life span. Use Process of Elimination to evaluate the answer choices. Eliminate (A) and (B) because *Maslow* and *Kohlberg* both developed hierarchies that are not necessarily sequential in nature. Keep (C) because *Erikson* is credited with his theory of psychosocial development continuing from birth through death. Eliminate (D) and (E) because *Piaget's* and *Freud's* theories of development both stop at adolescence. The correct answer is (C).

95. **D** The question asks into which concept the Kitty Genovese case sparked research. The case of Kitty Genovese has been a staple of psychology classes because there were many neighbors who heard Genovese scream while she was being stabbed to death, yet no one called for help because each assumed that someone else would call for help. This is known as the *bystander effect*, so (D) is correct. Eliminate (A) because *vicarious behavior* is another term of observational learning. Eliminate (B) because the *glass ceiling* is a term associated with feminism. Eliminate (C) because *racial segregation* had nothing to do with Genovese, who was white. Eliminate (E) because while this was a case pertaining to *violence against a woman*, it is not the reason for research that stemmed from the case. The correct answer is (D).

96. **A** The question asks what Bandura concluded was important to social learning in children from the famous Bobo doll experiment. The Bobo doll experiment proved how powerful and real observational learning is. Use Process of Elimination to evaluate the answer choices. Keep (A) because *observational learning* is consistent. Eliminate (B), (C), and (E) because *primary reinforcement, rewards,* and *shaping* are concepts of operant conditioning. Eliminate (D) because *concept learning* consists of learning categories of objects or examples, which has nothing to do with the Bobo doll experiment. The correct answer is (A).

97. **B** The question asks which of the following factors would Watson expect to most influence child behavioral development. Watson was a behaviorist who believed that a child's environment had a strong effect on behavioral development. Use Process of Elimination to evaluate the answer choices. Eliminate (A) because *morality* is harder to impart through environmental factors. Keep (B) because *imitation* is a common way of taking observations from the environment and implementing them directly into behavior. Eliminate (C) because *psychodynamic influences* are less involved with environmental factors. Eliminate (D) because while *psychosocial factors* are partially related to environmental factors in the social side of it, the psychological portion is internal. Eliminate (E) because *exploration needs* are curiosity driven, not necessarily behavior producing. The correct answer is (B).

98. **D** The question asks to which of the following statements would subjects take the longer amount of time to answer "true," according to Collins and Quillian. Collins and Quillian built the network model of semantic memory organization. Use Process of Elimination to evaluate the answer choices. Eliminate (A) because a shoe is directly tied to a type of clothing. Eliminate (B) because a ballet slipper is a type of shoe, and therefore directly related as well. Eliminate (C) for the same reason that a boot is a type of shoe and therefore directly related. Keep (D) because there are a couple of extra steps for the connection: a sandal is a shoe, and a shoe is a piece of clothing, so therefore a sandal is a piece of clothing. Eliminate (E) because a sandal is a type of shoe and therefore directly related. The correct answer is (D).

99. **A** The question asks which is true of the ossicles in the auditory system. Ossicles are the three little bones in the middle ear that vibrate to transmit sound from the air to the cochlea. Use Process of Elimination to evaluate the answer choices. Keep (A) because the *stapes* is the smallest of the three ossicles and the furthest toward the inner ear, which taps against the oval window. Eliminate (B) because the malleus, not the stapes, is closer to the tympanic membrane, which is closer to the outer ear. Eliminate (C) because they do not move in a *traveling wave* pattern; rather, they vibrate. Eliminate (D) and (E) because they are located in the middle ear, not the inner or outer ear. The correct answer is (A).

100. **C** The question asks which of the following types of tests is paired correctly with its form of memory testing. This question is testing the different types of recall: free, cued, and recognition. Use Process of Elimination to evaluate the answer choices. Eliminate (A) because an *essay test*, while sometimes started with a prompt, is largely using free recall. Eliminate (B) because a *language test* is either cued or free recall, depending on the task. Keep (C) because a *fill-in-the-blank test* is cuing a specific response with clues from surrounding words in the sentence. Eliminate (D) because a *multiple-choice test* is considered recognition, since a test taker must recognize the correct answer or recognize wrong answers to eliminate. Eliminate (E) because a *sentence completion test* is a cued recall exercise. The correct answer is (C).

101. **E** The question asks what type of behavior the bird displays. The question states that the bird was *hidden* but *makes a call of alarm* to alert its siblings of a predator. The bird displays *altruism* and places itself at *increased risk* in order to place its siblings at *decreased risk*. Use Process of Elimination to evaluate the answer choices. Eliminate (A) because *contact comfort behavior* is the physical and emotional comfort

an infant receives from physical interaction with its mother. There is no evidence of physical contact here. Eliminate (B) because *operant behavior* implies having a reward or a punishment, and there is not a guaranteed reward here, as none of the birds are safe yet. Eliminate (C) because *natural selection* is the concept that Darwin posited, in which beneficial adaptations and genetic variations within species dominate over time. Eliminate (D) because *irrelevant behavior* is one that disrupts a previous pattern of behavior temporarily. There is no evidence of a prior pattern of behavior in the question stem. Keep (E) because *inclusive fitness* is the Darwinian concept in which organisms develop behaviors in addition to genetics that aid in leaving the maximum number of offspring. By trying to save the siblings, this would mean more of the birds would be alive to preserve the species. The correct answer is (E).

102. **A**   The question asks which substance benzodiazepines work to enhance the effects of to relieve anxiety. Benzodiazepines act as a sedative by slowing the body's functions by increasing GABA. The correct answer is (A).

103. **B**   The question asks which theory represents the idea that people will alter their actions or beliefs so that their actions and beliefs agree with one another. When people experience tension between two competing actions or beliefs, often they will alter one of them so that both are more in line with each other. Use Process of Elimination to evaluate the answer choices. Eliminate (A) because a *risky shift* is a change in group attitude toward a greater chance for negative outcomes. There is no evidence for a *group* here, nor is there anything to suggest that people *alter their actions or beliefs* toward negative consequences. Keep (B) because *cognitive dissonance* refers to the tension between the conflicting beliefs or actions that is then reduced by the alteration. Eliminate (C) because the *Purkinje shift* is the tendency in low-light conditions to see longer wavelengths of light as darker, which has nothing to do with beliefs or actions. Eliminate (D) because the *self-serving bias* is a concept of attribution theory in which a person takes credit for good things that happen and blames others for bad things that happen. Eliminate (E) because *acceptance* does not address the alteration that takes place in the question stem. The correct answer is (B).

104. **A**   The question asks which concept Henry Landsberger discovered. Landsberger discovered the Hawthorne effect, in which subjects alter their behavior when they are aware they are being studied or observed. The correct answer is (A).

105. **A**   The question asks which of the following people argued that Kohlberg's moral stages were not directly applicable to females. Use Process of Elimination to evaluate the answer choices. Keep (A) because *Carol Gilligan* further divided post-conventional moral thinking into care-based (often found in women) and justice-based morality (often found in men). Eliminate (B) because *Diana Baumrind* theorized on parenting styles, not moral development. Eliminate (C) because *Matina Horner* researched motivation, intelligence, and achievement in women, coining the phrase "fear of success." Eliminate (D) because *Eleanor Maccoby* researched sex differences from a sociocultural standpoint, not a moral standpoint. Eliminate (E) because *Jenny Field* researched semantics. The correct answer is (A).

106. **D**   The question asks which of the following personality types is NOT associated with Alfred Adler's theory of personality. Adler's theory of personality is built on four different personality traits: *sanguine, choleric, melancholic,* and *phlegmatic.* With NOT questions, eliminate what IS true. Eliminate (A), (B), (C), and (E), which are all true. *Ectomorphic* personality is one of the principles of Sheldon's theory of personality, not Adler's. The correct answer is (D).

107. **C**   The question asks which of the social psychology tactics the woman used to sell her car. Since she *attempts to sell the car for $10,000 and then settles for $8,000* and she *only hoped to collect $8,000 in the first place,* she asked more than she was looking for with the aim of ending up with her desired price.

Use Process of Elimination to evaluate the answer choices. Eliminate (A) because *reactance* is a concept in which a person is reacting to unpleasant motivation, whether something would be taken away from them or something bad would happen if they chose a different option, thus limiting their decision-making. Eliminate (B) because the *foot-in-the-door* tactic is the opposite of what happened. A person would ask for a lower amount than they desire and then work their way upward. Keep (C) because the *door-in-the-face* tactic is to ask for more in the first place so that a later lesser amount sounds more agreeable. Eliminate (D) because the *guilt bias* is a self-control emotion or judgement, but this is in interpersonal interaction. Eliminate (E) because *false cooperation* is a relatively new concept that refers to what appears to be cooperation on the surface, but on a deeper look is actually a manipulation or con. The correct answer is (C).

108. **B** The question asks which of the following is the path of a received "message" through a single neuron. Use Process of Elimination to evaluate the answer choices. Since the message is received first through the *postsynaptic cell,* eliminate anything that does not start with this option: (A), (C), (D), and (E). The correct answer is (B).

109. **D** The question asks about which concept the symptom inventory provides information. The paragraph states that the *hypothesis is that a diet high in carbohydrates will help to alleviate the symptoms of depression.* The paragraph goes on to state that *the group being studied is a random group of depressed inpatients,* and that *every other day the subjects fill out a depression symptom inventory.* The depression symptom inventory therefore must have something to do with testing for the *dependent variable,* if the diet is the *independent variable* meant to have an effect on the subjects' symptoms. The correct answer is (D).

110. **D** The question asks which of the following is the most serious confounding variable in the experiment described in the paragraph. The paragraph states that the *hypothesis is that a diet high in carbohydrates will help to alleviate the symptoms of depression.* The paragraph goes on to state that *the group being studied is a random group of depressed inpatients,* and that *every other day the subjects fill out a depression symptom inventory.* A *confounding variable* is something that could alter the results of a study that the experimenters did not factor in. Use Process of Elimination against one another to compare which statement is the most problematic. In (D), the fact that some subjects are on antidepressants while others are not is clearly the most problematic, far above age, gender, and prior medical history. If some are receiving treatment other than the independent variable, the experiment is invalidated. The correct answer is (D).

111. **B** The question asks which of the following is NOT a dissociative disorder. With NOT questions, eliminate what IS true. Use Process of Elimination to evaluate the answer choices. Eliminate (A), (C), (D), and (E) because dissociative *amnesia,* dissociative *identity disorder,* dissociative *depersonalization disorder,* and dissociative *derealization disorder* are all dissociative disorders. However, keep (B) because *Multiple Personality Disorder* is an outdated term that is now called Dissociative Identity Disorder (DID). The correct answer is (B).

112. **A** The question asks what behavior therapy is most useful in treating. Behavior therapy works to teach better adaptive behaviors in place of maladaptive behaviors. Use Process of Elimination to evaluate the answer choices. Keep (A) because children tend to respond well to learning new behaviors without necessarily understanding the psychology behind the behaviors. Eliminate (B) because *paranoid schizophrenia* is best treated through medication and psychosocial therapy. Eliminate (C) because *depression* is a mood disorder and therefore better treated through medication and/or talk therapy. Eliminate (D) because *tardive dyskinesia* is treated through medication. Eliminate (E) because a *conversion disorder* is treated through a variety of psychotherapy, cognitive-behavioral therapy, physical therapy, among other treatments. The correct answer is (A).

113. **C**   The question asks what a child is able to appreciate who looks under a pillow for a lost toy, according to Piaget. The child is demonstrating *object permanence* because it knows that an object still exists even when it is hidden from view. The correct answer is (C).

114. **A**   The question asks why, according to Weber, the subject states the tones seem to be of the same intensity. The question states that the *subject is presented with two tones of differing intensities.* It goes on to say that the subject *states that the tones seem to be of the same intensity.* This is most likely because the percent difference in intensity was not enough to cross the just noticeable difference threshold. Use Process of Elimination to evaluate the answer choices. Keep (A) because this matches the prediction of the tones not being separated by the just noticeable difference. Eliminate (B) because location does not play a role in the JND; intensity does. Eliminate (C) because tones and intensity are two different scales that have nothing to do with each other. Eliminate (D) because the question does not give any evidence of motivational or attentional trouble. Eliminate (E) because response bias is not part of Weber's law. The correct answer is (A).

115. **B**   The question asks which theory Hermann von Helmholtz is famous for. He was a physicist who made significant contributions to the field of optics, most notably with his theory of color vision, or the trichromatic theory. The correct answer is (B).

116. **D**   The question asks how the structuralist school of psychology viewed consciousness. Structuralism, founded by Wilhelm Wundt, views consciousness as a series of experiences that are then strung together to create understanding of experience. Use Process of Elimination to evaluate the answer choices. Eliminate (A) because *three separate layers* alludes to the Freudian concept of the conscious, the preconscious, and the unconscious. Eliminate (B) because *a flow of ideas* is all right, but these ideas would be described as separate instances in structuralism. Eliminate (C) because genetics has nothing to do with consciousness, according to structuralists. Keep (D) because the *discrete sensations* refer to the series of experiences described above. Eliminate (E), which alludes to John Locke's *tabula rasa*. The correct answer is (D).

117. **E**   The question asks what the Whorfian hypothesis posits. The Whorfian hypothesis states that different cultures can express ideas such as color differently through language descriptors and cultural values. Use Process of Elimination to evaluate the answer choices. Eliminate (A) because *breeding seasons* has nothing to do with the Whorfian hypothesis. Eliminate (B) because the *diagnostic label* described in this choice seems more like a stereotype. Eliminate (C) because how *an eyewitness is questioned* has nothing to do with the Whorfian hypothesis, but rather may have to do with recall errors. Eliminate (D) because the Whorfian hypothesis is not connected with *schizophrenia*. Keep (E) because *language structure* is one of the factors of how speakers express ideas differently because of their *perceived reality* influenced by language structure. The correct answer is (E).

118. **C**   The question asks how the Oedipus and Electra complexes are resolved, according to Freud. The Oedipus complex in boys is the psychosexual urge to kill one's father and marry one's mother, a concept used to explain jealousy of the same-sex parent. This is resolved once the child identifies with the same-sex parent. Use Process of Elimination to evaluate the answer choices. Eliminate (A) because while the *latency stage* is the next stage after the phallic stage, the question asks about how the complexes are *resolved*, and one can move from one stage to the next while developing a fixation instead of resolving anything. Eliminate (B) because this is the opposite of what happens, and rather brings about the Oedipal complex instead of resolving it. Keep (C), as this matches the definition. Eliminate (D) and (E) because neither the *death instinct* nor the *ego* is part of the psychosexual stages of development. The correct answer is (C).

119. **E** The question asks why children often recall A, B, C, D, and X, Y, Z more readily than the letters in between. This phenomenon of recalling the first and last items more easily in a list is the definition of *primacy and recency effects*. The correct answer is (E).

120. **A** The question asks what an emotional response would involve, in order, according to Schachter and Singer. Remember that the Schachter-Singer theory of emotion involves cognition to interpret physiological arousal. Use Process of Elimination to evaluate the answer choices. Eliminate (B), (D), and (E) because the physiological reaction is the first piece of information to the individual. Since cognition must come before the experience of emotion to interpret the physiological reaction and environmental factors, eliminate (C). The correct answer is (A).

121. **A** The question asks which classic experiment indicated that behavioral traits could be at least partly determined by heredity. Use Process of Elimination to evaluate the answer choices. Keep (A) because *Tyron's experiment* with rats was a multi-decade experiment using breeding to develop rats that were genetically predisposed to being better or worse at completing a maze, which fits the concept of heredity having a partial determination on behavioral traits. Eliminate (B) because *Garcia's experiment with food aversion* relies on classical conditioning. Eliminate (C) because *Thorndike's puzzle boxes* helped prove the law of effect, that positive outcomes increase the likelihood of repeat behaviors. Eliminate (D) because *Von Frisch's experiment with honeybees* demonstrated that bees have color vision through classical conditioning. Eliminate (E) because *Tinbergen's experiment with stickleback fish* tested aggression, but was not necessarily focused on heredity. The correct answer is (A).

122. **A** The question asks about what a cross-sectional study is able to control for, as opposed to longitudinal design. A cross-sectional study often examines many different demographic groups at the same time, whereas a longitudinal study follows subjects over the course of a longer period of time, and usually has fewer subjects. Use Process of Elimination to evaluate the answer choices. Keep (A) because *cohort effects* occur when subjects of roughly the same age indirectly affect the results of a study due to common age-related factors. This is much more likely to happen in a longitudinal study, since the subjects will age with the study, whereas there can be much more age diversity in a cross-sectional study since the study lasts for a shorter amount of time. Eliminate (B) because *demand characteristics* is a term that denotes skewed results in an experiment due to experimenters' expectancies, which could happen in either design. Eliminate (C) because *experimenter bias*, a term that describes experimenters' altered behavior due to knowing who is receiving treatment vs. a placebo, could happen to either type of study. Eliminate (D) because the *Hawthorne effect* could happen in either type of study, depending on the setup. Eliminate (E) because *reactance*, a concept in which a person is reacting to unpleasant motivation which limits their decision-making, could happen in either type of study. The correct answer is (A).

123. **B** The question asks which of the following tests includes items that discriminate between groups but that seem lacking in face validity. Remember that *face validity* is the degree to which an experiment or assessment subjectively appears to test the variable or construct that it is supposed to test. Use Process of Elimination to evaluate the answer choices. Eliminate (A) because the *Thematic Apperception Test (TAT)* is a projection test to help show an individual's perception of interpersonal relationships. It subjectively does seem to test what it means to test. Keep (B) because the *Minnesota Multiphasic Personality Inventory (MMPI)* has many different uses, from personality tests to job screening, so the face validity is questionable here. Eliminate (C) because the *California Personality Inventory (CPI)* tests an individual's interpersonal behavior in social contexts, which seems to test what it is intended to test. Eliminate (D) because the *Q-sort* is a personality test to test cultural criterion of "truth," which sets out to study what it intends to. Eliminate (E) because *Rotter's Incomplete Sentence Blank* is a projective test that is used to study projections, as it would appear on face value. The correct answer is (B).

124. **C**   The question asks what wearing uniforms is found to promote. By wearing the same thing, individuals feel part of a larger group with less expressed individuality. Use Process of Elimination to evaluate the answer choices. Eliminate (A) because a *depressive affect* is a level of emotion, which likely is not directly connected to individual expression through uniforms. Eliminate (B) because *authoritarianism* is a method of governance that may restrict individuals' rights, but it is not directly related to wearing uniforms. Keep (C) because *deindividuation* is the lack of responsibility and inhibition directly as a result from an aroused state and/or loss of a sense of individuality. Eliminate (D) because *objective self-awareness* is a way of evaluating oneself against one's values, which may have nothing to do with a uniform. Eliminate (E) because *mental creativity* is not directly correlated with wearing uniforms. The correct answer is (C).

125. **D**   The question asks which term expresses how word order is determined in a sentence. Word order in a sentence is referred to as *syntax*. The correct answer is (D).

126. **D**   The question asks which of the following is a binocular cue used in depth perception. Use Process of Elimination to evaluate the answer choices. Eliminate (A) because *good continuation* is a Gestalt principle, not a binocular cue. Eliminate (B) because *interposition* is a monocular cue that allows an individual to judge proximity based on position. Eliminate (C) because *motion parallax* is a monocular cue that allows an individual to perceive change in position. Keep (D) because *disparity* is the way in which the right and left eyes view slightly different images. Eliminate (E) because *linear perspective* is also a monocular cue that helps show distance. The correct answer is (D).

127. **A**   The question asks which of the following groups of theorists offers stage models of development. Use Process of Elimination to evaluate the answer choices. Eliminate (C) and (D) because they do not contain Piaget, since Piaget created stages of cognitive development. Eliminate (B) because Kohlberg made stages of moral thought, not of *development*. Eliminate (E) because Adler did not make stages of *development*, but rather a theory of personality. This leaves (A), which contains Piaget, Erikson, and Freud. The correct answer is (A).

128. **E**   The question asks which of the following areas in the brain is the "master" of the endocrine system. The pituitary gland is the one that controls the endocrine system through secreting hormones. The correct answer is (E).

129. **B**   The question asks what the Acme Scale of Aggression has, according to the details of the question stem. The question states that *The Acme Scale of Aggression has a +0.10 correlation with four other standardized aggression scales*, meaning that it has a low external or concurrent validity. The question continues that *a correlation of +1.00 exists between the scores of any student who takes the Acme Scale of Aggression twice*. This means that it has a very high reliability rate since a perfect positive correlation of +1.00 means that repeated tests of a subject will yield the same results. Use Process of Elimination to evaluate the answer choices. Eliminate (A) because it does not have *high external validity*. Keep (B) because it has both a *low concurrent validity* and a *high reliability*. Eliminate (C) because *low face validity* would mean that it does not, on face value, test what it says it tests. Eliminate (D) because it does not have *moderate external validity* given its low correlation with the other four tests. Eliminate (E) because it does not have *low reliability*. The correct answer is (B).

130. **D**   The question asks which pattern of forgetting is likely to take place after learning new material, according to Ebbinghaus's forgetting curve. Forgetting happens quickly at first and then slows over time. Use Process of Elimination to evaluate the answer choices. Eliminate (A) because forgetting does not happen *gradually and consistently* as it slows over time. Eliminate (B) because this is the opposite of what happens. Eliminate (C) because *spontaneous recovery* is a classical conditioning term, not a memory term. Keep (D) because this matches that forgetting *happens rapidly at first and then gradually*. Eliminate (E) because forgetting is not an *all-or-nothing* process. The correct answer is (D).

131. **B** The question asks which of the following pairs of items is *incorrectly* associated. Use Process of Elimination to evaluate the answer choices. Eliminate (A) because *Dewey* was instrumental in founding the functionalist school of thought. Keep (B) because *Frankl* is associated with logotherapy, not cognitive psychology. Eliminate (C) because *Adler* is closely associated with individual psychology. Eliminate (D) because *Titchener* is associated with structuralism. Eliminate (E) because *James* is associated with the concept of stream of consciousness. The correct answer is (B).

132. **E** The question asks what research has proven that holding and interacting with infants enhances. Use Process of Elimination to evaluate the answer choices. Keep (A) because it is proven that interacting with infants enhances *motor development*. Keep (B) since research has proven that interacting with infants improves *physical development*. Since both of these statements are true, they must all be true. The correct answer is (E).

133. **D** The question asks which of the following children would probably acquire language the slowest. Use Process of Elimination to evaluate the answer choices. Eliminate (A) and (B) because research shows that children who are only exposed to one language acquire the one language quicker than their bilingual peers. Therefore, eliminate (E), since the prior statement disproves that all children acquire language at *precisely the same rate*. Finally, eliminate (C) because girls acquire language faster than boys. The correct answer is (D).

134. **D** The question asks which of the following stages an individual has recently entered into if he or she has just learned that water poured from a tube into a bowl maintains the same volume. Use Process of Elimination to evaluate the answer choices. Eliminate (A) because this is not a stage of Piaget's stages of development. Eliminate (B) because the *sensorimotor stage* happens during infancy. Eliminate (C) because the *preoperational stage* happens in young children and culminates in pretend play and egocentrism. Keep (D) because *conservation*, the term described in the question, is one of the milestones of the *concrete operational stage* of development, along with mathematical manipulation. Eliminate (E) because the *formal operational stage* is marked by moral development and abstract reasoning. The correct answer is (D).

135. **A** The question asks which concept Andrea has likely developed based on details in the question stem. The question states that *Andrea does not like to go to parties because she knows how people will conduct themselves*. She seems to have a preconceived notion about how people act at parties. Use Process of Elimination to evaluate the answer choices. Keep (A) because a *script* is a sequence of expected behaviors in a given situation, which matches the prediction of Andrea's preconceived notion of people's behavior at parties. Eliminate (B) because a *deduction* in psychology refers to reasoning from the general to the specific, and Andrea is not getting more specific here. Eliminate (C) because a *prototype* the "best" cognitive representation of something, and there is no evidence that Andrea's reasoning is the best. Eliminate (D) because a *heuristic* is a rule-of-thumb. The correct answer is (A).

136. **E** The question asks which of the following is a result of diffusion of responsibility. Diffusion of responsibility often happens in larger groups, in which individuals feel less responsible for a situation. Use Process of Elimination to evaluate the answer choices. Eliminate (A) because *cooperation* does not necessarily result in diffusion of responsibility if every member of the group is responsible for themselves and participates in the task. Eliminate (B) because the *two-person theory of psychotherapy* examines the real and perceived relationships with others, but this does not remove responsibility from the person. Eliminate (C) because *shyness* does not equate to diffusion of responsibility. One can be simultaneously shy and responsible. Eliminate (D) because *blaming the group for individual failures* suggests a self-serving bias rather than the diffusion of responsibility. Keep (E) because there is a tendency for individuals in a large group to not feel responsible and therefore *not to help others*. The correct answer is (E).

137. **B** The question asks what type of experimental technique is being described in the question stem. The question states that an experimenter is testing *heredity and learning*. The experimenter *takes a litter of cats and places each one with a different parent for rearing*. The litter *inherited very similar genes*, and *the observed differences between the cats could more easily be attributed to experience*. Use Process of Elimination to evaluate the answer choices. Eliminate (A) because a *hybrid design* adds different experimental designs together, but there is only one component of the design at play. Keep (B) because *cross fostering* is exactly what is happening, that the cats are placed with different parents for rearing. Eliminate (C) because *surrogate parenting* is a term in which a woman will carry a child for another couple and then relinquish parental responsibilities once the child is born. Eliminate (D) because *intentional design* is a marketing term. Eliminate (E) because *selective breeding* is breeding to develop selective phenotypical traits. The correct answer is (B).

138. **E** The question asks what Martin Seligman maintains that cognitive training can offset. Seligman is known for the theory of learned helplessness. The correct answer is (E).

139. **C** The question asks which of the following sensory systems involves the ganglion cells and the ciliary muscles. These are both found in the visual sensory system: ganglion cells are the final output from the retina; ciliary muscles change the shape of the lens during the accommodation reflex. The correct answer is (C).

140. **A** Which of the following individuals pioneered object-relations theory? Use Process of Elimination to evaluate the answer choices. Keep (A) because *Melanie Klein* in fact did pioneer object-relations theory. Eliminate (B) because *Carol Gilligan* further divided post-conventional moral thinking into care-based (often found in women) and justice-based morality (often found in men). Eliminate (C) because *Andrea Raring* does not have a major theory. Eliminate (D) because *Mary Ainsworth* posited attachment theory. Eliminate (E) because *Karen Horney* posited the theory that neurosis stems from anxiety from interpersonal relationships. The correct answer is (A).

141. **D** The question asks which of the following factors has the greatest influence on interpersonal attraction. The three greatest factors are proximity, shared values, and physical characteristics. Use Process of Elimination to evaluate the answer choices. Eliminate (A) because *similarity of needs* is not a factor of attraction. Eliminate (B) because *similarity of background* is not the same as similarity of *values*. Eliminate (C) because *polarity* would suggest opposition of some sort, and there is no law of attraction that opposites attract from a theoretical standpoint. Keep (D) because *proximity* means that people who interact with one another or who travel in the same spheres are more likely to become attracted to one another. Eliminate (E) because *emotional balance* is not related to attraction. The correct answer is (D).

142. **C** The question asks what individuals assess to decide on the relationship between words, according to Collins and Quillian. Collins and Quillian built the network model of semantic memory organization. Use Process of Elimination to evaluate the answer choices. Eliminate (A) because while *personal experience* can create semantic meaning, it is not the most important component of the network model. Eliminate (B) because the *acoustic similarity* of words does not mean they also have similar meaning. Keep (C) because *words' respective locations in semantic hierarchies* is a way of describing the network model. Eliminate (D) because *common characteristics between the words* does not necessarily connote semantic meaning. Eliminate (E) because the *parts of speech of the words* does not make them related semantically. The correct answer is (C).

143. **A** The question asks which concept can explain the idea that over-benefited people tend to feel guilty. Use Process of Elimination to evaluate the answer choices. Keep (A) because *equity theory* deals with whether interactions are fair to both parties involved, and inequity could cause guilt in this theory.

Eliminate (B) because *social exchange theory* weighs interpersonal interaction through risk and benefit, which does not explain guilt. Eliminate (C) because *gain-loss theory* is a model of interpersonal attraction. Eliminate (D) because *reciprocal interaction* is a social exchange that takes place in a back-and-forth manner, such as neighbors reciprocating favors for each other. Eliminate (E) because in *diffusion of responsibility*, individuals feel less responsible in situations in which there are others involved. The correct answer is (A).

144. **C** The question asks which of the following experimenters performed famous experiments on conformity EXCEPT. With EXCEPT questions, eliminate what IS true. Eliminate (A) because Stanley Milgram's experiment tested obedience through a teacher-learner experiment that administered perceived shocks to the learner. Eliminate (B) because Zimbardo's prison experiment focused on conformity through role playing. Keep (C) because Leon Festinger's experiment had to do with cognitive dissonance. Eliminate (D) because Solomon Asch's conformity experiment consisted of different lengths of lines for individuals to identify in the setting of confederates' incorrect statements. Eliminate (E) because Sherif's experiment has to do with intergroup conflict with limited resources. The correct answer is (C).

145. **B** The question asks what the double-blind experimental design is used to minimize. In the double-blind experimental design, neither the subjects nor the experimenters know who is receiving the treatment and who is receiving the placebo. Use Process of Elimination to evaluate the answer choices. Eliminate (A) because *cohort effects* occur when subjects of roughly the same age indirectly affect the results of a study due to common age-related factors. Keep (B) because the *experimenter bias* results when the experimenter might behave differently toward experimental groups, and the double-blind design would correct for this. Eliminate (C) because the *halo effect* is the concept of assuming other positive attributes based on another positive feature or characteristic. Eliminate (D) because *reactance* is a concept in which a person is reacting to unpleasant motivation, whether something would be taken away from them or something bad would happen if they chose a different option, thus limiting their decision-making. Eliminate (E) because the *Hawthorne effect* is the phenomenon that subjects behave differently when they know they are being observed. The correct answer is (B).

146. **A** The question asks that drugs what attempt to impact behavior generally try to do. Use Process of Elimination to evaluate the answer choices. Keep (A) because many drugs that alter behavior *hinder or facilitate the transmission of "messages" at the synaptic junction* by inhibiting or facilitating reception. Eliminate (B) because *action potential* is not something that can be sped up. Eliminate (C) because these drugs do not *increase the number of neurons*, but rather change how they are firing. Eliminate (D) because the *axon hillock* does not need to be stimulated for neurons to fire. Eliminate (E) because the *nodes of Ranvier* do not need to be stimulated for the neurons to fire. The correct answer is (A).

147. **C** The question asks what an individual with fluent aphasia would have difficulty with. Fluent aphasia has to do with Wernicke's area in the brain, which is responsible for speech production. Use Process of Elimination to evaluate the answer choices. Eliminate (A) because *understanding* would have to do with Broca's area of language comprehension instead. Eliminate (B) because individuals with fluent aphasia can *utter words,* but they may not make sense when strung together. Keep (C) because *creating a logical sentence* would be challenging for someone with fluent aphasia since they can create full sentences, but they often come out as "word salad," or nonsensical meaning. Eliminate (D) because *spelling* is not the issue, but rather it is logical meaning in sentences. Eliminate (E) because individuals with aphasia do not have memory issues; it is instead an issue of how they are able to understand or produce language. The correct answer is (C).

148. **E** The question asks what learned helplessness is associated with. Learned helplessness is the concept that an organism tries to avoid an aversive stimulus and fails to the point that they stop trying, even when the stimulus is escapable. Use Process of Elimination to evaluate the answer choices. Eliminate (A)

because *neuroticism* does not bring about learned helplessness, rather, higher anxiety levels. Eliminate (B) because *introversion* does not mean someone has an internal or external locus of control. Eliminate (C) because *androgyny* is a term that relates to male and female characteristics exhibited in an individual. Eliminate (D) because *femininity* has nothing to do with learned helplessness. Keep (E) because an *external locus of control* is an important contributing factor to the individual believing they cannot escape from the aversive stimulus because it is beyond their control, which then allows them to stop trying. The correct answer is (E).

149. **A**   The question asks which of the following factors facilitates accurate recall of a list of words from the short-term memory EXCEPT. With EXCEPT questions, eliminate what IS true. Keep (A) because *acoustic similarity among the items* has been shown to be more difficult to recall in the short-term memory. Eliminate (B) because it is true that *meaningful* information facilitates better recall at all parts of the working memory. Eliminate (C) because it is true that *concrete items* are easier to remember in the short-term memory than abstract concepts. Eliminate (D) because it is true that *lack of similarity between items* facilitates accurate recall. Eliminate (E) because it is true that the greater the *subject's investment*, the greater the individual's accurate recall. The correct answer is (A).

150. **C**   The question asks what Mr. C's gracious behavior would most likely be interpreted as by a psychoanalyst. The question states that *Mr. C is passed over for a promotion at work for the fifth year.* It continues to state that *Instead of showing his anger and frustration, Mr. C responds by being the first to congratulate the promoted worker.* Psychoanalysis would most likely classify the behavior as a subconscious defense mechanism. Use Process of Elimination to evaluate the answer choices. Eliminate (A) because *repression* usually manifests itself as not remembering traumatic events that have happened so that the individual is not reminded of the event. Eliminate (B) because *undoing* would involve doing some sort of opposite behavior that would cancel out destructive thought or behavior. The behavior is not something that Mr. C did in this case, but rather something that happened to him, so there is not a way to "cancel" or "undo" the outcome here. Keep (C) because a *reaction formation* occurs when an individual behaves in the opposite way in which he or she thinks or feels. By *being the first to congratulate the promoted worker*, Mr. C is acting in the opposite way of his feelings. Eliminate (D) because *sublimation* involves turning socially unacceptable impulses into socially accepted ones. There is not an unacceptable impulse present in the question stem, so this defense mechanism is not applicable. Eliminate (E) because *denial* is to deny that a person is feeling the way they are feeling, and there is no evidence that he denies he is feeling the way he does. The correct answer is (C).

151. **E**   The question asks which of the following individuals is associated with the discovery of secure versus insecure infant attachment. Use Process of Elimination to evaluate the answer choices. Eliminate (A) because *Matina Horner* researched motivation, intelligence, and achievement in women, coining the phrase "fear of success." Eliminate (B) because *Anna Freud* posited that every child should be recognized as their own autonomous self. Eliminate (C) because *Karen Horney* posited the theory that neurosis stems from anxiety from interpersonal relationships. Eliminate (D) because *Diana Baumrind's* theory is about parenting styles. Keep (E) because *Mary Ainsworth* posited attachment theory, which encompasses secure versus insecure attachment. The correct answer is (E).

152. **B**   The question asks which of the following is a negative symptom of schizophrenia. Positive symptoms are delusional or disorganized, while negative symptoms are muted affect or behavior. Use Process of Elimination to evaluate the answer choices. Eliminate (A) because *delusions* are positive symptoms. Keep (B) because a *flat affect* is a muted expression of emotion. Eliminate (C) because *hallucinations* are delusional and therefore positive symptoms. Eliminate (D) because *neologisms* are made-up words or new uses of old words, which would most likely appear in disorganized speech, a positive symptom. Eliminate (E) because *disorganized behavior* is a positive symptom. The correct answer is (B).

153. **B** The question asks which is true about the sentence, *Two bears and a donkey lived happily ever after.* Use Process of Elimination to evaluate the answer choices. Eliminate (A) because *deep structure* is the greater abstract meaning of a sentence, but the replacement of the animals changes its meaning. Keep (B) because the word *bears* is made up of two *morphemes,* the smallest components of meaningful language. *Bear* and *-s* both contain meaning as the animal and the suffix that denotes plurality. Eliminate (C) because *lived* has semantic meaning, but so do the rest of the words since each word gives meaning. Eliminate (D) because sentences are structured on *syntactical* rules, not *phonological* rules. Eliminate (E) because sentences rely on *syntax* and cannot exist without it. The correct answer is (B).

154. **A** The question asks the sentence, *Two bears and a donkey lived happily ever after,* uniquely exhibits which of the following, according to Chomsky's work. Use Process of Elimination to evaluate the answer choices. Keep (A) because the *surface structure* of a sentence refers to the specific words used to represent a concept, and each of these words contributes to that specific representation. Eliminate (B) because the *deep structure* is the greater abstract meaning of a sentence. Eliminate (C) because the *semantic differential* is a scale that rates connotations and levels of meaning, which is not unique to this sentence. Eliminate (D) because *morphemes* are the smallest components of meaningful language, none of which are unique to this particular sentence. Eliminate (E) because *phonemes* are the smallest units of sound, and none of these are unique to this sentence. The correct answer is (A).

155. **D** The question asks what Bartlett found about memory. Bartlett found that memory is largely reconstructive. Eliminate (A) because *procedural* memory is responsible for motor coordination and doing tasks. Eliminate (B) because *episodic* memory is recall of events. Eliminate (C) because *declarative* memory is another word for *explicit* memory, which is the recall of events and information that can be recalled. Keep (D) because *reconstructive* is consistent with Bartlett's work. Eliminate (E) because *sensory* memory comes directly from sensory input into the working memory. The correct answer is (D).

156. **E** The question asks which of the following figures is known for developing field theory. Field theory, which studies the patterns of interaction between individuals and the entire environment or community, was developed by Kurt Lewin. The correct answer is (E).

157. **B** The question asks which of the following brain areas would most likely be used for complex problem-solving. Use Process of Elimination to evaluate the answer choices. Eliminate (A) because the *occipital lobe* is primarily responsible for vision. Keep (B) because the *frontal lobe* is responsible for logic, problem-solving, and other complex tasks that make humans unique. Eliminate (C) because the *cerebellum* is responsible for voluntary movement, balance, and coordination. Eliminate (D) because the *hypothalamus* is responsible for homeostasis and regulation. Eliminate (E) because the *hippocampus* serves many functions of emotion, learning, and memory as well as serving as part of the limbic system. The correct answer is (B).

158. **C** The question asks what group polarization is. It is a tendency for a group to become more extreme in its viewpoint. Use Process of Elimination to evaluate the answer choices. Eliminate (A) because the group does not necessarily need to have a *common enemy* to become extreme in a viewpoint. Eliminate (B) because the group that becomes extreme is a complete unit; there are not two groups, but rather the individuals within the group reinforce each other in a consensus of sentiment. Keep (C) because the group would *feel strongly about the dominant viewpoint.* Eliminate (D) because while an *ingroup* may *identify an outgroup,* it does not have to be the case to become more extreme in a viewpoint. Eliminate (E) because group polarization requires members to reinforce and agree with one another, not to have *deadlock,* or disagreement, *during decision making.* The correct answer is (C).

159. **D** The question asks which of the following types of statistics to test his results for statistical significance and then draw conclusions about his population. Use Process of Elimination to evaluate the answer

choices. Eliminate (A) because *correlations* cannot show causation and therefore cannot be used to draw conclusions. Eliminate (B) because *frequency distributions* show how frequently an event occurs, which will not show statistical significance of a result, necessarily. Eliminate (C) because *descriptive statistics* do not deal with statistical significance. Keep (D) because *inferential statistics* matches the definition described in the question. Eliminate (E) because while *referential statistics* allows psychologists to make inferences, they are usually mathematical likelihoods of scenarios happening. The correct answer is (D).

160. **A** The question asks what Edward Tolman's theory of motivation postulated. Tolman posited that behavior can be motivated from a variety of stimuli, not simply needs, but also curiosity, attitudes, changing conditions, and goals. Use Process of Elimination to evaluate the answer choices. Keep (A) because *expectancy* and *value* could motivate an organism to act. Eliminate (B) because *motivation* is not solely based on *need*. Eliminate (C) because *success* is not part of Tolman's theory. Eliminate (D) because while *drive* might be a motivation, *habit* is not a necessary part of Tolman. Eliminate (E) because *ability* and *practice* are not underlying motivations. The correct answer is (A).

161. **B** The question asks what two-year-old Billy is most likely bothered by. Think of the different theories of development that could aid in evaluating answer choices. Use Process of Elimination to evaluate the answer choices. Eliminate (A) because the *Oedipus complex* happens during the phallic stage, which is roughly around ages 3–6. Keep (B) because *separation anxiety and stranger anxiety* would be supported by both Ainsworth's experiments of attachment theory as well as Erikson's Autonomy vs. Shame and Doubt, The marker to transition from Trust vs. Mistrust to Autonomy vs. Shame and Doubt is stranger anxiety. Eliminate (C) because *castration anxiety* is a fear of repercussion for acting on incestuous inclinations during Freud's phallic stage of development. Eliminate (D) because while *separation anxiety* works, *trust anxiety* should be resolved already according to Erikson's Trust vs. Mistrust stage, which generally happens roughly from ages 0–18 months. Eliminate (E) because *expression anxiety* is not a term used for development, and *mobility anxiety* is applicable to aging adults who fear losing mobility and freedom. The correct answer is (B).

162. **A** The question asks why a woman might choose not to work, according to Matina Horner. Use Process of Elimination to evaluate the answer choices. Matina Horner researched motivation, intelligence, and achievement in women, coining the phrase "fear of success," which matches (A). The correct answer is (A).

163. **D** The question asks which of the following is true of schizophrenia. Use Process of Elimination to evaluate the answer choices. Eliminate (A) because schizophrenia does not discriminate between *class*. Eliminate (B) because while there are *biological* factors to schizophrenia, it is not *entirely* so. Eliminate (C) because *strong social history* would likely receive more support, and therefore might have a better chance of recovery than others without such a support system. Keep (D) because *reactive* schizophrenia is more severe than *process* schizophrenia at the onset, but reactive schizophrenia also has a better prognosis than process schizophrenia. Eliminate (E) for the same reason as (D). The correct answer is (D).

164. **C** The question asks at which of the following cognitive states most five-year-old children should be, according to Piaget. Use Process of Elimination to evaluate the answer choices. Eliminate (A) because *accommodational* is not one of Piaget's stages. Eliminate (B) because the *sensorimotor* stage is for infants. Keep (C) because the *preoperational* stage encompasses young children roughly ages 3–6, so a five-year-old would fit into this category. Eliminate (D) because the *concrete operational* stage involves school children, who are too old. Eliminate (E) because the *formation operational* stage happens in adolescence. The correct answer is (C).

165.   **A**   The question asks which of the following is referred to as white matter in the brain and spine. *Nerve fibers made of axons* are referred to as white matter. The correct answer is (A).

166.   **E**   The question asks how to obtain a random sample of students in a lecture hall. Use Process of Elimination to evaluate the answer choices. Eliminate (A) because *students who raise their hands* are volunteering, which could create the self-selection bias. Eliminate (B) because selecting by a characteristic is not *random*. Eliminate (C) for the same reason as (B); randomization should be done mathematically. Eliminate (D) because the students have *volunteered* and are thus not randomly selected. Keep (E) because *every fifth student* is the most mathematical, systematic selection proposed, which would be the best attempt at randomization. The correct answer is (E).

167.   **C**   The question asks what the knowledge used to categorize and understand new stimuli is best known as. The question states that *In general, people attach concepts and attributes to items and events*. Use Process of Elimination to evaluate the answer choices. Eliminate (A) because an *algorithm* is a series of deductions until an answer is reached. This is how math works, but it is not necessarily how humans understand new stimuli. Eliminate (B) because a *heuristic* is a rule-of-thumb estimation, which sometimes can help with new stimuli, but it can also lead to incorrect conclusions. A heuristic is also not a person's knowledge set. Keep (C) because a *schema* is a person's mental "filing cabinet," so to speak, in which the "folders" classify and organize information based on attributes and concepts. Eliminate (D) because a *mental set* is a framework for thinking about a problem, making it easier to solve similar problems, but can inhibit in other situations. It is not the knowledge set itself. Eliminate (E) because *metacognition* is thinking about thinking, which does not refer to a knowledge set. The correct answer is (C).

168.   **D**   The question asks what a sign stimulus serves to trigger. A sign stimulus triggers a reaction, usually one that is innate. Use Process of Elimination to evaluate the answer choices. Eliminate (A) because a *homing mechanism* is a way for animals to place themselves in space. Eliminate (B) because a *variable-interval ratio* is a reward schedule, and the reaction to the stimulus is not done for reward, but rather innately. Eliminate (C) because a *simple reflex* is a monosynaptic reflex. Keep (D) because a *fixed action pattern* is a mostly innate reaction that results in the same behavior every time the stimulus is presented. Eliminate (E) because a *pheromone reaction* is a chemical reaction that animals release into the air to elicit a response from other animals of the same species. The correct answer is (D).

169.   **B**   The question asks which of the following exemplifies the illusion of control. The *illusion of control* is a person's tendency to overestimate their ability to control what is around them. Use Process of Elimination to evaluate the answer choices. Eliminate (A) because *a teacher who believes she influences her students* is likely correct that her students model behavior via observational learning and learn more explicitly from her as well. Keep (B) because *superstitious behavior* is behavior that is meant to induce an outcome, even when there might not be any correlation between the behavior and the outcome. Eliminate (C) because practicing *positive imagery* to remain calm is helping to gain control of one's emotions, which in turn may impact the boy's performance. Eliminate (D) because the *string around her finger* is both a physiological and visual cue to remember to do something. Eliminate (E) because *punishment is a deterrent* to undesired behavior. The correct answer is (B).

170.   **A**   The question asks which of the following statements about sensations is false. Use Process of Elimination to evaluate the answer choices. Keep (A) because *Meissner's corpuscles* are sensory nerve endings that are sensitive to *mechanical* stimuli, not *temperature* stimuli. Eliminate (B) because it is true that *the organ of corti is the technical name for the ear*. Eliminate (C) because *papillae* is the formal name for taste buds. Eliminate (D) because the *tympanic membrane* is the formal name for the eardrum. Eliminate (E) because the *olfactory bulb* is located at the base of the brain. The correct answer is (A).

171. **D** The question asks which of the following most effectively lessens group conflict. Use Process of Elimination to evaluate the answer choices. Eliminate (A) because the F in an *F-scale* test stands for fascist, and it measures the authoritarian personality in a variety of different dimensions of personality. Therefore, different situations could elicit different dimensions of personality, and high scores in the different dimensions would not necessarily *lessen* group conflict; it might even make certain situations worse. Eliminate (B) because *groupthink* may make it seem as if there is consensus among members; it might actually be that individual dissenters did not feel comfortable speaking up, or that there was hostility against alternative approaches or viewpoints. Eliminate (C) because while a *charismatic leader* might inspire some, it does not necessarily lessen conflict. Keep (D) because a *superordinate goal* gives individuals a common goal to work toward, leading them to work together instead of in conflict with one another. Eliminate (E) because *similarity of individuals in the group* does not mean the group will have less conflict. The correct answer is (D).

172. **C** The question asks what Harlow called his conclusion that with every novel problem it took the monkeys less time to learn how to solve it. The question states that *in a series of learning experiments... Harlow asserted that monkeys gained a sort of cumulative knowledge about solving problems.* Use Process of Elimination to evaluate the answer choices. Eliminate (A) because *higher-order conditioning* is a form of classical conditioning, and there does not seem to be evidence of association here. Eliminate (B) because *simultaneous conditioning* is also a classical conditioning concept. Keep (C) because *learning to learn* is the act of gaining knowledge or skills through study or a series of experiences, which matches the description. Eliminate (D) because there does not seem to be any evidence of *trained anticipation* in the description. Eliminate (E) because the description never mentions the learning to be *instinctive*. The correct answer is (C).

173. **C** The question asks which concept the details of the question stem exemplify. The question states that *A city has different-sounding sirens for police, fire, and hospital vehicles.* The question continues that *each of these vehicles can emit varying patterns of the sirens.* Already, there seems to be a lot of different siren sounds in this city. The question continues to state that *regardless of the type of siren heard...the cars all know to pull to the right and clear the way.* It seems that the type of siren does not matter, rather that all sirens have the same effect. Use Process of Elimination to evaluate the answer choices. Eliminate (A) because *stimulus-response theory* simply suggests that behavior is a series of responses to stimuli, but this doesn't explain the lack of discrimination between the types of stimuli in the question. Eliminate (B) because *stimulus discrimination* is the opposite of what is happening here: there would rather be a different reaction to each type of stimulus. Keep (C) because *stimulus generalization* means that multiple related stimuli produce the same reaction. Eliminate (D) because *forward conditioning* would have to do with the timing of classical conditioning presentation. Eliminate (E) because there are not any rewards or punishments listed in the question. The correct answer is (C).

174. **E** The question asks which of the following is NOT central to psychoanalytic theory. With NOT questions, eliminate what IS true. Use Process of Elimination to evaluate the answer choices. Eliminate (A) because *aggression* is an id-related instinct that humans try to control. Eliminate (B) because *libido* is Freud's concept of psychic energy that comes from sexual urges. Eliminate (C) because *free association* is a method of accessing the subconscious in psychoanalytic theory. Eliminate (D) because *transference* is the concept of transferring feelings and emotions to another person or object, often toward the therapist. Keep (E) because *animus* is a concept of masculine expression in Jungian psychoanalytic theory, which is somewhat of an offshoot from its Freudian roots and *not* a central concept of psychoanalytic theory. The correct answer is (E).

175. **D** The question asks what the vestibular sacs in the inner ear are essential for. The vestibular sacs are essential for physical balance and equilibrium. The correct answer is (D).

176. **A**   The question asks what type of recall device Robin used based on the description. The question states that Robin *successfully remembered all the frozen foods, and then all the snack foods*. She is essentially breaking the items into related groups. Use Process of Elimination to evaluate the answer choices. Keep (A) because *clustering* breaks items into related groups. Eliminate (B) because while *chunking* has to do with remembering things in groups, it has to do more with location and physical grouping. Eliminate (C) because *mnemonics* are devices to help remember each item, such as the first letter of each item creating a word, such as ROY G. BIV to remember the rainbow. Eliminate (D) because Robin never used *imagery* to imagine the items. Eliminate (E) because *mediation* is a way to describe the relationship between an independent and a dependent variable. The correct answer is (A).

177. **B**   The question asks what happens to the meaning that a child initially gives to a word, according to Vygotsky. Vygotsky states that the child's understanding of a word will *undergo change* as the child learns more nuance of the word through experience. The correct answer is (B).

178. **A**   The question asks what the Bayley Scales of Infant Development do. The Bayley Scales of Infant Development measure cognitive, language, motor, adaptive, and social-emotional development in children 0–42 months of age. Use Process of Elimination to evaluate the answer choices. Keep (A) because by monitoring cognitive development, the test could help to identify cognitive developmental delays. Eliminate (B) and (C) because the test does not measure *intelligence,* but rather development. Eliminate (D) because this test has nothing to do with *school placement*. Eliminate (E) because *cognition* and cognitive development are not the same thing. The correct answer is (A).

179. **C**   The question asks which of the following is an obsessive-compulsive disorder that involves pulling out one's own hair. The name of this disorder is trichotillomania. If you did not know this term, use Process of Elimination to evaluate the answer choices. Eliminate (A) because *Pick's disease* is a type of dementia, and would therefore fall under neurocognitive disorders, not obsessive-compulsive disorders. Eliminate (B) because *dysthymia,* also known as persistent depressive disorder, is a depressive disorder, not an obsessive-compulsive disorder. Eliminate (D) because *conversion disorder* falls under somatic symptom and related disorders, not obsessive-compulsive. Eliminate (E) because *follicle phobia,* called trichophobia, is a phobia and therefore an anxiety disorder, not an obsessive-compulsive disorder. The correct answer is (C).

180. **B**   The question asks what one of the few gender differences seems to be, according to Maccoby and Jacklin. Maccoby and Jacklin found that females tend to have greater verbal ability, while males tend to have greater visual/spatial ability, though this is still debated. Use Process of Elimination to evaluate the answer choices. Eliminate (A) because this is the opposite of their findings, that there is *better visual ability in girls*. Keep (B), which is consistent that there is *better spatial ability in boys*. Eliminate (C) because the assertion that there seems to be *more compassion in girls* is a myth, not a fact. Eliminate (D) because the scientists never found anything specifically about *science skills in boys*, only spatial abilities. Eliminate (E) as well because *better mathematical skills in boys* is a stereotype and myth, even though it is related to better *spatial ability*. The correct answer is (B).

181. **E**   The question asks what the limbic system is crucial for regulating. The limbic system is crucial in regulating *emotion*. The correct answer is (E).

182. **D**   The question asks for what Rochel Gelman criticized Piaget's cognitive stages. Rochel Gelman's research into cognitive development questions the broad stages, especially those of preoperational and concrete operational stages and their milestones, that this process actually might be more fluid. Use Process of Elimination to evaluate the answer choices. Eliminate (A) because Gelman does not dispute the stages *ending at adolescence*. Eliminate (B) because Piaget never used *unnatural testing instruments*. Eliminate (C) because Piaget did not focus on *gender* in his development. Keep (D)

because *underestimating preschoolers' ability* would fall in the timeline of the preoperational stage, and therefore might need some reframing. Eliminate (E) because Gelman's research is earlier in cognitive development than *adolescence*. The correct answer is (D).

183. **B** The question asks when a subject would most quickly find the letter "C," according to feature detection theory. Feature detection theory posits that features are more easily detected when noise around them is reduced, so similar looking letters would create more noise while different looking letters would create less. Use Process of Elimination to evaluate the answer choices. Eliminate (A), (C), (D), and (E) because "Q" and "O" are both round looking letters and therefore closer in appearance to "C," creating more noise. Keep (B) because "M" and "T" are both linear instead of curved, which would create less noise to locate the curve of a "C." The correct answer is (B).

184. **B** The question asks which of the following figures introduced the logic theorist, the first computer model of human problem solving. Allen Newell, Herbert Simon, and Cliff Shaw first introduced the logic theorist in 1956. The correct answer is (B).

185. **C** The question asks which of the following tests allows unconscious motivation, particularly the need for achievement, to be expressed. Use Process of Elimination to evaluate the answer choices. Eliminate (A) because the *Minnesota Multiphasic Personality Inventory (MMPI)* has many different uses, from personality tests to job screening, but it primarily tests personality type, not *motivation*. Eliminate (B) because the *Goodenough Draw-A-Person Test* examines nonverbal intelligence to screen for behavioral and/or emotional disorders, not *motivation*. Keep (C) because the *Thematic Apperception Test (TAT)* is a projection test to help show an individual's perception of interpersonal relationships, and this can show *motivation*, particularly *the need for achievement*. Eliminate (D) because the *California Personality Inventory (CPI)* tests an individual's interpersonal behavior in social contexts, which does not focus on *achievement*. Eliminate (E) because the *Q-sort* is a personality test to test cultural criterion of "truth," which is a *perception*, not a *motivation*. The correct answer is (C).

186. **D** The question asks which theory Milgram used to explain urbanities' tendency to be less social than country dwellers. Use Process of Elimination to evaluate the answer choices. Eliminate (A) because *social loafing* happens within group interactions, regardless of demographic or locale. Eliminate (B) because *inoculation* is a process of changing someone's attitude, which does not rely on a person's location. Eliminate (C) because *social facilitation* is also a phenomenon that happens within a group, regardless of dwelling space. Keep (D) because *stimulus-overload* refers to the increased stimuli urbanites experience in a city, making them want to shut out stimuli when they can, and this can lead to less social behavior. Eliminate (E) because *self-monitoring* is not specific to a location. The correct answer is (D).

187. **A** The question asks what Abraham Maslow is well known for. Maslow was a humanist whose most recognizable contribution was the Hierarchy of Needs. Use Process of Elimination to evaluate the answer choices. Keep (A) because while it is vague, it is true that he was a *forerunner of the humanist movement*. Eliminate (B) because he did not create *cognitive-behavioral therapy*. Eliminate (C) because Carl Rogers, another humanist, created *client-centered therapy*. Eliminate (D) because Maslow did not have anything to do with *object-relations theory*. Eliminate (E) because the *archetype concept* has to do with self-concept and perception, not with humanism. The correct answer is (A).

188. **A** The question asks which parenting style produces the most well-adjusted children, according to Diana Baumrind. Baumrind's parental types are authoritarian, authoritative, and permissive, in decreasing levels of severity and strictness. Use Process of Elimination to evaluate the answer choices. Keep (A) because *authoritative* parenting was considered the most effective, balancing rules with allowing the child freedom to make decisions on their own as well. Eliminate (B) because *authoritarian* parenting

consists of rigid rules that do not allow the child much freedom, making the child more prone to rebelling or developing another maladaptive set of coping mechanisms. Eliminate (C) because *permissive* parenting often is not structured enough for the child to feel secure, which can lead to adjustment issues later on. Eliminate (D) because *attached* is a term that is more associated with Ainsworth's Strange Situation experiments and attachment theory. Eliminate (E) because not all are true. The correct answer is (A).

189. **B**   The question asks which of the following sensory system components is said to "accommodate." Ciliary muscles change the shape of the *lens* during the accommodation reflex. The correct answer is (B).

190. **C**   The question asks which of the following areas is analyzed for activity in lie detector tests. Use Process of Elimination to evaluate the answer choices. Eliminate (A) because the *central nervous system* consists of the brain and the spinal cord, which controls one's interpretation of an environment, but is not receiving or directing somatic signals directly. Eliminate (B) because the *somatic nervous system* is responsible for movement, and most people are not moving during lie detector tests. Keep (C) because the *sympathetic nervous system* is the body's involuntary response to stressful or dangerous situations, so feelings of nervousness would fall under this system. Eliminate (D) because the *parasympathetic nervous system* works to slow the heart rate and conserve energy, which is the opposite of what happens when someone becomes nervous. Eliminate (E) because *EEG patterns* show waveforms emitted from the brain. The correct answer is (C).

191. **B**   The question asks which theory of forgetting would support the outcome if the two groups recalled the numbers equally as accurately, according to the details of the question stem. The question stem states that *Subjects…attempt to remember the social security number of the person sitting next to them.* The question continues that *half the subjects were told to put their heads down on their desks for 3 minutes* while *the other half are told to solve math problems for 3 minutes.* Both groups are completing different tasks here, but for the same amount of time. Use Process of Elimination to evaluate the answer choices. Eliminate (A) because *interference theory* would suggest that the group doing math problems would perform worse since the activity of manipulating numerical equations should interfere with their recall. Keep (B) because *trace theory* suggests that there has been encoding to remember information in the brain already, so the intermediary action would not necessarily harm the encoding. Eliminate (C) because *proactive inhibition theory* is the idea that previously learned material may hinder subsequent learning, which is not present here. Eliminate (D) because *proactive interference theory* would mean that they would perform worse on a later task after having learned a first task. Eliminate (E) because *association theory* suggests that a subject creates an association between a stimulus and a response, such as in classical conditioning. The correct answer is (B).

192. **E**   The question asks what Harlow found in experiments with social isolation in monkeys EXCEPT. Monkeys in this experiment exhibited abnormal behavior well into their adult lives. With EXCEPT questions, eliminate what IS true. Eliminate (A) because it is true that *socially isolated adult females did not exhibit normal maternal behavior.* Eliminate (B) because it is true that *adult males did not exhibit normal sexual behavior.* Eliminate (C) because *exposure to peer pressure is an important factor in developing mature behavior.* Eliminate (D) because *being reared with other young monkeys provides positive socialization.* Keep (E) because in all the experimentation, nothing took the place of the monkeys' *biological parents.* The correct answer is (E).

193. **E**   The question asks which kind of scale can best organize the data in the question. The question states that *Five hundred undergraduates were asked to report their favorite television show from a list of 100 different shows.* Use Process of Elimination to evaluate the answer choices. Eliminate (A) because an *ordinal* classifies data into ordered classes, but it does not appear that there is a hierarchy in the shows

from the question details. Eliminate (B) because an *interval* scale shows numerical values of distance between any two adjacent attributes. Eliminate (C) because an *F-scale* refers to a personality test, which is irrelevant here. Eliminate (D) because a *ratio* can show relationships between two or more values, but it might not be the most useful to show overall popularity. Keep (E) because a *nominal* label is one that groups categories and other nonquantitative values, such as comedy, drama, etc., which could be useful in providing data for this study. The correct answer is (E).

194. **D** The question asks what the set of all possible moves a chess player could make would be an example of. Use Process of Elimination to evaluate the answer choices. Eliminate (A) because *functional fixedness* is the notion of using an object only for its intended purpose. Eliminate (B) because a *heuristic* is a mental rule-of-thumb that actually might lead the player to a narrowed mindset instead of viewing all the options in the list. Eliminate (C) because someone with a *mental set* would likely approach the moves from one particular set of parameters instead of listing all possible moves. Keep (D) because *a problem space* is the entire range of possible solutions to a problem, which is what the player has created. Eliminate (E) because *inductive reasoning* is a method of creating generalizations based on prior information or anecdotal evidence. The correct answer is (D).

195. **A** The question asks which of the following factors would NOT increase the likelihood that the speaker will convince the audience, based on the details of the paragraph. With NOT questions, eliminate what IS true. The paragraph states that *A speaker is attempting to convince the audience of listeners that a particular theory of evolution is correct.* The paragraph continues that *The audience consists of 500 adult men and women.* The most effective route of persuasion is the central route, which has to do with the quality of the message that is delivered. Use Process of Elimination to evaluate the answer choices. Keep (A) because the speaker *confidently [telling] the audience it will be convinced* is NOT part of the central or peripheral routes of persuasion. Therefore, this approach is less effective because it is not concerned with *content* or *speaker*. Eliminate (B) because a *debate with an opponent* would appeal to the central route persuasion because it is about the content of the message. Eliminate (C) because while the speaker being *similar to the audience* is a peripheral route of persuasion, it still may have some power in persuading the audience. Eliminate (D) because whether the *speaker is perceived as an expert* is another variable in persuasion. Eliminate (E) because *anecdotal information* is part of the central route of delivering a convincing message. The correct answer is (A).

196. **B** The question asks which of the following statements would be true of the description, according to the sleeper effect. The paragraph states that *A speaker is attempting to convince an audience of listeners that a particular theory of evolution is correct.* The paragraph continues that *The audience consists of 500 adult men and women.* The most effective route of persuasion is the central route, which has to do with the quality of the message that is delivered. The sleeper effect is a delay in the effectiveness of a message because of a discounting or negative cue from either the message or the presenter. Use Process of Elimination to evaluate the answer choices. Eliminate (A) because *individuals in the audience who do not pay close attention* are neither the message nor the presenter. Keep (B) because *a speaker with low credibility* would be a negative cue that could discount the message at first. Eliminate (C) because *following the majority opinion* has nothing to do with a negative cue from the message or the messenger. Eliminate (D) because *individuals who previously had no opinion on the topic will be convinced* suggests that there was no sleeper effect, that the message worked immediately. Eliminate (E) because the *passage of time* would do the opposite with a sleeper effect; the negative cue would make it seem unconvincing at first, but then become *more* convincing with time. The correct answer is (B).

197. **D** The question asks what the rat pressing the bar three days later is an example of, based on details of the question stem. The question states that *A rat is conditioned to press a lever for food* and is *rewarded with food every time.* This shows a continuous reward schedule. The question continues to state that

the experimenter stops rewarding the rat for this behavior and eventually the rat stops pressing the bar altogether. Continuous reward schedules tend to have a medium to fast extinction rate, but that behavior could have a spontaneous recovery over the passage of time. Use Process of Elimination to evaluate the answer choices. Eliminate (A) because *incidental learning* is unplanned learning or a byproduct of planned learning. Eliminate (B) because *latent responding* is a delay between the stimulus and the response, and there is no stimulus that the rat is reacting to here. Eliminate (C) because *positive transfer* is an improved learning process because of prior learning, of which there is none described. Keep (D) because *spontaneous recovery* is the reappearance of a behavior after extinction. Eliminate (E) because *systematic desensitization* is a form of diminishing a reaction to a stimulus. The correct answer is (D).

198. **B** The question asks during which of the following periods is an individual likely to display the most stereotypical sex-typed behavior. Use Process of Elimination to evaluate the answer choices. Eliminate (A) because *adolescence* would fall under Erikson's stage of Identity vs. Role Confusion, which is focused on finding a sense of one's true self. Keep (B) because *young adulthood* would fall under Erikson's stage of Intimacy vs. Isolation, in which individuals seek intimate relationships with others, both platonically and romantically. It would therefore be fitting to exhibit sex-typed behavior during this stage of life. Eliminate (C) because *middle adulthood* focuses on Generativity vs. Stagnation, in which finding fulfilling work or purpose in life is the focus. Eliminate (D) because *old age* would be focused on Integrity vs. Despair, finding deeper meaning and wisdom from one's life. Eliminate (E) because while Freud refers to childhood as a series of psychosexual development, there is no one stage in which children outwardly exhibit sex-typed *behavior*. The correct answer is (B).

199. **A** The question asks which of the following is associated with Jung's analytical therapy. Use Process of Elimination to evaluate the answer choices. Keep (A) because *dream analysis* is closely associated with Jung's analytical theory. Eliminate (B) because *transference* is a Freudian defense mechanism in which the individual transfers feelings for one person onto another, usually the therapist. Eliminate (C) because *focus on libido* was a Freudian concept of seeking pleasure and following sexual desires or urges. Eliminate (D) because Freud also used *hypnosis* quite frequently to access the subconscious. Eliminate (E) because Freud coined *defense mechanisms* to explain individuals' reactions, thoughts, and behaviors. The correct answer is (A).

200. **D** The question asks which of the following figures pioneered the concept of the inferiority complex. The psychologist who pioneered this term was psychoanalyst Alfred Adler. The correct answer is (D).

201. **C** The question asks what happens to the study. The question states that *A study requires that a group of college undergraduates be present for a problem-solving workshop every other Saturday.* The question goes on to state that *Eventually, a number a students who want to attend fall football games drop out of the study.* Use Process of Elimination to evaluate the answer choices. Eliminate (A) because *cohort effects* occur when subjects of roughly the same age indirectly affect the results of a study due to common age-related factors. Eliminate (B) because the *social desirability bias* describes how individuals will monitor their behaviors to paint a positive picture to those around them, but there does not appear to be anything about the students wanting to impress each other in the question. Keep (C) because *selective attrition* is the idea that some participants in a study are more likely to drop out than others. Eliminate (D) because it is unclear that the study used *nonrandom sampling* to assemble the initial group. Eliminate (E) because *reactance* is a concept in which a person is reacting to unpleasant motivation, whether something would be taken away from them or something bad would happen if they chose a different option, thus limiting their decision-making. The correct answer is (C).

202. **E** The question asks which concept would be illustrated by the example of a married couple's disagreement over why the husband rarely cleans up the house. Use Process of Elimination to evaluate the answer choices. Eliminate (A) because the *false consensus bias* would mean that there was some sort of

consensus, but there is a disagreement here. Eliminate (B) because *base-rate fallacy* is the tendency to ignore statistics and use irrelevant data, which is not present in this scenario. Eliminate (C) because *reciprocal interaction* refers to an exchange between two individuals doing a similar, mutually beneficial action, and that is not the case here. Eliminate (D) because the *fundamental attribution error* attributes one characteristic or behavior to the person's overall being or personality. The wife never says the husband is a bad person because he rarely cleans up the house. Keep (E) because the *actor-observer attributional divergence* because the attribution for a behavior may be divergent based on whether the person is the one doing the behavior or the one observing the behavior. Here, the wife is observing the behavior and attributing it one way while the husband is the doer of those actions and attributes the behavior another way. The correct answer is (E).

203. **E**   The question asks what Vicky is likely suffering from given the information in the question. The question states that *After a serious head injury, Vicky could not remember the events that led up to the accident.* The fact that Vicky *could not remember* suggests an amnesia of some sort. Use Process of Elimination to evaluate the answer choices. Eliminate (A), (B), and (C), which are not amnesia-related conditions. The question states that she could not remember *the events that led up to the accident*, meaning she could not remember events before the accident. This is *retrograde amnesia*. The correct answer is (E).

204. **D**   The question asks which of the following is the central source of conflict in Freud's revised psychoanalytic theory. Use Process of Elimination to evaluate the answer choices. Eliminate (A) because the *libido* was a part of Freud's original theory. Eliminate (B) because Freud's theory always included the id, the ego, and the *superego*. Eliminate (C) because the *secondary process* is a logical way of thought, usually associated with the ego, and was always a part of Freud's theory. Keep (D) because *Eros and Thanatos* are the revised life and death instincts, respectively. Eliminate (E) because the *pleasure principle* existed in Freud's original theory of the instinct to seek pleasure and avoid pain. The correct answer is (D).

205. **C**   The question asks which of the following has been most closely related to heart disease. Heart disease is most closely linked to higher anxiety levels due to higher chronic stress. Use Process of Elimination to evaluate the answer choices. Eliminate (A) because an *internal locus of control* would most likely lessen a person's anxiety levels since they feel in control of their actions and outcomes. Eliminate (B) because while *authoritarianism* may lead to increased rules, regulations, and potentially stress, it is not inherently bound to do so. Keep (C) because *chronic stress* is a combination of psychological and physiological factors. Chronic stress can lead to elevated blood pressure, which is a common risk factor for heart disease. Eliminate (D) because *introversion* does not indicate that someone is experiencing high levels of stress, but rather that they choose to recharge themselves through solitary or small group activities as opposed to large groups. Eliminate (E) because *conscientiousness* causes people to more often than not be organized and put together, but not necessarily stressed. The correct answer is (C).

The Princeton Review®

1. NAME
Enter your last name, first name initial (given name), and middle initial if you have one.
Omit spaces, apostrophes, Jr., II., etc.

Last Name only (Family Name or Surname) - First 15 Letters | First Name Initial | Middle Initial

DO NOT USE INK

Use only a pencil with soft, black lead (No. 2 or HB) to complete this answer sheet.
Be sure to fill in completely the space that corresponds to your answer choice.
Completely erase any errors or stray marks.

BE SURE EACH MARK IS DARK AND COMPLETELY FILLS THE INTENDED SPACE AS ILLUSTRATED HERE: ●
YOU MAY FIND MORE RESPONSE SPACES THAN YOU NEED. IF SO, PLEASE LEAVE THEM BLANK.

(Answer grid: questions 1–115, each with options A B C D E)

2.
YOUR NAME: _____
(Print)   Last Name (Family or Surname)   First Name (Given)   M.I.

MAILING ADDRESS: _____
(Print)   P.O. Box or Street Address

City _____ State or Province

Country _____ ZIP or Postal Code

CENTER: _____
City   State or Province

Country _____ Center Number   Room Number

SIGNATURE: _____

3. DATE OF BIRTH
Month | Day | Year
○ Jan.
○ Feb.
○ Mar.
○ April
○ May
○ June
○ July
○ Aug.
○ Sept.
○ Oct.
○ Nov.
○ Dec.

4. LAST FOUR DIGITS OF SOCIAL SECURITY NUMBER
(U.S.A. Only)

5. REGISTRATION NUMBER
(from your admission ticket)

6. TITLE CODE
(on back cover of your test book)

7. TEST NAME (on back cover of your test book)
_____

FORM CODE (on back cover of your test book)
_____

8. TEST BOOK SERIAL NUMBER
(number in upper right corner of front cover of your test book)

SIDE 2

SUBJECT TEST

COMPLETE THE CERTIFICATION STATEMENT, THEN TURN ANSWER SHEET OVER TO SIDE 1.

BE SURE EACH MARK IS DARK AND COMPLETELY FILLS THE INTENDED SPACE AS ILLUSTRATED HERE: ●.
YOU MAY FIND MORE RESPONSE SPACES THAN YOU NEED. IF SO, PLEASE LEAVE THEM BLANK.

116 Ⓐ Ⓑ Ⓒ Ⓓ Ⓔ	148 Ⓐ Ⓑ Ⓒ Ⓓ Ⓔ	180 Ⓐ Ⓑ Ⓒ Ⓓ Ⓔ	212 Ⓐ Ⓑ Ⓒ Ⓓ Ⓔ
117 Ⓐ Ⓑ Ⓒ Ⓓ Ⓔ	149 Ⓐ Ⓑ Ⓒ Ⓓ Ⓔ	181 Ⓐ Ⓑ Ⓒ Ⓓ Ⓔ	213 Ⓐ Ⓑ Ⓒ Ⓓ Ⓔ
118 Ⓐ Ⓑ Ⓒ Ⓓ Ⓔ	150 Ⓐ Ⓑ Ⓒ Ⓓ Ⓔ	182 Ⓐ Ⓑ Ⓒ Ⓓ Ⓔ	214 Ⓐ Ⓑ Ⓒ Ⓓ Ⓔ
119 Ⓐ Ⓑ Ⓒ Ⓓ Ⓔ	151 Ⓐ Ⓑ Ⓒ Ⓓ Ⓔ	183 Ⓐ Ⓑ Ⓒ Ⓓ Ⓔ	215 Ⓐ Ⓑ Ⓒ Ⓓ Ⓔ
120 Ⓐ Ⓑ Ⓒ Ⓓ Ⓔ	152 Ⓐ Ⓑ Ⓒ Ⓓ Ⓔ	184 Ⓐ Ⓑ Ⓒ Ⓓ Ⓔ	216 Ⓐ Ⓑ Ⓒ Ⓓ Ⓔ
121 Ⓐ Ⓑ Ⓒ Ⓓ Ⓔ	153 Ⓐ Ⓑ Ⓒ Ⓓ Ⓔ	185 Ⓐ Ⓑ Ⓒ Ⓓ Ⓔ	217 Ⓐ Ⓑ Ⓒ Ⓓ Ⓔ
122 Ⓐ Ⓑ Ⓒ Ⓓ Ⓔ	154 Ⓐ Ⓑ Ⓒ Ⓓ Ⓔ	186 Ⓐ Ⓑ Ⓒ Ⓓ Ⓔ	218 Ⓐ Ⓑ Ⓒ Ⓓ Ⓔ
123 Ⓐ Ⓑ Ⓒ Ⓓ Ⓔ	155 Ⓐ Ⓑ Ⓒ Ⓓ Ⓔ	187 Ⓐ Ⓑ Ⓒ Ⓓ Ⓔ	219 Ⓐ Ⓑ Ⓒ Ⓓ Ⓔ
124 Ⓐ Ⓑ Ⓒ Ⓓ Ⓔ	156 Ⓐ Ⓑ Ⓒ Ⓓ Ⓔ	188 Ⓐ Ⓑ Ⓒ Ⓓ Ⓔ	220 Ⓐ Ⓑ Ⓒ Ⓓ Ⓔ
125 Ⓐ Ⓑ Ⓒ Ⓓ Ⓔ	157 Ⓐ Ⓑ Ⓒ Ⓓ Ⓔ	189 Ⓐ Ⓑ Ⓒ Ⓓ Ⓔ	221 Ⓐ Ⓑ Ⓒ Ⓓ Ⓔ
126 Ⓐ Ⓑ Ⓒ Ⓓ Ⓔ	158 Ⓐ Ⓑ Ⓒ Ⓓ Ⓔ	190 Ⓐ Ⓑ Ⓒ Ⓓ Ⓔ	222 Ⓐ Ⓑ Ⓒ Ⓓ Ⓔ
127 Ⓐ Ⓑ Ⓒ Ⓓ Ⓔ	159 Ⓐ Ⓑ Ⓒ Ⓓ Ⓔ	191 Ⓐ Ⓑ Ⓒ Ⓓ Ⓔ	223 Ⓐ Ⓑ Ⓒ Ⓓ Ⓔ
128 Ⓐ Ⓑ Ⓒ Ⓓ Ⓔ	160 Ⓐ Ⓑ Ⓒ Ⓓ Ⓔ	192 Ⓐ Ⓑ Ⓒ Ⓓ Ⓔ	224 Ⓐ Ⓑ Ⓒ Ⓓ Ⓔ
129 Ⓐ Ⓑ Ⓒ Ⓓ Ⓔ	161 Ⓐ Ⓑ Ⓒ Ⓓ Ⓔ	193 Ⓐ Ⓑ Ⓒ Ⓓ Ⓔ	225 Ⓐ Ⓑ Ⓒ Ⓓ Ⓔ
130 Ⓐ Ⓑ Ⓒ Ⓓ Ⓔ	162 Ⓐ Ⓑ Ⓒ Ⓓ Ⓔ	194 Ⓐ Ⓑ Ⓒ Ⓓ Ⓔ	226 Ⓐ Ⓑ Ⓒ Ⓓ Ⓔ
131 Ⓐ Ⓑ Ⓒ Ⓓ Ⓔ	163 Ⓐ Ⓑ Ⓒ Ⓓ Ⓔ	195 Ⓐ Ⓑ Ⓒ Ⓓ Ⓔ	227 Ⓐ Ⓑ Ⓒ Ⓓ Ⓔ
132 Ⓐ Ⓑ Ⓒ Ⓓ Ⓔ	164 Ⓐ Ⓑ Ⓒ Ⓓ Ⓔ	196 Ⓐ Ⓑ Ⓒ Ⓓ Ⓔ	228 Ⓐ Ⓑ Ⓒ Ⓓ Ⓔ
133 Ⓐ Ⓑ Ⓒ Ⓓ Ⓔ	165 Ⓐ Ⓑ Ⓒ Ⓓ Ⓔ	197 Ⓐ Ⓑ Ⓒ Ⓓ Ⓔ	229 Ⓐ Ⓑ Ⓒ Ⓓ Ⓔ
134 Ⓐ Ⓑ Ⓒ Ⓓ Ⓔ	166 Ⓐ Ⓑ Ⓒ Ⓓ Ⓔ	198 Ⓐ Ⓑ Ⓒ Ⓓ Ⓔ	230 Ⓐ Ⓑ Ⓒ Ⓓ Ⓔ
135 Ⓐ Ⓑ Ⓒ Ⓓ Ⓔ	167 Ⓐ Ⓑ Ⓒ Ⓓ Ⓔ	199 Ⓐ Ⓑ Ⓒ Ⓓ Ⓔ	231 Ⓐ Ⓑ Ⓒ Ⓓ Ⓔ
136 Ⓐ Ⓑ Ⓒ Ⓓ Ⓔ	168 Ⓐ Ⓑ Ⓒ Ⓓ Ⓔ	200 Ⓐ Ⓑ Ⓒ Ⓓ Ⓔ	232 Ⓐ Ⓑ Ⓒ Ⓓ Ⓔ
137 Ⓐ Ⓑ Ⓒ Ⓓ Ⓔ	169 Ⓐ Ⓑ Ⓒ Ⓓ Ⓔ	201 Ⓐ Ⓑ Ⓒ Ⓓ Ⓔ	233 Ⓐ Ⓑ Ⓒ Ⓓ Ⓔ
138 Ⓐ Ⓑ Ⓒ Ⓓ Ⓔ	170 Ⓐ Ⓑ Ⓒ Ⓓ Ⓔ	202 Ⓐ Ⓑ Ⓒ Ⓓ Ⓔ	234 Ⓐ Ⓑ Ⓒ Ⓓ Ⓔ
139 Ⓐ Ⓑ Ⓒ Ⓓ Ⓔ	171 Ⓐ Ⓑ Ⓒ Ⓓ Ⓔ	203 Ⓐ Ⓑ Ⓒ Ⓓ Ⓔ	235 Ⓐ Ⓑ Ⓒ Ⓓ Ⓔ
140 Ⓐ Ⓑ Ⓒ Ⓓ Ⓔ	172 Ⓐ Ⓑ Ⓒ Ⓓ Ⓔ	204 Ⓐ Ⓑ Ⓒ Ⓓ Ⓔ	236 Ⓐ Ⓑ Ⓒ Ⓓ Ⓔ
141 Ⓐ Ⓑ Ⓒ Ⓓ Ⓔ	173 Ⓐ Ⓑ Ⓒ Ⓓ Ⓔ	205 Ⓐ Ⓑ Ⓒ Ⓓ Ⓔ	237 Ⓐ Ⓑ Ⓒ Ⓓ Ⓔ
142 Ⓐ Ⓑ Ⓒ Ⓓ Ⓔ	174 Ⓐ Ⓑ Ⓒ Ⓓ Ⓔ	206 Ⓐ Ⓑ Ⓒ Ⓓ Ⓔ	238 Ⓐ Ⓑ Ⓒ Ⓓ Ⓔ
143 Ⓐ Ⓑ Ⓒ Ⓓ Ⓔ	175 Ⓐ Ⓑ Ⓒ Ⓓ Ⓔ	207 Ⓐ Ⓑ Ⓒ Ⓓ Ⓔ	239 Ⓐ Ⓑ Ⓒ Ⓓ Ⓔ
144 Ⓐ Ⓑ Ⓒ Ⓓ Ⓔ	176 Ⓐ Ⓑ Ⓒ Ⓓ Ⓔ	208 Ⓐ Ⓑ Ⓒ Ⓓ Ⓔ	240 Ⓐ Ⓑ Ⓒ Ⓓ Ⓔ
145 Ⓐ Ⓑ Ⓒ Ⓓ Ⓔ	177 Ⓐ Ⓑ Ⓒ Ⓓ Ⓔ	209 Ⓐ Ⓑ Ⓒ Ⓓ Ⓔ	241 Ⓐ Ⓑ Ⓒ Ⓓ Ⓔ
146 Ⓐ Ⓑ Ⓒ Ⓓ Ⓔ	178 Ⓐ Ⓑ Ⓒ Ⓓ Ⓔ	210 Ⓐ Ⓑ Ⓒ Ⓓ Ⓔ	242 Ⓐ Ⓑ Ⓒ Ⓓ Ⓔ
147 Ⓐ Ⓑ Ⓒ Ⓓ Ⓔ	179 Ⓐ Ⓑ Ⓒ Ⓓ Ⓔ	211 Ⓐ Ⓑ Ⓒ Ⓓ Ⓔ	

The Princeton Review®

NOTES

NOTES

NOTES

NOTES

NOTES

NOTES

NOTES

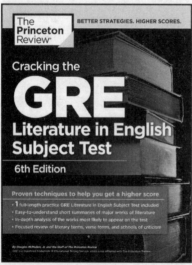
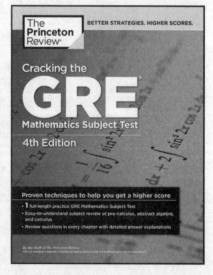